Applied Policy Research

Garland Reference Library of Social Science
Volume 1051

Applied Policy Research

Concepts and Cases

Peter J. Haas
San José State University

J. Fred Springer
University of Missouri–St. Louis
E.M.T. Associates, Inc.

Garland Publishing, Inc.
A member of the Taylor & Francis Group
New York & London
1998

Library of Congress Cataloging-in-Publication Data

Haas, Peter J. (Peter Jerome)
Applied policy research : concepts and cases / Peter J. Haas, J. Fred Springer.
p. cm. — (Garland reference library of social science : v. 1051)
Includes bibliographical references and index.
ISBN 0-8153-2092-2 (alk. paper). — ISBN 0-8153-2093-0 (pbk. : alk. paper)
1. Policy sciences. 2. Evaluation research (Social action programs) I. Springer, J. Frederick. II. Title. III. Series.
H97.H3 1998
320'.6—dc21 97-50533
CIP

Printed on acid-free, 250-year-life paper
Manufactured in the United States of America

For my parents,
—Peter J. Haas

and

For Nathan and Locke,
—J. Fred Springer

CONTENTS

PREFACE

The purpose of this book is to give students of program evaluation, policy analysis, research methods, and public administration insight and experience in conducting and consuming policy research. The book lays particular emphasis on the research needs of public agencies and is therefore particularly appropriate for courses in public administration and public policy curricula. The preponderance of existing texts in the field aspire primarily to introduce readers to theoretical and conceptual aspects of research and generally lack extensive reference to "real life" situations and applications.

One of the recurring headaches for instructors of research-related courses in public administration is making the theoretical content of the subject matter lifelike to students. Some policy-research–related texts contain at least a few examples that are intended to illustrate theoretical principles of analysis and evaluation. As a rule, however, these examples are thinly drawn and abstract. This text is intended to provide full-fledged, richly detailed case studies that draw the student into as real a research situation as possible in a variety of contexts.

In our experience, an immense gap exists between research as it is practiced and the theory expounded in textbooks. This gap is not merely the conventional gulf between "theory" and "practice"; it represents a failing of prevailing theory itself. As a rule, both the demand for information and the accessibility of information among public programs are quite different in practice from those prescribed by prevailing theoretical texts.

As a result, students unfamiliar with the practice of research and its many applications among public agencies frequently struggle in courses intended to familiarize them with the research process. Whereas texts often belabor topics such as cost-benefit analysis, experimental designs, and multiple regression, such concepts are only infrequently invoked in day-to-day policy research. Students may finish a course in research but lack any confidence in their ability to really do policy research in a public agency context. Once employed, some may wonder why they learned so many techniques they never really use.

Part of our approach is to demystify policy research in several ways. Our perspective recognizes that traditional policy analysis or program evaluation approaches are rarely applicable in their pure forms to the applied analysis of public policy concerns. Therefore, the first four chapters of this text set out a practical approach to tackling policy research problems that does not force frequently idealistic and obscure research concepts onto complex public programs and policies. These chapters also emphasize the importance of the decision context in which research products are created and used.

In point of fact, much if not most research into public programs is much more dependent on qualitative techniques, such as observation, interviews, case studies, and reasoned analysis than on high-powered number crunching and statistical analysis. Even when such quantitative techniques are employed, they are typically offered as a complement to more pedestrian (but still useful) approaches.

Does this perspective imply, then, that real policy research is mundane in comparison to the more far-flung conceptual approaches of theoretical texts? Nothing could be further from the truth. Whereas the construction and manipulation of sophisticated research design and techniques would seem to render policy research to the level of a technical exercise, real policy problems are frequently far more engaging on a substantive level.

Part Two of this text offers a set of case-study situations, each drawn from real instances of policy research, that provide students with the opportunity to consider and then learn how to grapple with the challenges posed by the information needs of public programs and agencies. Each case study focuses on a different type of information need and a different type of public agency. The case studies are designed to be of value both as examples of how to do policy research and as opportunities for students to advance their own knowledge, skills, and experiences with such research.

Another way in which public administration texts directed at research topics potentially alienate and/or mislead student readers is through overemphasis on national level policy problems. Although the overwhelming majority of employment (and applied research) opportunities for public administration students are at state, local, and nonprofit agencies, many texts use federal government agencies and national policy problems as examples to illustrate concepts and theories. The information needs, and resources for research, of state and local governments differ markedly from those of the national government. Many students are also interested in managing nonprofit organizations. The cases described here arise from broadly representative backgrounds, including local, state, and nonprofit agencies as well as federal-state-local intergovernmental "hybrids."

Each case study chapter includes the following: (1) a detailed description of a policy research problem; (2) a discussion of the unique challenges posed by the problem; (3) a description of the policy research techniques used; (4) a summary of the outcomes or conclusions associated with the research as it was conducted; and (5) conclusions about the implications or lessons for policy research. Additionally, each case study chapter includes exercises and discussion questions for classroom use.

Many of the case studies explore our experiences with conducting policy research for agencies, programs, and policies connected to the field of the prevention and treatment of substance abuse. Although every policy area has unique characteristics with respect to research, these case studies explore this field from the standpoint of a variety of types of programs, institutional settings, and research designs representative of many other policy arenas. It has been our experience that this field is one of the more challenging for policy researchers—and therefore pedagogically useful and appropriate.

As noted earlier, the text also provides (in the first four chapters) a straightforward introduction to the field of policy research, such that it can be adapted as a free-standing text. This introduction includes a suggested process for organizing and conducting policy research from start to finish. The text also addresses topics not commonly found in other texts, such as means by which policy research arises, as well as the varying roles played by policy researchers in the policy process.

The final chapter is a summary of the lessons that may be drawn from the case studies. Because it reflects our opinions about some of the questions raised during the rest of the text, we suggest that this chapter be read after the rest of the book is completed.

If you are a student, you are probably enrolled in a course with a name like *Program Evaluation*, *Policy Analysis*, or *Research Methods*. Perhaps you are enrolled in more than one of these courses at the same time, or have taken several of them in the past. If so, you may have noticed that the subject matter in these areas frequently overlaps. For example, both a program evaluation textbook and a research methods textbook will typically devote at least one chapter each to experimental research designs. (Experimental research designs are sometimes used by public administrators to emulate the logic of laboratory experiments in the physical sciences.) Such texts may also demonstrate the use of regression and other advanced statistical techniques in addressing research problems.

One reason that these courses and their textbooks tend to address common themes is that in many ways they are all concerned with the same task: reducing uncertainty or providing information for decision makers in the public arena. Whether one regards the task as "evaluation" or "analysis" or "research" is of little concern to decision makers, who generally need and demand *useful* information. Of course, when a person is learning how to produce and analyze useful information, it makes sense to break the task into manageable parts, such as program evaluation, research methods, and the like. But when thrust into the role of assisting decision makers, we have found that the usefulness and appropriateness of such terms is more apparent than real. Providing the appropriate information requires all the skills and knowledge one has, but labeling the process in the long run is of little value.

The goal of this text is to give you experience in the process of producing useful information for public decision makers by presenting you with a series of case studies that show how the research was conducted. These case studies are intended to provide a complement, and perhaps a foil, to more general theories and concepts of producing information for decision makers. Because research challenges in the real world tend to be unique, you won't always be able to directly apply what you've learned in class to the case studies. But the cases may help you understand how and why research is typically conducted in the public sector.

You will walk through eight situations, each representing a different type of information need and decision-making "client." The focus of each case study is not primarily on techniques, which you will learn with the aid of other texts and perhaps other courses. Rather, the case studies will give you the opportunity to apply what you've learned to "real life" and to see how the reality of policy research affects the evaluation-analysis-research process. In each situation, you will become familiar with the process of actually doing research for a real issue or problem faced by a public agency. You'll have to think about the best way to go about providing useful information.

ACKNOWLEDGMENTS

This book represents the lessons of many years of teaching and scholarly research, as well as participation in innumerable policy research projects on the part of both authors. With respect to the latter, the contribution made by Joël Phillips, President of Evaluation, Management, and Training, Inc. (EMT) deserves special recognition. His vision of "management-based" evaluation is at the core of the approach to policy research espoused in this text. He helped provide both authors with extensive experience in applied policy research. Additionally, he was instrumental in the design and implementation of several of the research projects described in the case studies in this book. In sum, this book could not have been written without the support, assistance, and contributions made by Joël and his staff at EMT.

Other individuals have also provided the authors with invaluable assistance. Among those deserving special appreciation are the following: Robert Rotz at the Joint Legislative Audit and Review Commission of the Commonwealth of Virginia; Mary Buuck at the Workshop in Political Theory and Policy Analysis at Indiana University; Susan Stroud with EMT; Steve Van Beek at San Jose State University; and Harold I. Haas, Professor Emeritus at Lenoir-Rhyne College. David Estrin, Senior Editor at Garland Publishing, Inc., is to be thanked for his fervent commitment to and support of this project. The helpful comments and suggestions offered by several anonymous reviewers with Garland are also acknowledged. Peter Haas wishes to acknowledge the inspiration, support, and guidance supplied by Larry Baas and Albert Trost at Valparaiso University, Steve Brown and John J. Gargan at Kent State University, and Gordon Whitaker and Deil S. Wright at the University of North Carolina at Chapel Hill.

Fred Springer wishes to thank Richard W. Gable at the University of California-Davis as both mentor and friend. His professional and personal example has been a beacon of commitment and caring in all aspects of life.

PART I

Principles of Policy Research

CHAPTER 1

Introduction to Policy Research

Popular views of the workings of American government are characterized by diverse and sometimes contradictory stereotypes—politicians in smoke-filled rooms, bumbling bureaucrats putting rules and regulations before content, and "rational" technocrats who coldly pursue numbers and logic to the exclusion of people. This book addresses a similar image—that of the policy analyst whose highly technical studies and advice influence the decisions of politicians and administrators and devour tax dollars.

Although policy analysts may not top the list of popular stereotypes of government workers, policy research has some harsh critics. Former U.S. Senator William Proxmire's political calling card was his weekly Golden Fleece award, with which he criticized particularly useless studies. From a different perspective, however, many practitioners of policy research lament that their studies gather dust because decision makers are reluctant to heed their sound advice (Kress and Springer 1988).

As is frequently the case with public arguments, selective evidence and understanding are in part responsible for these contradictory positions. One of our major purposes in writing this book was to provide a more balanced, practical, and realistic understanding of how policy research is accomplished and how it influences public decisions. This discussion may not enflame political passion the way the more hyperbolic commentary of advocates and detractors does, but it will lead to a more realistic understanding of the role of research-based information in public decisions. This perspective should be particularly useful to students and practitioners of politics and public administration.

In keeping with a focus on the ways in which policy research is really produced and used in public decision making, we will emphasize studies that focus on policies and programs at the state or local level. Multimillion-dollar studies by the federal government make excellent fodder for critics of policy research, but they are not typical of most policy research. The work of the policy analyst is usually done at a more modest level, financed by a small budget and limited resources in either of two less visible settings: in state, county, or municipal government, or in the nonprofit sector that implements many policies. The cases and discussion presented in this text reflect this local and programmatic milieu in which most public employees and decision makers operate.

This chapter is the first of four that introduce some general principles of policy research. We begin by addressing five fundamental questions:

- *What is policy research?* How does policy research differ from other social research? What is its relation to commonly used terms like *policy analysis* or *program evaluation?*
- *How is policy research conducted?* What basic procedures, methods, and activities are used in policy research?
- *Who does policy research?* What kinds of jobs do policy researchers hold? What kinds of organizations do they work in?
- *Why do policy research?* What purposes, mandates, and incentives motivate policy researchers?
- *Does policy research improve public decision making?* Who uses policy research and why?

What Is Policy Research?

Although the formal title of the activity varies considerably, many employees (and consultants) of public agencies engage in something called "policy research." *Policy research* is a catch-all term embracing the many information-gathering and processing activities that public agencies engage in to facilitate decision making (Putt and Springer 1989).

Textbooks often refer to policy research activities as *policy analysis, program analysis,* or *program evaluation.* Sometimes these terms (or others) are used to correspond to the temporal sequence of the analysis. For example, Patton and Sawicki (1993:257) draw a distinction between *ex-*

ante evaluation—analyzing policies, programs, and projects before they are undertaken—and *ex-post evaluation*—evaluation after programs have been implemented. One might associate ex-ante evaluation with the term *policy analysis* and ex-post evaluation with *program evaluation.* Similarly, Dunn (1994) establishes an elaborate framework of types of policy analysis based largely on whether the analysis occurs before or after implementation of a given decision.

Although such distinctions help identify specific types of policy research, the demand by decision makers for policy research information occurs before, during, *and* after implementation of specific programs (Dunn 1994). Demand for policy research occurs as often as not directly in the middle of full-scale implementation efforts. The case studies in this text clearly demonstrate that policy research occurs at a variety of points in the policy process. One of the distinguishing characteristics of policy research is this situational nature. Would-be analysts must be prepared to engage in research at any time during the policy process, and under a variety of conditions because policy researchers do not themselves define the research problems they investigate. Rather, they seek to identify problems as they are perceived by others in a specific policy or problem situation (MacRae and Wilde 1979).

Carley (1980:29) provides a useful distinction between two kinds of policy research: Analysis *for* policy is applied policy research; it is intended to be used by decision makers to improve policies or programs. Analysis *of* policy is more concerned with illuminating the causes and effects of policies and programs, without the purpose of directly affecting policy decisions. These are essentially academic studies of policy problems and are usually conducted in the public interest to promote knowledge about policy-relevant subjects.

This text focuses on *applied* policy research that is requested by and provided for decision makers. As a rule, applied policy research is concerned with *policy manipulable* factors. MacRae and Wilde (1979) point to the importance of producing *actionable* research, research that can be used as the basis for action by decision makers. By keying into aspects of programs and policies that can actually be manipulated or altered, policy researchers can help ensure the usefulness of their efforts.

How Is Policy Research Conducted?

Policy research employs a number of methods, techniques, and tools that have been drawn together over the past decades because of their utility in analyzing public problems and issues. These methods may seem disparate, but when properly applied they share the common characteristic of helping to reduce uncertainty for decision making in public settings. The case studies in Part Two of the text contain examples of six research tools:

- Interviewing
- Survey research
- "Case studies" including site visits and observation
- Secondary data analysis
- Sampling
- Quasi-experimental research

Other techniques occasionally used by policy researchers but not covered in this text include experimental research; cost-benefit and cost-effectiveness analyses; and forecasting. Our decision to focus on the techniques exemplified in this text reflects in part our conviction that they are among the most commonly invoked in applied policy research projects in day-to-day practice.

Despite the plethora of scholarly publications concerning the "science" of policy analysis, no monolithic, universally acknowledged standards, guidelines, or rules of conducting policy research exist. Thus, the discretion of the policy researcher frequently determines which policy research methods to use, as well as when and how (Dunn 1994:5). In most cases, the information needs associated with a given policy problem or issue will require the use of *multiple* methods, rather than the exclusive use of one method. One common mistake of the inexperienced analyst is to rely too heavily on the technique one knows best. Surveys, for example, are frequently used as policy research tools but often provide no useful policy insights. (We, like many of our peers, have fallen prey to overreliance on surveys.) Patton and Sawicki (1993:11) caution against this "toolbox" mentality, arguing that "the problem should dictate the methods, not vice versa." In fact, the problem should dictate the entire approach to the research process. Different kinds of problem situations or policy issues connote a different research process and products.

Detailed discussion of how to design and implement specific research methods or approaches (such as survey research, field studies, quasi-experiments, cost-benefit analysis, and statistical analysis) is beyond the scope of this book, although references are provided for readers who want to pursue these topics. Numerous texts and a large body of literature address research methods and techniques. Our primary intent is to help you understand the decision setting when you make choices about method, implement specific methods, or interpret the data and other results produced by specific methods.

Who Does Policy Research?

One of the dark and dirty secrets of public administration may be that nearly every kind of public employee engages in policy research at one time or another. One of the reasons *policy research* has a negative connotation is that many public administration students and practitioners sometimes fear and abhor classes concerning policy research. (If students knew how likely it is that they, too, will engage in policy research, they might be scared into entering other professions!) Nevertheless, although policy research is commonly practiced in certain contexts, policy researchers lack a unique identifying label, in part because of the multitude of organizational settings in which they work.

The most obvious examples of public administrators engaging in policy research occur in federal agencies with such names as General Accounting Office and Congressional Research Service. But these relatively large research-focused agencies are the exception rather than the rule. In fact, students seeking employment as policy researchers should know that, without doubt, the greatest number of opportunities exist at the state and local level. Nearly every state government boasts an equivalent to the federal agencies. California, for example, has the Office of the Legislative Analyst, and Virginia has the Joint Legislative Audit and Review Commission. Some city governments also have this type of analytic capacity—the City of San Jose has the Office of the Policy Analyst mandated in its city charter.

However, even taking the many state and local "analysis" agencies into account still overlooks the majority of policy research activity in the United States. Nearly every legislator, legislative committee, and task force relies on the work of policy researching staff. More important, public administrators in nearly every state and local agency routinely engage in policy research activities. Often these policy researchers have titles like *legislative analyst, program analyst,* or *management analyst,* but equally often they do not. Additionally, managers and other staff from nonprofit, government-funded agencies (such as some Planned Parenthood chapters) also engage in policy research.

Individuals who excel at policy research generally possess a considerable amount of technical skill. As Putt and Springer (1989:8) note, "Policy research draws on a broad spectrum of techniques for information collection and analysis, including adaptation of the scientific model of experimentation, applications of economic analysis to program costs and benefits, surveys of individuals, statistical analysis of large data sets, personal observation and more." Students planning careers in policy research-related fields should plan on acquiring skills and experience in as many techniques, methods, and approaches as possible.

Not every public administrator must excel at policy research, but few can perform at their best without a general understanding of it. Because the demand for the information generated by policy research is so great, and because the need for independent sources of information is so frequent, a great deal of policy research is contracted out to consulting firms, private research organizations, or individuals known as consultants. When contracts are awarded to conduct policy research on behalf of a public agency, the managerial staff of that agency become clients or *consumers* of policy research. Although some public administrators typically find themselves on the consuming end of the research process, they cannot be informed consumers if they have not developed policy research skills.

Whether a particular research project is undertaken directly by a public agency or by a consulting firm, policy research—except for the smallest projects—is frequently the product of a team of researchers. This cooperative effort is often achieved by division of research tasks according to the expertise of the team members. For example, a research project might include a leader with lead responsibilities and authority, a statistician/methodologist, a subject specialist, a data processing specialist, and, of course, graduate students and interns, who frequently round out the team.

Working on a policy research team is a challenging yet enjoyable experience. A typical project is conducted according to tight deadlines, which impose an atmosphere of pressure and the need for long hours of work. Policy research teams often develop an exhilarating esprit de corps as they get to know one another's personalities, strengths, and weaknesses.

Why Do Policy Research?

One obvious reason for conducting policy research is that it can improve the quality and effectiveness of public programs and agencies. That is somewhat of a truism, however. Here are some *real* reasons many public administrators get involved in policy research:

1. Policy Research Is the Law

Many public programs must be evaluated at legislatively mandated intervals. In fact, many of the research projects described in the case studies in Part Two were initiated as the result of some legislative requirement. Legislative mandates for evaluation generally reflect a concern for accountability for expenditures, but they are also intended to provide information that will improve programs and policies. These legislative mandates mean that careers in public administration are quite likely to draw individuals into policy research, either as planners of and participants in research projects, or as consumers and users of such research.

2. Policy Research Is Interesting

Granted that it may be an acquired taste for some, but most policy research is conducted at the cutting edge of some of the most important challenges that modern government faces. Policy research frequently tackles questions like:

- *Are "workfare" programs successful at reducing dependence on public welfare?*
- *Are drug treatment programs effective in addressing the drug problem?*
- *Do programs like Head Start offer a solution to educational inequities?*
- *Does raising the drinking age help reduce automobile accident fatalities?*
- *How should government deal with the increasing cost and declining availability of health care?*

3. Policy Research Is Influential

If policy research is indeed influential, then so are those who conduct it. The unspoken goal of many involved in policy research is to have an impact on public programs and policy. That is a legitimate and honorable motivation, but it begs a question: Just how influential really is policy research?

When policy research was first applied to public policy issues, particularly in the 1960s and 1970s, some observers felt that techniques like cost-benefit analysis would supplant the democratic political process. They feared that policy research technocrats, using quantitative methods of analysis, would make important policy decisions at the expense of the influence of elected officials and citizens. For a variety of reasons, policy research never achieved the kind of influence its supporters envisioned and its detractors decried (Putt and Springer 1989:14–16). Perhaps the most important reason is that the American political process proved much more critical of policy researchers' findings and recommendations than many had imagined.

The apparent inability of policy research to change public policy quickly and decisively leads some cynics to question its overall effectiveness and usefulness. For some, there is a logical conclusion of such cynicism: If everything boils down to questions of politics, why bother to conduct research? Such a pessimistic outlook overlooks the impact that policy research often has on modern government. Many public programs, projects, and policy have been profoundly changed by the influence of policy research. By filling a vacuum of experience and expertise, policy research can serve as an effective guide to decision makers, and it has done so for many state and local matters decided in the absence of more politicized issues.

This is not to say, however, that neophyte policy researchers should naively cling to the notion that their efforts must rapidly change the world in order to be worthwhile. The role of policy research in affecting policy is frequently subtle, its impacts incremental rather than dramatic. Policy research is perhaps best regarded as "facilitating policy decisions, not displacing them" (Putt and Springer 1989:64). Policy researchers need to bear in mind that they are but one source of information to decision makers. Optimizing the influence of that one source requires conscious and specific effort. The case studies in Part Two are intended to provide experience in developing useful information that will affect decision making, and the principles in the next three chapters lay the groundwork for an understanding of those cases.

4. Policy Research Can Represent Vocational and/or Economic Opportunity

For those who want to pursue a career in government, a canny strategy is to acquire policy research skills and experience. Policy research skills are nearly always in demand, and an individual with such skills can frequently find desirable employment with state or local government, even during hiring freezes. In government as in the private sector, information is valuable, and those who can help procure and analyze it are often in demand.

Conducting research *per se* may be only an instrumental vocational goal, because a stint as a policy research specialist can be of immense value to one's professional development. Indeed, conducting policy research often exposes one to, and lends, valuable expertise in the work of many agencies. It is not uncommon for erstwhile policy researchers to jump from agency to agency when their skills and experience become evident to the managers of those agencies.

With any luck, those who begin their careers as analysts will become familiar with many different kinds of agencies and potential career paths. Their analytic skills, as well as written and oral communications skills will be developed and noticed by those with a need for the same. It is no accident that the career of many a department head or director has begun in the ranks of the analysts.

Another avenue of economic opportunity in the field of policy research resides in work as a consultant. As noted earlier, much of the demand for policy research information is met by consulting firms and individual consultants. Consulting in policy research is difficult, demanding work that is not for everybody, but it offers a great deal of opportunity for skilled researchers. Working for a consulting firm can provide the same kind of exposure and experience as working for a public agency and can also familiarize one with the work of many agencies. Some career paths meander from consulting contracts to work with state, local, or federal agencies and back again. Some individuals start their careers by working for large consulting firms and then branch out on their own. Several of the case studies in this book were conducted under the auspices of consulting contracts.

Does Policy Research Improve Public Decisions?

For many, this is the bottom-line question concerning the topic of this book. Research unquestionably consumes resources, and cost-conscious decision makers and citizens want to know if they get any bang for their research buck. Indeed, many would agree with Senator Proxmire that it has been difficult to justify much of the research conducted with public funds. Even some policy analysts would agree that research findings and recommendations that are ignored are wasted tax dollars.

Our response to these critics is that asking whether policy research improves public decisions is a poorly phrased question. If the implied criterion is whether study recommendations were adopted wholeheartedly and implemented immediately, the answer will almost invariably be no. This criterion produces that answer because it is based on an unrealistic view of public decision making.

Public decisions in the United States political system *should not be dictated* by technical studies and reports. Information is, of course, a necessary ingredient in public decisions, but different actors and interests will interpret and value it differently. Policy research is but *one* ingredient in a complex decision-making stew that includes the biases inherent in institutional procedures, the influence of cultural norms, the political clout of specific interests, and more. Therefore, a more realistic assessment of the impact of research on decisions must be based on a more subtle understanding of the influence process than whether a recommendation is adopted or rejected.

From this perspective, subsequent decisions in this book will argue that well-done policy research improves public decisions in many ways, including the following:

- *Policy research reduces the uncertainty in public decisions in a variety of ways.* For example, public decisions often involve judgments about how large groups of people will be affected, or what large groups need. This information is beyond the personal experience or knowledge of any one decision maker or group of decision makers. Research is necessary to inform decisions that otherwise would be guesses or pure expressions of personal preferences.
- *Policy research increases the logical clarity and consistency of decision makers' understanding of policies or programs.* Public decisions are often characterized by drift (Kress, Koehler, and Springer 1981) that occurs when decision makers lose sight of overall policy purpose or program design in the heat of day-to-day decisions and situations. Policy analysis can bring the logic of policies and programs back into focus.
- *Policy research can bring new perspectives and understanding of public problems and responses to decision makers.* These new insights thereby affect future decisions.

- *Policy research can improve the quality of public debate by making evidence a part of the decision calculus.* An enlightened public is more likely to support conclusions consistent with the findings of policy research.

In summary, policy research leavens the dough of public decisions by bringing evidence and clarity to the decision-making recipe. The process of influence is not simple or straightforward: "Policy research . . . is not expected to produce solutions, but to provide information and analysis at multiple points in a complex web of interconnected decisions [that] shape public policy" (Putt and Springer 1989:16).

The remainder of Part I addresses the interconnection between the information provided by policy research and the process and substance of public decisions.

Overview of this Book

Policy Research and Public Decisions is presented in two parts. Chapters 2, 3, and 4 make up Part I, which presents a brief discussion of policy research and a framework for understanding and implementing its application to public decisions. Chapter 2 explains how different kinds of issues, problems, and situations require different kinds of policy research activities and products. Understanding the various roles of policy research is fundamental to understanding how to apply the research methods and techniques used by public administrators.

Chapter 3 focuses on the conditions you can expect to face in conducting policy research in the "real world." The point of this chapter is to familiarize you with the difficulty of applying "textbook" knowledge to challenging research situations in the here and now.

Chapter 4 presents a practical approach to designing and implementing policy research that is informed by the concepts described in the first three chapters. The model for conducting policy research emphasizes the information needs of the decision maker and the importance of multiple information sources.

Part Two presents eight case studies that describe and assess actual examples of policy research. These cases were selected to demonstrate how a variety of methods were applied in diverse policy settings. A number of these studies address topics related to policy or programs concerning drugs and drug-related problems. This policy context reflects the authors' recent research activity, but the lessons are also applicable to many other policy areas.

Each case study includes six components:

1. A detailed description of a policy research problem
2. A discussion of the unique challenges posed by the problem
3. A description of the policy research techniques used
4. A summary of the outcomes or conclusions associated with the research as it was conducted
5. Conclusions about the implications or lessons for policy research
6. Exercises and discussion questions for classroom use

Chapter 13 is an overview, and it presents some concluding thoughts on the lessons to be learned from the cases in Part II.

Discussion Questions

1. Based on class readings and experience, describe the differences, if any, between policy analysis, program evaluation, research methods, and policy research. If they differ, state whether, in your opinion, the differences are important. Explain your reasoning.
2. Describe an example of a familiar piece of policy research. Who conducted it? Why was it initiated? What impact, if any, did it have on decision making?
3. Is policy research interesting? Why or why not?
4. How important is policy research in influencing government programs? Cite an example of such influence.

Assignments and Activities

1. Pick one government agency with which you are familiar. Find out which unit conducts policy research for the agency and what job titles are given to individuals who engage in policy research activities.
2. Identify an example of a public decision that was influenced by policy research. Why do you think the policy research was important?

CHAPTER 2

Strategies for Policy Research in Context

Decision makers need information but they need specific kinds of information that is prepared in forms they can digest and use and that is provided in a timely manner. Moreover, the information needs of decision makers at the national level differ from those of officials at the state and local government levels. Although policy research is conducted in a wide variety of situations, each situation requires a unique research strategy. It is also true, however, that policy researchers need a guide, a common approach to their task, complex and varied though it may be. This chapter attempts to provide such a guide by synthesizing several popular approaches to policy research and linking them to a common purpose: meeting the information needs of decision and policy makers. Given this purpose, our approach to policy research will focus on three main points:

- Identifying the major information needs and information utilization capabilities in a given policy problem
- Designing and implementing appropriate and feasible research strategies
- Communicating usable information to decision makers

The chapter begins with a brief introduction to three common models or approaches that are representative of the ways students are taught to do policy research. Each approach offers important insights, but none is broad or flexible enough to serve as a general model for practicing policy researchers. In essence, each model assumes that policy research problems are more clearly and narrowly defined than they are in the real world.

The Policy Analysis Approach

One of the more popular and time-honored research strategies (and one many students may be familiar with), is sometimes called the *rational model* or the *policy analysis process* (see, for example, MacRae and Wilde 1979; Starling 1988; Quade and Carter 1989; Dunn 1994). There are a number of variations on this strategy, but their general outline often resembles the six steps suggested by Patton and Sawicki (1993:3):

1. Verify, define, and detail the problem.
2. Establish evaluation criteria.
3. Identify alternative policies.
4. Evaluate alternative policies.
5. Display and select among alternative policies.
6. Monitor policy outcomes—then repeat the process as necessary.

One need not be an experienced researcher to see that this six-step strategy is very similar to the basic scientific method of research. This strategy likens policy alternatives to a scientist's hypotheses, or focused research questions. The policy researcher, like the scientist appraising rival hypotheses, must evaluate policy alternatives and choose the best available option. To do so, the researcher, again like the scientist, collects data and analyzes them.

This strategy, or model, is called "rational" because when properly applied it is supposed to yield the best or optimal policy response to a given problem. However, even its most ardent advocates acknowledge that using the model will not necessarily yield an optimal decision. One important reason for the frequent failure or inapplicability of the policy analysis approach is that the issues that confront public agencies are rarely of a form that is amenable to the straightforward application of the rational model. For example, consider the following policy situation:

> The director of a large social service agency is concerned about the effectiveness of several related programs that are supposed to pro-

vide training and, ultimately, employment for economically disadvantaged citizens in urban areas. Some of the programs involve the ostensibly cooperative effort of several agencies, but personnel from these agencies are feuding. The director suspects these programs are working as well as they could or should be, but she cannot say this with certainty. She also has no firm idea why the programs are—or are not—working well.

How can the director (or a policy researcher assigned to the problem) apply the principles of the rational model to this situation? The problem is vague and does not represent a clear-cut choice between alternative policies. Moreover, the agency is in the middle of a presumably institutionalized policy process—not at the beginning, when policy alternatives would perhaps be clearer. Therefore, the answer to the above question is that the rational model would be very difficult to apply in this situation. Yet, in the absence of information and understanding from some sort of policy research, the agency may be churning away vast sums of public money that could be more effectively used.

This is not an atypical example. As Dunn (1994:146) observes, *most* important policy problems are similarly "ill structured," entailing one or more of these characteristics:

- lack of clear definition and parameters
- lack of clear alternatives
- involvement of multiple decision makers and stakeholders

To the extent that their problem is ill structured, decision makers will tend to be less amenable to traditional policy analysis techniques. Nevertheless, many policy research theoreticians cling to the rational model as the best available approach.

The Program Evaluation Approach

A second general model for conducting policy research might be called the evaluation model. Compared with the rational policy analysis model, the evaluation model is a bit less uniformly disseminated—that is, theorists tend to emphasize different aspects of the same general approach (see, for example, Weiss 1972; Nachimas 1979; Rutman and Mowbray

1983; Fitz-Gibbon and Morris 1987; Mohr 1988; Bingham and Felbinger 1989; Dunn 1994: 403–422; Patton and Sawicki 1993:362–397). Typically, evaluation models are supposed to help identify the impact or outcomes of specific public programs. As one theorist states it, "the crux of [program evaluation] is a comparison of what *did* happen after implementing the program with what *would have* happened had the program never been implemented" (Mohr 1988:2–3; emphasis supplied). Bingham and Felbinger (1989:12) outline a typical program evaluation model:

1. Identify the goals and objectives of the program or policy in a manner that can be evaluated.
2. Construct an impact model of what you expect of the impact of the program or policy.
3. Develop a research design . . . that is driven by an appreciation of the literature that suggests these expectations.
4. Measure the phenomena of interest.
5. Collect the data and analyze the results.

The evaluation model is actually quite similar to the policy analysis model—both frequently involve measurement of the attainment of policy goals and objectives. Both frequently imply use of traditional social science methods to determine causal relationships.

The models differ in that the evaluation model does not always prescribe the comparison of various policy or program alternatives, as does the policy analysis approach. Moreover, most applications of the evaluation model focus on selecting an appropriate research design—one that will enable the isolation and identification of the impacts or effects of a specific program or policy to see whether the program "worked." For example, one famous policy experiment compared the test scores of an experimental group of disadvantaged children enrolled in the Head Start program with those of a control group who received no special education (see, for example, Weikart 1984). The experiment seemed to "prove" that the program worked, although subsequent analyses cast some doubt on that finding. The doubt stemmed in part from the fact that preschoolers' gains in educational attainment that were evident when they completed the Head Start program typically disappeared during their elementary school years.

The traditional program-evaluation model encounters numerous problems when applied to "real world" policy problems. Some relate to the requirement that the analysis must focus on previously identified program goals. As noted earlier, program goals may be unclear, controversial, or multiple—that is, programs may serve different goals for different people with a stake in them. For some, Head Start gains after preschool may justify the program. For others, nothing less than lasting gains are acceptable. The difficulties of tying evaluation closely to program goals have led some evaluators to suggest a model they call "goal-free evaluation" (Scriven 1972).

Other "real-world" application problems stem from the emphasis the traditional evaluation approach places on rigorous research designs like those used by the classic "experimental" model, including the need for control groups that receive no program services. Such requirements are unrealistic for two reasons. First, most policy research settings and budgets allow only "quasi-experiments," approximations of experiments that raise difficult issues of accuracy and interpretation. Experiments also raise ethical questions because establishing control groups means denying services to persons who are in need (see, for example, Boruch et al. 1985:172, and Fitz-Gibbon and Morris 1987: 12–13).

The focus on goals, or "outcomes," raises another problem in the application of the traditional evaluation model. Determining *whether* an outcome was realized says little about why it was realized, or *what might be done* to improve goal attainment. Lack of goal attainment does not necessarily mean the program concept is poor; it may simply mean the program was poorly implemented. Information useful for program-level decision makers must include information about the program activities and procedures themselves—what policy researchers often call "process information." Note that the results obtained from the Head Start evaluation do little to explain why the program's effect was apparently short lived.

One popular variation on the program evaluation approach is outcomes measurement. Hatry, Winnie, and Fisk (1981) state that the key to effective evaluation of the programs of state and local governments is development of appropriate measures or indicators of program performance. This approach places relatively less emphasis on experiments and control groups and relies more on measuring and monitoring the outcomes (or "outputs") associated with programs and policies. For example, the City of Sunnyvale, California, uses an advanced, comprehensive system of output measures for each city department and service. Sunnyvale incorporates these measures in its evaluations of the efficiency and effectiveness of many city programs.

As useful as such measurements can be, they do not always provide the type of information decision makers need. A program may not deliver outcomes that are accurate reflections of its quality or impact. Educational programs, for example, tend to have diffuse, long-term goals that defy ready measurement. Even when programs do deliver measurable outcomes, collecting such information tends to proceed independently of necessary links to program inputs, structure, and implementation. Knowing how much output a program produced in a month is not very helpful in the absence of knowledge about *why* it produced that particular level of output.

Because of the inadequacies and frequent inappropriateness of the traditional evaluation model, some scholars have argued for a more qualitative approach to program evaluation (see, for example, Guba 1978; Patton 1980; Herman et al. 1987).

The Hypothesis Testing or Statistical Analysis Approach

A third approach to policy research problems emphasizes the scientific method of hypothesis testing, frequently by means of statistical analysis. This approach, which is espoused by many "research methods" texts, tests specific hypotheses through manipulation of policy-relevant variables by means of a variety of relatively sophisticated statistical methods. A primary goal of most research methods texts, of course, is teaching statistical concepts, but they often suggest that policy research should be conducted using the hypothesis-testing approach (see, for example, Welch and Comer 1988; Matlock 1993; Meyer and Brudney 1993; Giventer 1996). O'Sullivan and Rassel (1995:3–5), for example, state that policy research should conform to the following approach:

> After the research question and study's purpose are stated, a preliminary model should be built. . . . Models consist of elements and relationships. . . . By the time they are ready to collect the data the investigators should be satisfied that they have included the relevant elements in the model. The included elements and their relationships become important components of decisions about which data to collect and how to analyze them.

Such research models are then used to generate more specific hypotheses—theories about how research elements are related. Statistical analysis and/or

TABLE 2.1

A Comparison of the Relative Merits of Quantitative and Qualitative Data and Analysis

Qualitative methods	Quantitative methods
Permit study of selected issues in depth and detail	Use standardized measures and predetermined responses
Provide details about limited numbers of people or cases	Facilitate comparison and generalizations to larger populations
Can provide detailed descriptions about situations, events, interactions, and observed behaviors	Are of limited use in providing contextual information

Source: Michael Patton, *How to Use Qualitative Methods in Evaluation* (Newbury Park, Calif: Sage Publications, 1987).

hypothesis testing are frequently appropriate and necessary in policy research, but this approach tends to overemphasize the value of hypothesis testing in many policy research situations. Proving or disproving a particular hypothesis is likely to be of limited use (if any) in the context of much broader policy research questions. Many policy problems simply do not generate cogent "models" or attendant hypotheses. Moreover, the data to support hypothesis-testing statistical methods are frequently lacking.

Another problem with a statistical orientation to policy research is that it tends to engender the "tool box" approach to policy research criticized earlier in this chapter. For example, many "research methods" texts focus on survey research methods simply because surveys are a mainstay of academic social science research. Surveys can be, and often are, appropriate and useful, but not when researchers rely on them to such an extent that they generate less-than-useful results.

Policy researchers need to be sensitive to the limitations of strictly quantitative analysis because its application may not provide decision makers with the kinds of information they need. Patton's (1987) extensive writings about the relative merits of quantitative versus qualitative data in the context of policy research are summarized in Table 2.1.

A strictly quantitative approach to policy research can emphasize standardized data at the expense of rich, contextual information that more qualitative methods may provide. In policy research conducted for decision makers, quantitative data nearly always need to be complemented with qualitative information.

Weaknesses Shared by All Three Models

Theoreticians have proposed three models—policy analysis, program evaluation, and hypothesis testing/statistical analysis—as prescriptions for conducting policy research. All three share the following shortcomings:

- Each assumes a more limited set of information needs than decision makers usually really have. Decision makers need more than just information about policy alternatives, formal program goals, or focused research hypotheses. Decision makers need information on a broad range of issues, from simple information on program functioning or citizen perceptions, to complex models of future economic possibilities. This information will be consumed in varying environments in which it will be treated with varying degrees of credibility and interpreted from differing perspectives.
- Each is generally prescriptive, stating how researchers *should* structure their analyses, or how the decision process *should* operate. These are reasonable standards for an analyst to keep in mind, but they fail to emphasize the reality of what analysts *can* do in more realistic circumstances. Hence each approach is an imperfect guide to practice.
- Each focuses on logical processes or research techniques that meet technical criteria for research, *rather* than on the substance of the problems being addressed. The practicing policy researcher needs to know how to adapt technique to substance and circumstance.

In sum, although the policy analysis, program evaluation, and hypothesis testing/statistical analysis models may work well in certain situations, they are clearly less readily applicable in others. It is rarely self-evident when these models are applicable, or how to apply them in less than optimal conditions. What would-be policy researchers need is a more adaptable model for tackling the information needs of decision makers and public agencies. The model needs to be adaptable both to different kinds of situations and to the complexities of public programs and policies.

These needs function as a straightforward beginning point for an alternative approach to structuring policy research challenges, one based largely on the concept of shaping policy research methods to match the *information needs* of decision makers. This approach is situation-based policy research.

Situation-Based Policy Research

A useful model for tackling policy research problems must be based on a more complete understanding of how the information needs of decision makers differ in various situations. This means that policy research must be consumer or client based: the goal must be to serve the expressed needs of the person or agency requesting the information. Although policy research that serves other needs—such as "the public interest"—is occasionally commissioned by various institutions or government agencies, policy research in public administration is almost always commissioned by agencies or individuals with more specific information needs. In any event, a situation-based approach assumes that the policy researcher is working for a client, as either an "insider" (subordinate or peer) or an "outsider" (evaluator or contractor). Policy researchers must bear in mind that "*the ability to respond to information needs of others is a central skill in policy research*" (Putt and Springer 1989:80, emphasis added). The principle to remember is that *successful policy research begins with and depends upon recognizing the specific information needs of the client.*

Patton (1987:8–9) observes that the following questions ought to be answered when policy researchers consider their data collection options and strategies:

1. Who is the information for and who will use the findings of the [research]?
2. What kinds of information are needed?
3. How is the information to be used? For what purposes is [research] being done?
4. When is the information needed?
5. What resources are available to conduct the [research]?

The answers to these questions should have a profound impact on the methods policy researchers use to serve the needs of decision makers.

Who Will Use the Information?

The kinds of information administrators need will not satisfy the information needs of legislators. Similarly, sponsors of academic research stress methodologically rigorous products whereas public administrators, who operate under strict time constraints, demand information that is generally accurate and reliable—even if it does not absolutely conform to the most rigorous scientific standards. In each case, the research must be appropriate for the client's needs.

What Kinds of Information Are Needed?

This is perhaps the most important issue policy researchers must resolve before designing the specific research activities they will carry out. The implications of this question are therefore discussed in detail in a later section.

How Will the Information Be Used?

The purpose for the policy research will help determine the kinds of information that should be presented. Generally, information that is to be used to guide actual decision making will be both broader in scope and more detailed than basic "academic" research. It will be broader in the sense that it will address a wider range of subjects (rather than focusing on specific hypotheses, for example) and more detailed in that it will frequently delve into operational details of policies and programs.

When Is the Information Needed?

If the information generated by policy research is to be used, it must be timely. As noted earlier, policy research for decision makers is typically conducted under strict time constraints. These constraints limit the choices policy makers have when they plan their data collection and analysis activities.

What Resources Are Available to Conduct the Research?

The resources available to policy researchers are almost always quite limited, especially when the research is conducted within a government agency. Limited resources may be be reflected in limited options, putting the "perfect" or most desirable approach to analyzing a policy or program beyond the reach of the policy researchers. For example, the most desirable way to evaluate a statewide program with sites across a state may be to visit every site periodically, yet travel and staff time may be too expensive to support this activity. Policy researchers frequently must compromise the demands of scientific rigor in order to stay within the limitations of their resources.

Types of Information Needs

Before designing the specific research activities they will carry out, policy researchers must determine the kinds of information the client needs. Policy analysts typically encounter five types of information needs: exploration, description, causation, estimation, and choice (Putt and Springer 1989:86). These five categories are not always mutually exclusive because in practice most problems may fit into more than one category. Nevertheless, a potentially valuable means for establishing a client's expressed needs is to consider the research problem in the context of one or more of these categories. Many problems do fit better into one category than another, and working through the categories is a useful way of thinking about information priorities and linking them to research techniques.

The following sections describe each type of policy research problem and the tools and methods commonly associated with it. The discussions include references to sources that deal in depth with policy research methods and techniques. Several techniques that are not well documented in existing literature are discussed in greater detail in the text that follows. Each type of problem concludes with a discussion of the related end products. Practically speaking, the most obvious end product of policy research is the written report, but the style, format, and content of reports vary with the different types of problems.

Exploratory Research Problems

Even with the glut of information that now pervades many public policy issues, many public agencies confront problems that are inherently unclear. Decision makers, like the hypothetical welfare agency director mentioned earlier in this chapter, sometimes are even uncertain whether they truly face a problem that can be addressed by means of public action.

In such situations, public administrators may be confronting *exploratory research problems,* which are characterized by an overall lack of developed knowledge about an issue or problem. Exploratory policy research may be able to shed light on an emerging problem or policy opportunity. By nature, therefore, such research is commonly diffuse and open ended.

Appropriate Strategies and Methods

Policy researchers called upon to do exploratory research tend to choose flexible research strategies and methods. Rigid strategies, such as the policy analysis and program evaluation models discussed earlier, are likely to be insufficient for the scope of exploratory problems when used alone and may be of little value in revealing an emerging problem or opportunity.

The typical exploratory research project incorporates several methods, not just one. This is appropriate since exploratory research projects focus as much on problem *identification* as they do on problem *solving*. The following methods may be used in an exploratory effort:

- *Interviews with selected individuals* One unheralded yet truly vital technique of applied policy research is the interview. In fact, interviews with knowledgeable officials, line and staff agency employees, agency clientele, and other relevant individuals are the bread and butter of nearly every piece of policy research. Interviews are an excellent, if not the sole, source of information about such important topics as policy or program background and history, implementation and processes, political factors, and other essentially *qualitative* areas of interest. Most theories of policy research have paid little attention to the central role interviews play in shaping and contributing to policy research, and relatively little has been written about interviewing techniques in this context. Murphy (1980) provides an introduction to the subject, and Gordon (1992) explores the topic of interviewing technique.
- *Surveys of selected populations* Surveys are one of the most overused policy research tools, but they nevertheless are frequently useful in an exploratory research context. Surveys can be a low-cost means of exploring the attitudes, opinions, and knowledge of a specific and/or geographically dispersed target population. Unlike public opinion polls, where the population of interest is the general public, policy research surveys focus on populations with some specific perspective on a policy or program, such as clientele groups; other jurisdictions; and agency employees, managers, or supervisors. In an exploratory research context, a survey could establish whether a knowledgeable group believes a problem exists or could reveal the group's knowledge and perceptions of a particular problem. In addition to the instruction provided in most research methods texts, many useful guides to conducting surveys in the policy research context exist, including Fowler (1984), Fink and Kosecoff (1985), Lavrakas (1987), Miller and Miller (1991), and Folz (1996).
- *On-site observation and site visits* Another underrecognized tool for policy research is actual observation of programs in action in

the field. Such observation, even if it is not systematic (and is therefore "unscientific") can lead to valuable insights about why a program is or is not working well. In exploratory policy research, site visits are often part of the process of familiarizing the researcher with the policy or program terrain. For guides to conducting site visits and on-site observation, see, for example, Patton (1987) and Murphy (1980).

- *Analysis of existing data* Depending on the clients many different kinds of existing data can be used to help clarify an exploratory issue or problem. Government and private agencies collect a wide variety of policy-relevant data on an ongoing basis. In the exploratory research context, such data can be assembled and analyzed to help clarify an issue or problem. The gathering of information about the related policies and programs of neighboring or comparable jurisdictions also falls under this category. For example, U.S. Census data can be disaggregated and analyzed to illuminate discussions about various social problems in a given community.
- *Literature reviews* Although policy research problems tend to be unique, they also tend to fall into patterns that repeat past efforts. The odds are that if one agency is encountering a problem and seeking relevant policy research, some other agency might have conducted a similar study in the past. Scholarly literature may be another source of insight into an exploratory research problem. Those engaged in applied policy research can expect to spend a few days in the library tracking down such studies. Some agencies maintain their own small libraries of particularly relevant literature, which can facilitate the literature review. Contemporary online databases that search for relevant literature also make the task of literature review much less onerous.

The End Product of Exploratory Policy Research

A report associated with a primarily exploratory research project is usually open ended and lacks specific recommendations. A narrative style will enable the researcher to "tell a story," dividing the larger issue into its constituent parts. An exploratory report may be light on statistical analysis, although it may contain a significant amount of descriptive statistical information collected during the course of the project. Substantively, the emphasis of the report will typically be on defining the "policy envelope" (Patton and Sawicki 1993:17) of an issue or problem. The policy envelope refers to the boundaries of an issue: which aspects of the problem, for example, are policy manipulable, and which are beyond the scope of the decision maker's authority or influence? The report may help decision makers choose whether further research, action, or inaction is the most appropriate response to the supposed problem.

Descriptive Information Problems

Descriptive policy research addresses a plethora of information needs. First and foremost, descriptive research helps answer the question "What's going on?" Despite the ongoing flood of data that surrounds contemporary public agencies, decision makers—particularly legislators and chief executives—are frequently in the dark about major policy issues. Descriptive information can provide a baseline for understanding a particular problem or issue.

In the case of the hypothetical welfare program director discussed earlier, a lack of basic information about programs and policy was evident. Before this director could take definitive action to improve the effectiveness of the programs in question, she needed descriptive information about how the various programs were working. Policy research can supply this sort of information in a systematic, unbiased, objective manner. Putt and Springer (1989:92) note that "descriptive research provides [decision makers] with information about phenomena they cannot possibly observe themselves."

Appropriate Strategies and Methods

Descriptive information can be either quantitative or qualitative in nature. Many clients benefit from both types of information, which means that the research strategy must incorporate methods for collecting both.

QUANTITATIVE DESCRIPTIVE RESEARCH AND DESCRIPTIVE STATISTICS Primarily quantitative methods of descriptive policy research include surveys, cost analysis, and analysis of existing data. Quantitative data are likely to be analyzed using descriptive statistics, rather than more sophisticated analytic statistics.

- *Surveys* Surveys conducted as part of descriptive policy research projects are likely to be much more focused than those associated with more exploratory projects: "While exploration provides a basic understanding of issues, description is more focused and involves more precisely determining empirical characteristics of aggregate phenomena" (Putt and Springer 1989:91–92). For example, surveys may be conducted as part of descriptive research into social service needs, the extent of drug and alcohol abuse problems, or victimization rates in urban areas.

- *Cost analysis* A commonly demanded piece of descriptive information is the cost of policies, programs, and their constituent elements. Decision makers frequently require accurate assessments of the cost of policy alternatives, program modifications, and other potential changes.
- *Analysis of existing data* As is the case with exploratory research, descriptive research frequently employs the use of existing data sources. Many agencies collect such information in the course of their daily operations. Hospitals, for example, collect extensive information about their patients.
- *Descriptive statistical methods* The term *descriptive statistics* refers to a group of statistical methods used to provide information about the characteristics and conditions of large populations. Such methods may include simple concepts like the mean, median, and standard deviation, graphs and charts, as well as more esoteric measures. Surveys, cost analysis, and analysis of existing data are all potential sources of descriptive statistics.

The terms *descriptive research* and *descriptive statistics* are somewhat misleading to the uninitiated in that they imply that policy phenomena are merely and objectively "described." In fact, most descriptive research actually represents fairly sophisticated and pointed *analysis* in addition to description. For example, descriptive research concerning the level of law enforcement efforts in various neighborhoods of a large city will inevitably address the issue of which neighborhoods receive the most services, and it will probably endeavor to answer why they receive such services. Thus description can promptly segue into analysis. Policy researchers need to remember that few, if any, of the descriptive statements they offer will be regarded as merely "descriptive" by their clients or other interested parties.

QUALITATIVE DESCRIPTIVE RESEARCH AND REASONED ANALYSIS Quantitative information of adequate scope and quality may not be available or appropriate for descriptive policy research. In that case, policy researchers turn instead to more qualitative techniques, and they apply reasoned analysis to the data they collect.

- *Structured and semi-structured interviews* Interview data can be an invaluable source of descriptive information, as it often is in exploratory analysis. Interviews are particularly well adapted for gathering information about policy and program processes. Although interviews are usually considered a descriptive technique, they also provide a basis for *explanation* of how and why programs do or do not work. As Murphy (1980:3) points out, decision makers often need to "find out what's going on," and carefully selected and conducted interviews can help them do so.

  A structured interview consists of a standardized schedule of interview topics and questions that is administered in a similar way to each respondent. Semi-structured interviews are designed to give the interviewer more latitude to explore topics of interest as they emerge. In descriptive policy research, interviews are likely to be more structured than those employed in exploratory research because the problem or issues being addressed are themselves usually more definite in the descriptive context.
- *Site visits and observation* A series of field visits to the sites of a program or policy area are often a part of descriptive research. Whereas in exploratory research such visits are usually informal and casually designed, sites in descriptive research projects are more carefully selected and on-site activities rigorously circumscribed.

FIGURE 2.1.

Example of Program Process Flow Chart (FNL Program)

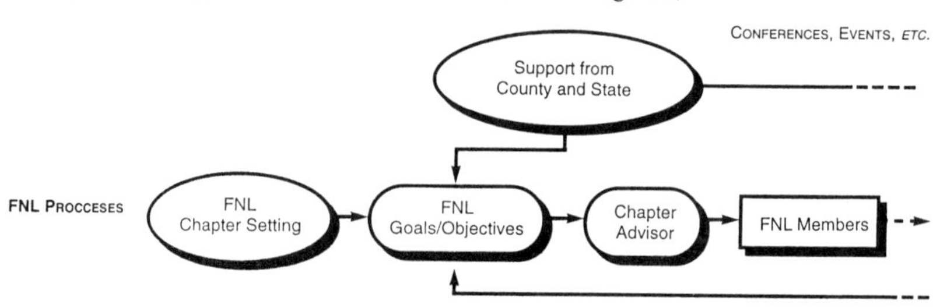

- *Reasoned analysis* Qualitative data collected by means of the above-listed techniques are not merely published verbatim in a descriptive policy research report. Like descriptive statistical information, descriptive qualitative information is analyzed—albeit frequently without as rigorous a methodology. Policy researchers wring insights out of qualitative information using a variety of resources, including their experience with similar programs and related issues, their intuition ("hunches" and educated guesses about policies and programs), and comparisons with other agencies and/or jurisdictions.
- *Process analysis* Process analysis, a specific form of reasoned analysis, can take many forms, but it usually begins with a flow chart of the elements that comprise the typical policy or program. Pressman and Wildavsky's (1975) classic study of a federal-local grant program in Oakland, California, centered in large part on an analysis of the unlikely series of events that would have to occur for the program to succeed. Although there are no specific guidelines for conducting a process analysis, many policy research studies use this technique to convey to decision makers the complexity and interdependent components of government programs. Figure 2.1 is an example of a program process flow chart developed for an evaluation of the California Friday Night Live (FNL) program. The diagram indicates the events and resources, the key program elements and processes of an effective drug prevention in California. The flow chart is only the linchpin of the typical process analysis. Other techniques and data sources are typically used to flesh out how well the program processes work and interact with one another.

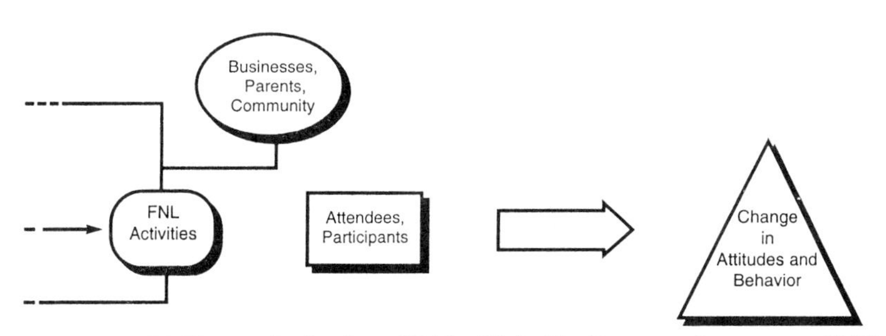

EMT. 1996. Evaluation of Friday Night Live Program. Sacramento: EMT

FIGURE 2.2.

Example of a Logic Model (Project SCAN)

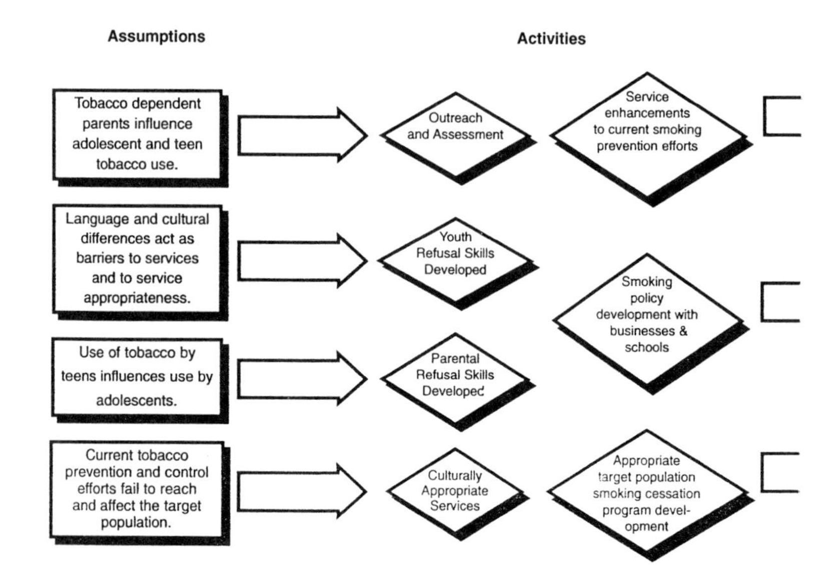

- *Logic models* Another technique that might be used in conjunction with a process analysis or evaluation is the logic model, a series of logical "if-then" statements about the interdependence of program processes and desired outcomes. By focusing attention on these logical relationships, policy researchers can identify weak (or strong) links in the design of a program or policy. Figure 2.2 provides an example of a logic model developed in conjunction with the evaluation of an antitobacco program for teenagers. The logic model for this tobacco prevention program (Project SCAN) clarifies the links between assumptions the program is based on, actual program activities, and the desired intermediate and long-term outcomes. The figure suggests that the desired long-term outcomes for the program (including significant drops in the initiation of tobacco use by youths) are contingent upon the validity of program assumptions and the completion of various program activities.

The End Products of Descriptive Policy Research

Descriptive research reports are likely to be more structured than exploratory products, although a narrative format is still possible. Among the

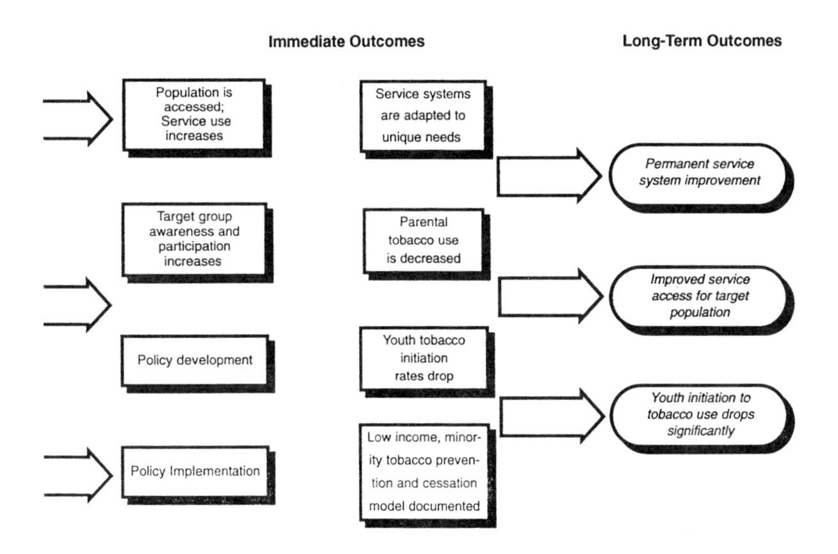

possible ways of structuring these reports are divisions based on (1) program or policy components and subcomponents, (2) specific issues and subissues, and (3) data source or method.

Substantively, descriptive reports can address a wide range of concerns. The objects of description may be processes and procedures, explanations of problems and/or solutions, the nature and extent of such problems, and a host of other topics. The substance of descriptive reports commonly includes a great deal of statistical information, displayed both in tables and in graphs and charts.

Causal Research Problems

Causal research problems address issues of policy effects, outcomes, and impacts. "Policies," as Pressman and Wildavsky (1975:xxiii) note, "imply theories." Policies and their constituent programs are often designed to create change, solve problems, improve conditions, help people, and so on. Causal policy research is intended to disclose how effective a policy or program is in achieving its stated purposes, goals, and objectives. Unfortunately, that undertaking can be quite problematic. Policies are implemented amid an active environment of other forces, including social, economic, administrative, and political influences that may also have an impact on the target of public policies. Nevertheless, causal research seeks to disentangle these outside influences and measure the impact of policies and programs as precisely as possible.

Appropriate Methods and Strategies

EXPERIMENTAL DESIGN Causal research problems are the most likely candidates for structured and statistically rigorous policy research methods. To the extent that ideal conditions exist—particularly the ability to use control groups—experimental methods may be appropriate. In less ideal circumstances, various compromises on the experimental approach may be necessary. In the ideal situations where it can be used, the program evaluation approach to policy research is best suited for conducting causal policy research. Specifically, various forms of experimental designs can help identify and measure program impacts, outcomes, or effectiveness.

Three notable kinds of experimental designs are true or "classical" experiments, quasi-experiments, and pre-experiments. The design and implementation of such experiments is one of the more thoroughly documented aspects of policy research (see, for example, Mohr 1988; Bingham and Felbinger 1989; Sylvia et al. 1985; Langbein 1980; Weiss 1972). Most public administration curricula include the study of experimental designs.

Although experimental designs, particularly true experiments, are ideal for the purposes of establishing causality, they are rarely practical in policy research. Typical designs randomly assign individuals to control and experimental groups, in the same manner as laboratory experiments. Such designs are difficult to implement amid the ongoing milieu of public agencies, for three reasons:

- Random assignments frequently cannot be made because of legal, ethical, or moral prohibitions on treating equals unequally.
- The expense of creating experimental conditions is frequently prohibitive.
- Designing and implementing experimental designs can be time consuming and costly.

REGRESSION ANALYSIS AND OTHER STATISTICAL CONTROL APPROACHES When conditions for creating experimental designs to establish policy causality are less than favorable, statistical control methods may be appropriate. Multiple regression is one statistical technique that can sometimes disentangle the effects of several influences on policy outcomes. For example, a study of the effect of aggressive policing on victimization rates in 60 neighborhoods used multiple regression to control for the impact of other variables, such as neighborhood income levels, racial composition, and population density (Whitaker et al. 1985).

Other statistical techniques that can be useful in establishing causal relationships include logit and probit analysis, discriminant analysis, and various forms of time series analysis. However, even statistical approaches to establishing policy causality are fraught with difficulty in the context of analyzing public policies and programs. Any statistical approach to policy research is highly dependent on sufficient amounts of high-quality data. In this regard, two factors tend to make statistical analysis in policy research difficult to implement.

- The impact of public programs is frequently difficult or impossible to measure because such programs tend to have vague, multiple, and even conflicting goals and objectives.
- The cost and administrative difficulty of obtaining adequate data is often prohibitive.

Statistical approaches to causal policy research may be avoided for yet another reason: They require a relatively sophisticated and receptive audience to be understood and accepted. Esoteric statistical models can alienate even the most well-educated audiences.

Analysis of Proximal Indicators of Policy Impact Using both experimental and statistical control designs is infeasible in many instances; in such cases, a compromise approach to causal analysis may be the method of choice. Particularly useful when appropriate measures of policy or program impact and/or effectiveness are unavailable, the analysis of proximal indicators can substitute for, or complement, more rigorous alternatives.

In this approach, a "proximal" policy impact indicator is chosen to represent a factor considered to be a necessary precursor to the ultimate success of a program. As a rule, such indicators precede policy outcomes in temporal sequence. For example, directly measuring the effectiveness of human service programs such as education, treatment, counseling, and case management is often difficult or impossible. However, if proximal factors to such services can be identified, the effectiveness of the program can be indirectly measured or verified. In the case of an education program, for example, proximal factors that are "necessary precursors" to successful outcomes might include the presence of qualified instructors; appropriate curricula and educational materials; and students' attendance at the program. In the absence of such factors, effective education probably could not transpire.

Measurement of proximal indicators is not necessarily an exclusively quantitative technique. The process analysis approach described earlier, based on interviews and observations of program procedures, may also help generate understanding of causal relations. Such qualitative approaches may have to suffice as sources of information about proximal indicators of program impact. The weakness of such an approach, obviously, is that it does not directly measure program impacts. Proximal factors are typically necessary for desirable program impacts, but they are rarely sufficient. The reality is, however, that policy researchers often must measure what can be measured, not what should be measured.

SUMMATIVE VERSUS FORMATIVE EVALUATION Policy research directed toward isolating the impact or outcomes associated with public programs is sometimes referred to as *summative evaluation* (Herman et al. 1987; Rossi and Freeman 1989). This type of evaluation is not appropriate in all cases. When public programs or policies are newly inaugurated, for example, ascribing specific outcomes or ascertaining how effective they are may be particularly difficult or even impossible. In addition, programs that lack clear and measurable goals, organization, or activities—as many do—may be inappropriate for summative evaluation (Herman et al. 1987:17).

An alternative approach to evaluating programs and policies under such conditions is known as *formative evaluation* (Herman et al. 1987; Rossi and Freeman 1989). Formative evaluation focuses on "providing information to planners and implementers on how to improve and refine a developing or ongoing program" (Herman et al. 1987:26). In practice, because decision makers so often want to know how to "improve an ongoing program," many policy research projects end up using formative evaluation strategies and techniques. Even evaluations with an otherwise summative focus will tend to incorporate elements of formative evaluation (Herman et al. 1987:26).

Formative evaluation also frequently seeks to identify effects of program efforts, but compared with more summative studies, formative evaluation tends to search for more immediate (proximal) program outcomes that can be used to get an early start on improvements in program implementation and/or design. Herman and her colleagues (1987:26) offer a comparison between the emphases in formative and summative evaluation (see Table 2.2).

The End Products of Causal Policy Research

Causal policy research reports tend to emphasize a display of statistical information—tables, graphs, and charts that depict findings gleaned from quantitative analyses. One danger is that the putative strength of the causal policy report—its definitive statistical analysis—may also be its weakness because its technical sophistication may overwhelm the intended audience. The organization of the causal report is often keyed to its central methodological effort. However, if the use of policy research is to be maximized, structuring the report around more substantive concerns may be a wise move. In other words, rather than flaunting its methodological elegance, policy research should be organized to emphasize its answers to the important questions it addresses. Moreover, policy researchers must measure only what they can.

TABLE 2.2

Comparison of Formative and Summative Research Emphases

Element	Formative Evaluation	Summative Evaluation
Decision maker	Program developers, managers, and implementors	Policymakers
Data collection	Clarification of problems and progress	Documentation of outcomes
Primary role of evaluator	Collaborator	Judge
Typical methodology	Qualitative and quantitative (emphasis on former)	Primarily quantitative
Frequency of data collection	Ongoing	Limited by design
Requirements for credibility	Understanding of program	Scientific rigor

Source: Adapted from Herman et al. (1987:26).

Estimation Research Problems

Estimation policy research seeks to help decision makers anticipate and plan for future events by providing accurate information about the upcoming policy environment. Putt and Springer (1989:98) note that decision makers generally ask two questions about the future:

1. What will happen if no action is taken with respect to a particular issue?
2. What effect will a policy have on a particular issue?

To help answer these questions, estimation research specializes in forecasting. If policy research is supposed to reduce uncertainty for decision makers, perhaps no single form of uncertainty is more critical than that represented by the future. Unfortunately for policy researchers, the value of estimation research is matched by its difficulty.

Appropriate Methods and Strategies

Among the most critical of estimation problems are future economic conditions, such as anticipated revenues, expenditures, and unemployment. Forecasts about such variables have important implications for many other policy decisions. Although most methods and strategies used in estimation policy research are quantitative, some qualitive methods can also provide valuable information.

QUANTITATIVE FORECASTING TECHNIQUES Forecasting methods are primarily quantitative and steeped in technical issues. Quantitative forecasting techniques include relatively simple methods like moving averages and exponential smoothing, as well as more complicated methods like autoregressive and econometric models (see, for example, Box and Jenkins 1969; Gass and Sisson 1974; Ascher 1978).

QUALITATIVE FORECASTING TECHNIQUES Nonquantitative approaches to policy estimation issues may also be used. Such approaches include the *Delphi technique,* which employs panels of expert or knowledgeable individuals, and *scenario writing,* in which knowledgeable individuals discuss likely or desired future conditions (see, for example, Linstone and Turroff 1975; Dunn 1994:242–249).

The End Products of Estimation Policy Research

Estimation policy research tends to be more narrowly focused than other types of policy research. Particularly when based on quantitative forecasting methods, this type of research usually attempts to forecast future values of policy-relevant variables.

Choice Policy Research Problems

When decision makers face a clear choice among a number of future policy or program alternatives, they may ask researchers to provide an analysis that will enable comparison.

Appropriate Methods and Strategies

The policy analysis or rational model discussed in Chapter 1 is clearly well suited to issues of choice. Critics of this approach, contend, however, that decision makers rarely face such clear-cut decision points and alternatives. Rather, they point to the messy, poorly defined nature of most policy problems, such as that faced by the hypothetical welfare director at the beginning of this chapter. Nevertheless, the policy analysis process is one of the more salient approaches to policy research espoused by theorists (for examples, see, Patton and Sawicki 1993; MacRae and Wilde 1979; Hatry et al. 1987; Carley 1980).

The key to conducting choice analysis is establishing basis of comparison for evaluating policy alternatives. The difficulty of this task lies in finding criteria that are at once measurable, practical to collect, and politically acceptable. If the criteria a policy researcher adapts for a choice analysis are not embraced by the client/decision maker, key political actors, or the public, the resulting analysis will be of dubious value. Two primary methods are used to compare policies in choice analysis:

Economic Cost-Benefit Analysis The most popular criterion for comparing policies is cost. The appeal of economic analysis is that cost represents a single, universal, and concrete criterion for evaluating policy alternatives. Cost-benefit analysis is a prominent form of economic analysis for this purpose. However, it is frequently controversial in that concerned parties often disagree on the value of various costs and benefits. Another methodological issue concerns the use of discounting—placing less value on future benefits—because the rate selected has an impact on the most desirable policy alternative. Cost-benefit analysis appears to have lost luster as a decision-making aid, and its use at the state and local level is poorly documented, if not rare. For an introduction to cost-benefit methods, see, for example, MacRae and Wilde 1979; Gramlich 1990; Weimer and Vining 1992: 259–311; Patton and Sawicki 1993: 187–226.

NONECONOMIC ANALYSIS Some advocates of choice analysis recommend using multiple criteria to evaluate policy alternatives. Such criteria could include administrative, technical, and political considerations, and they need not necessarily be totally quantitative. Use of a Goeller scorecard—a matrix of alternative choice criteria—involves rank ordering of policy alternatives for various criteria rather than hard and fast economic evaluation (Patton and Sawicki 1993:249–357). However, little evidence exists to suggest that either policy researchers or decision makers rely on such matrices to any great extent.

The End Products of Choice Policy Research

Reports based on choice analysis are usually organized according to the policy alternatives that were considered, often with a separate section devoted to each alternative. Ideally, a cost-benefit analysis identifies a clear preferred choice among the alternatives. Cost-benefit analysis can also be used more heuristically, as a means of shedding light on trade-offs inherent among policy alternatives.

Multiplism and Multiple Information Needs

The typology that has been discussed in this chapter provides a useful heuristic device for diagnosing the kinds of information decision makers need. Little, if anything, is known about the extent to which decision makers actually require each kind of information. What is known, however, is that decision makers usually require data that transcends specific categories of information. To ensure that the information they provide meets the needs of decision makers, policy researchers combine strategies and methods that are complementary and mutually reinforcing.

Plural Information Needs

Clients require mutually reinforcing analysis of data for several reasons. First, many clients express a need for information that will not fit neatly into one of the research problem types or will overlap two or more types. For example, a program director may want to know how effective a specific program is (a causal problem), yet may also need to know *why* it is—or is not—working (a more descriptive policy research problem). Another client may present a research problem that is primarily exploratory but that includes some specific descriptive information requirements, such as a survey.

A second issue is reliability. In the context of evaluating or analyzing public policy issues, single sources of information are rarely reliable enough to support an entire policy research project. Even the most exacting quantitative techniques—regression analysis, for example—frequently generate results with great amounts of error or uncertainty. This is due in large part to the inexact measures that may be needed in examining the effects and other aspects of public programs. Furthermore, highly structured techniques like regression cannot reflect the full complexity of a policy problem.

A third issue is validity. Specific types of data collection and analysis techniques can detract from the usefulness of policy research if one or more concerned parties or stakeholders in the policy process attacks their validity solely on methodological grounds. A survey, for example, may be vilified because the instrument is somehow biased. Cost-benefit analysis may be assailed because stakeholders disagree about how to measure intangible costs and benefits. Virtually every research application is subject to criticism of some kind.

The Advantages of Multiplism

Cook (1985) argues that these challenges of policy research require "multiplism"—a number of strategies for increasing both the scientific validity *and* the usefulness of policy research. Mutiplism includes the following:

- Operationalization of multiple policy-related measures
- Using multiple methods for a single policy research project
- Policy research that includes multiple interconnected studies
- Synthesis of initially separate research findings
- Use of the perspective of multiple stakeholders to formulate research questions and approaches
- Use of multiple theoretical and value frameworks to interpret research questions and findings

The research strategies implied by the concept of multiplism tend to weigh against selecting a single research perspective, such as those contained in the policy analysis or program evaluation perspectives, and toward more practically oriented strategies. Cook states (p.38) that

> the fundamental postulate of multiplism is that when it is not clear which of several options for question generation or method choice is "correct," all of them should be selected so as to "triangulate" on the most useful or the most likely to be true. If practical constraints prevent the use of multiple alternatives, then at least more than one should be chosen, preferably as many as span the full range of plausible alternative explanations.

Cook (pp. 46–47) sees three potential benefits from multiplism: (1) it can increase the validity and objectivity of research findings by promoting multiple perspectives to problems and issues; (2) it can provide more comprehensive pictures of how policies work (or don't work); (3) it can promote more value-conscious, debate-centered research that is more useful because it acknowledges valuative differences among policy stakeholders.

Incorporating Multiplism in Policy Research Strategies

The multiplistic perspective maintains that research should not be based entirely on a single measure, method, or perspective. Thus research strategies that seek to increase and diversify these components of the research process are likely to yield benefits. This is particularly true in policy research where the following kinds of situations are frequently encountered.

- Decision makers need multiple types of information, and multiple research approaches are necessary to meet those needs;
- Multiple types of data are relevant and available to provide information (e.g., agency records, client opinions, staff perceptions);
- Policies have multiple objectives, or complex objectives that are represented by multiple indicators;
- Policies address complex problems that have been researched in multiple ways;
- Multiple stakeholders with differing concerns are involved in policy deliberations.

Dunn (1994:10) observes that it is rarely possible to incorporate the full range of multiplistic techniques into a policy research project. He notes, however, that using the multiplistic approach will usually result in fewer "preventable errors that result from the analyst's own limited perspectives of a problem." In any event, policy researchers routinely incorporate elements of multiplism—frequently on an intuitive rather than a strategic basis—because they sense that decision makers need more expansive information than can usually be provided by one method or data source.

Discussion Questions

1. What are the differences and similarities among policy analysis, program evaluation, and statistical analysis/hypothesis testing as approaches to conducting policy research?
2. Which model of policy research (policy analysis, program evaluation, or statistical analysis/hypothesis testing) do you think is most likely to be useful to decision makers?
3. Which kind of decision makers do you think make the most use of policy research? Why?
4. Why can't every decision be based on policy analysis?
5. Why can't every program be evaluated using the "program evaluation" approach?
6. Why is descriptive information so important to many decision makers?
7. What's the difference between causal and choice information needs? Are there any circumstances under which the two can be identical? Why or why not?
8. Why are quantitative methods often not sufficient to satisfy the information needs of decision makers?
9. How might multiplism be applied to a research project?

Assignments and Activities

1. Using your library or visiting local agencies, try to find examples of real-world policy research. (Avoid journal articles and books intended for scholarly audiences.) Which model of policy research do they follow?
2. Using the same sources you located in Assignment 1, find examples of policy research that exemplify as many of the following as possible: quantitative and qualitative methods; formative and summative evaluation; multiplism.
3. Looking at the policy research you have located, describe the type (or types) of policy information it provides (exploratory, descriptive, causal, choice, or estimation).
4. Ask a local public administrator, politician, or other policy maker to discuss a problem he or she perceives. What kind of policy research information (exploratory, descriptive, causal, choice, or estimation) does the decision maker need?

CHAPTER 3

Policy Research and the Policy Process

Previous chapters in this book have emphasized that policy research is situational. It is different from research conducted in universities or in the laboratory partly because the policy analyst must respond to his or her environment in a variety of ways. As has been pointed out in previous discussions, the questions a policy analyst must address emerge from the concerns and problems of policy makers. The analyst must identify and clarify these problems so they can be the basis for focused research. Similarly, the methods of data collection available to the policy analyst are determined to a great extent through the budget resources that the client is willing to make available and by the availability of information in the environment. A program with good records, for example, presents a different research context than does one with incomplete or inaccurate records. Finally, the conclusions and findings that will be useful for a particular piece of policy research depend to a great extent on the ability and willingness of policy makers and policy implementers to act upon recommendations. Coming up with useful findings depends as much on insightful assessment of the ability to use the findings as it does on skills in analyzing the data themselves, without interpretation.

Accordingly, it is extremely important that policy analysts develop skills in assessing the decision context in which their studies will be used. This chapter focuses on this context and the important ways in which it can shape policy research. The discussion begins with a look at the way in which decisions are made in public settings and how information can reasonably be expected to affect these decisions. This discussion will include a description of the components of a decision system which would structure the production and use of policy research in public decision making.

The second section in the chapter outlines the relationship between policy research and various stages in the policy-making process. Although policy decisions cannot be easily classified by phase, it is useful to think about a cycle that begins with planning, goes through the decision and policy-making stage, advances to the implementation and maintenance of actual programs, and concludes with the evaluation of those programs. Analysis of the experience of program implementation can then feed back into future planning.

The third part of the chapter addresses more specifically the varieties of ways in which policy research may be accomplished in public organizations. Specifically, the discussion contrasts the use of agency employees with the use of outside consultants to produce policy research. Either option has its own advantages and disadvantages. The discussion includes a description of the ways in which agencies write requests for outside policy research consultation.

Information and Decisions

The rational model of policy analysis and decision making presented in Chapter 2 is based on the assumption that data and information are an important consideration when making decisions. However, a little reflection on what it means to make a decision suggests that this is not necessarily, and possibly not typically, the case. Other factors enter into any choice situation. For instance, preferences of the decision maker or the decision maker's supporters (the voters for an elected official, for example) are critical factors in the decision-making process. Decision makers are guided by their own objectives and views of the "good society," as much as by evidence about the way things are, or about how to get where they would like to go. In short, ideology is an important part of politics; the way people see the world and the way they would like it to be are important ingredients in any decision-making process.

Another part of the decision calculus will be the decision maker's perception of the consequences for his or her own career and personal goals. The astute policy analyst must be aware not only of the public purpose of the decision but also of this individual dynamic.

Public decisions are also affected by the constraints of the institutional setting. Organization theorists have long recognized the importance of standard operating procedures in determining decisions in organizational settings. Put simply, decisions are often made because of organizational inertia—things are done the way things are done. Budget constraints, available resources, and the talents of the people working in an office are internal institutional constraints on the kinds of decisions public decision makers will make. The preferences and capabilities of other organizations with which the decision making agency must work will place similar external constraints on feasible decisions.

It is important to recognize that all of this complexity in the public decision-making setting means that decisions are not the monolithic and broad-reaching dictums that some naively expect in public settings. Citizens may think of politicians and public decision makers as powerful people who make important and far-reaching policy decisions that affect all of our lives. In fact, even the highest-ranking government officials express "a fairly general reluctance to admit making decisions of any substance" (Weiss and Bucuvalas 1980:38).

Policy and program decisions are made in a highly fragmented and pluralistic system. High-level decision makers may set general directions and overall objectives, but these directions are fine-tuned through the many decisions of lower-ranking administrators and program managers who typically have great discretion in fashioning their particular local activities. As Putt and Springer (1989:23) stated, this conceptualization of decision making in a policy setting means that policy research has relevance at multiple points in the decision process, rather than being confined to addressing centralized, comprehensive policy questions.

Transforming Data into Usable Information

The various elements of the decision context must be taken into consideration by the policy analyst in the process of transforming data into usable information. This process and the way it occurs lie at the heart of the difference between policy research and other types of research that may be carried out in the laboratory or at a research university.

Data are the raw material of the data collection component of any research project. In very concrete terms, data may be the coded responses of citizens who have answered a telephone survey. These coded responses are literally the numbers represented in the computerized data file ready for statistical analysis. Other forms of data are the attendance records of people enrolled in a publicly supported GED course for school dropouts, the attendance records of high school students participating in a school's dropout-prevention program, the criminal offenses in the record of an offender being prosecuted in a selective prosecution program funded as part of a national demonstration project, or any one of many public record sources used to document the work accomplished in a program or the effects of a program.

Data may be structured or relatively unstructured. In public settings, records kept by agencies—such as numeric responses to questionnaires, or counts and categorizations—are an important source of data for policy studies. Data may also be the less structured narrative records of public proceedings, or the interview responses of staff in a program, or the verbatim dialogue recorded in a focus group session. These actual narrative accounts become the raw representation of reality from which policy analysts may construct information. Unfortunately, for a number of reasons, data have limited utility for most people in a position to use them to make public decisions.

Public Decision Makers Are Not Social Scientists

Few public decison makers have been trained to understand or interpret data. In a consulting experience of one of the authors, the client was a hearing officer in an administrative law court. The consulting task was to explain to the hearing officer how differing technical experts for two sides of a case could arrive at opposite conclusions using the same data. At one point in the proceedings, the judge burst out with frustration. The point was clear: The judge, who had the responsibility for making the decision in the case, was not technically competent to weigh the differing interpretations of the information. This is often the case in public decision making.

Decision Makers Are Aware of Complexity

Public decision makers often have an intuitive insight into the limitations of data in their raw form. Public policy is multifaceted. People have varying interests in the outcome of a single policy, and social science measures by their nature tend to reflect only some of these interests. Decision makers often sense that the question being answered is not necessarily the one in which they are most interested. Decision makers are often aware of the complexity of the context in which policy is being implemented, and social science technique (particularly quantitative technique) is ill-suited to reflecting the comprehensive and encompassing concerns of decision makers and their constituencies.

Decision Makers Want to Know the Human Implications of Study Results

Decision makers are often interested in what might be called the human side of research findings. They often want to know how a general pattern of findings, such as increased earnings for participants in a welfare-to-work program, translates into real life stories. For example, an aggregate increase in income may be statistically significant but may not make a meaningful difference in the actual quality of life for the individuals receiving the increase. Indeed, in some instances, the trade-offs in terms of lost medical benefits, extra expenses for child care out of the home, and other costs may actually lower the quality of life for program participants even though they show a statistical improvement in nonassisted income levels. The data themselves will not reflect such human implications of study results.

Decision Makers Want Interpretations, Not Raw Findings

Public decision makers are busy people, with many demands on their time. They have neither the time nor the inclination to study social science data closely and draw their own interpretations. In short, they need intermediary assistance between the data and their interest in the data. They need an analyst to interpret the data according to their perspective and interest and to tell them what the data say about their concerns and priorities. This process of translating raw findings into a meaningful result is the process of transforming data to information. Information, as used here, is interpretable and relevant to the concerns of the decision makers who are expected to use it.

As will be evident in the case studies in the last half of this book, the process of transforming data into information is complex. First, the policy analyst must pose the "right" research questions—those that are relevant within the decision-making context—recognizing what is feasible within the constraints of the context and addressing the policy objectives held by relevant decision makers. Next, the skillful analyst must select, from a wide array of available quantitative and qualitative techniques (see Chapter 4), the techniques most appropriate for analyzing data and providing answers to the research questions that have been posed. This is the exclusive bailiwick of the analyst in many circumstances. In most instances, consumers of information will not question the policy analyst's choice of techniques because they have not been trained to do so. The case studies in Part Two show how policy analysts choose among the various scientific methods available to them.

Packaging the Information

A significant part of the transformation between data and information in the policy setting is in the presentation of the findings and interpretations of the study. This packaging does not mean introducing bias or hiding results, but rather communicating the information in such a way that it is understandable and relevant for the decision context. Although written reports are a necessary and traditional part of the information production process, they are not sufficient to achieve effective production of policy relevant information. The history of policy analysis is replete with examples of final reports that sit on shelves and gather dust. Indeed, this is one of the most frequently repeated criticisms of policy analysis in the public setting—it produces findings that are not used. In fact, reports have many shortcomings as a means of providing information to decision makers. As stated earlier, decision makers are busy people, and they simply do not have time to read long reports. Short executive summaries may partially overcome this shortcoming, but they frequently do not give the fullness of understanding that makes excerpted findings and recommendations convincing.

If policy research information is to be used effectively, the production of information must be multifaceted. Analysts must recognize that there are different audiences within any one decision setting and that these audiences need different kinds of communication (Morris et al. 1987). The following sections discuss some of the major avenues policy analysts must consider and use.

Compendia of Information and Findings

One important product of policy analysis studies can be a detailed and easy-to-use compendium of data findings and interpretations. In several of the larger research projects in which we have been involved, it was effective to produce additional volumes beyond the final report that essentially listed frequency distributions of survey results, tables conveying important findings in the study, and very brief narrative interpretations of these results. These supporting volumes, which in some instances ran hundreds of pages, covered specific types in greater detail, and are packaged to become a reference for staff and parties who have an interest in the program or policy under study.

A notable example was a study conducted for the California Fair Political Practices Commission, which produced an 89-page final report and executive summary that highlighted recommendations and supporting evidence. The study consumed six months and involved many databases and analyses that could not be fully reported in the final report format. Accordingly, a set of supporting volumes that ran 600 pages in length was attached, one for each major area of responsibility for the commission. These included reports on each of the study components that were conducted, such as surveys of campaigns regulated under the commission's finance regulations, interviews with lobbyists subject to the lobbyist regulation provisions, and studies of reports by campaign finance contributors. Follow-up discussion with staff in the Fair Political Practices Commission indicated that these volumes had many uses for several years following the study. New staff members read them to become familiar with the various functions and impacts of the commission. Staff members used them as background and evidence when they participated in decision-making discussions. In sum, although the visible recommendations of the evaluation study in the final report drew considerable political opposition and typically were not implemented, many of the underlying premises for those recommendations eventually found their way into commission policy through staff members' more protracted study and use of the supporting volumes.

Formal Oral Presentations

For policy makers, formal oral presentations of results can be an extremely effective means of communication. In our work as policy analysts, we have often provided interim and final oral presentations, complete with overheads and focused handouts, to succinctly emphasize the most important and relative findings and implications of a piece of policy work. These presentations are suitable for a variety of audiences, and they can be tailored to the particular interests of each. Oral presentations have several advantages:

1. They place the study results on the formal meeting agenda of the policy makers, a place in which they will certainly get their attention.
2. They allow the analysts to emphasize and explain the important implications of the study in a way that is understandable to the consumers of the information.

3. Very importantly, they allow policy makers to question the analysts and to ask for elaborations, alternative scenarios, and explanations of how the results were produced. This sense of responsiveness to the policy makers' concerns can be extremely important in making the information relevant to them.

Informal Discussions

The building of cooperative and effective communications between analysts and policy makers is a potentially important avenue for the effective transformation of data to information. The analyst knows the data and can make the evidence and implications of these data part of the ongoing decision-making discussions concerning a program or a policy. In some instances, policy analysts are close enough to the program that they can attend many regularly scheduled staff or management meetings and be available as a resource with information and a perspective that is not present among the managers themselves. Managers are often consumed by the day-to-day decisions necessary to managing the program, and they may not have the time or perspective to stand back and see issues in a larger context. As a spokesperson who is respected and trusted, the analyst can become an important part of the informal management discussion concerning a program, its status, and what ought to be done to improve the program.

Forms, Records, Procedures

In some instances, the product of a piece of policy research can be procedures recommended for the continued implementation of a program or policy. For example, a program that is in need of information on client needs in a changing environment may require a simple procedure for monitoring the characteristics and status of clients and for using this information to guide program activities. Policy analysts may work with staff to develop forms and ways of using forms that will meet these needs. In other words, the outcome of a piece of policy research can sometimes be a concrete change in the operating procedures of the program or agency.

Formal Reports

Although formal reports may have received too much emphasis as the sole product of policy research in the past, their place as a policy research product cannot be minimized. Formal reports create a lasting documentation of the results of a study. They become part of the formal organizational record that can be reused in the future. They provide credibility and accountability because they can be accessed in policy discussions.

In sum, the process of communicating policy results and of transforming data into useful information must recognize the realities of the decision-making process in public settings. The process of communication must be relevant to the individual aspirations and objectives of important members of the policy-making body. It must be justifiable and credible in an evidentiary sense, making maximum use of the credibility of the scientific method as well as appealing to the "common sense" of policy makers. And, it must recognize that useful policy information is consistent with institutional constraints on policy action and must address those constraints when necessary. The skills that are relevant for creating useful policy information go beyond the technical skills of the researcher. An amalgam of research and policy knowledge is what makes the role of the policy analyst both fascinating and challenging.

Decision Systems

With the growth of policy analysis in government agencies, there have been attempts to institutionalize the creation and use of information in public decisions. These attempts have occurred at federal, state, and local levels, and they take on a variety of forms and degrees of rigor. When these efforts are conscious and focused on the intent to generate and use policy information in governmental decisions, they typically share some general characteristics. Robert Mowitz (1969) has described some successful attempts to institutionalize the use of policy analysis as "decision systems." Simply put, a decision system as defined by Mowitz is a *set of organized roles and decision procedures* that incorporate data and information into planning and evaluation of public decisions. These roles and procedures are organized so that information to assess need and governmental performance is regularly produced and regularly communicated to decision makers at explicit points in the decision process. These points may be legislative hearings, points in the budget setting and allocation process, or points in the annual cycle of program review and recommendations within an agency. All explicit decision systems, however, share the characteristic of regularity and have explicit roles assigned to the production of data and its translation into useful information.

Figure 3.1 displays a generic structure for a decision system. In practice, the roles in institutions and databases in institutionalized decision systems vary, but the layout in Figure 3.1 is useful for identifying the general attributes of institutionalized uses of policy analysis. Its major components are a database, information development, information application, planning, and policy decisions.

A Database

Figure 3.1 has on the far left a box labeled *Database.* Institutionalized decision systems will generate and maintain ongoing files containing a continuing stream of data in the policy or program areas covered by the system. The content of the box indicates that a comprehensive database will include indicators of the program system's capacity and commitment in terms of fiscal resources and work or system outputs.

A complete database will include some monitoring system for keeping score of the programmatic and policy outcomes generated by decisions in the system. This includes both indicators of need and demand or the status of society with respect to the problems and circumstances addressed by the decision system. It will also include indicators of outcome or impact of programs, the degree to which they reach their explicit objectives with respect to improving society, and (at the program level) be the means of keeping track of the outputs and impacts of specific programs so that program management and the knowledge of specific program-level effectiveness can be monitored.

At this point, it is important to reflect on the earlier discussion about the distinctions between data and information. The database itself is simply a set of common indicators ideally maintained over time so that trends and changes can be observed and related to changes in policy, program effort, or resources. As with any database, however, the data do not speak for themselves. In relatively sophisticated decision systems, data are often published in terms of trends, figures, and graphics in annual reports. Nevertheless, policy makers need to have these data interpreted and applied to the particular circumstances in which they are making decisions.

Information Development

The second column in Figure 3.1 represents the necessary procedures and roles in a fully developed decision system dedicated to carrying out the transformation of data to information. The figure bifurcates the informa-

FIGURE 3.1

Components of a Decision System

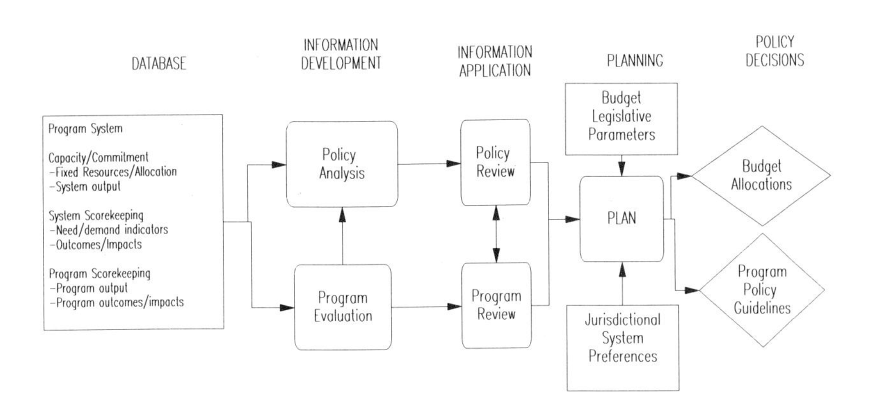

This diagram describes the components of an idealized decision system. Note that various forms of policy research are integrated into the decision process.

tion development process into policy analysis and program evaluation. As noted earlier in this text, this is an arbitrary distinction, with no exact dividing point. However, the policy analysis category recognizes the use of data to develop information that will be of interest to higher-level policy makers who make policy of a broad geographic scope, such as the Congress or state legislatures.

Information development represents the study of specific implementation and outcomes of local programs that carry out general policy. For example, policy analysis may be concerned with the aggregate economic and social consequences of changes in welfare laws to encourage welfare recipients to enter the work force. Program evaluation might look at one local effort to implement this policy (a county-level program designed to put mothers who are on welfare into an educational and training program that will place them in jobs). The two levels are linked because the policy cannot be carried out without the program, and the program is engendered by the policy. However, differing data sources, analytic techniques, and levels of generalization and findings will be produced by these different approaches. They complement one another in ways that will be discussed later in this section.

The important point about the information development component is that roles for personnel must be specifically created and supported in order to develop this information. These people may be analysts in a state department of finance assigned to developing information on the effectiveness of programs and relating it to the cost. They may be analysts in administrative departments who generate regular annual reports based upon databases maintained in those departments. They may be outside consultants who are brought in for a particular assignment to develop information relevant to a concern of a policy-making body. (The advantages and disadvantage of having insiders and outsiders fill this role are discussed further in subsequent sections.)

Information Applications

The third component illustrated in Figure 3.1 contains boxes representing policy review and program review functions. This column is distinct from the information development phase because it involves the use of information in a systematic review of programs and policies for which decision makers are responsible. Again, in an institutionalized decision system, this phase will be represented by specific required points of deliberation (meetings, hearings, and decisions that must be made, in all of which information from the database will be presented for the consideration of policy makers). For example, in the state of California, the legislature has created an independent research office called the Office of the Legislative Analyst. This office is responsible for conducting research triggered by any proposed piece of legislation that has fiscal implications for the state. The office will assess the need and demand for the policy, program, or benefits authorized by the legislation. It will assess the capacity of the proposed program efforts to produce these benefits, and it will assess the cost benefits of these efforts. All of this information is a required part of committee deliberations that will make recommendations for or against the bill's passage. The process of review is therefore built into the legislative procedure.

Planning

The fourth column, planning, represents a step that is highly formalized in some decision systems but is really a part of the information application process in less formalized or rigorous decision systems. For agencies that develop an annual plan, or for statewide or nationwide processes such as setting the budget, the plan can be a comprehensive written statement of objectives and intended activities. The point here is that in a decision system this plan is informed by the database and by the information developed from it and its application to policy and programmatic concerns.

Plans are part of a formal process of reconciling information-based and desirable objectives and activities in a policy area with resource and legislative parameters and with the preferences of political constituents and other supporters. The development of a plan recognizes that recommendations based on evidence are not the only considerations that go into a political planning process.

Policy Decisions

The final column reminds us that a plan is simply a stated set of objectives or a stated set of intentions on paper. Making plans into policy requires the specific allocation of resources and the specific guidance of action. This involves decisions like budget allocations from the level of the nation and state to specific agencies and offices.

Program policy guidelines are specific statements of program-level objectives that are indicated by policy, with relative degrees of explicitness as to the steps to be taken to achieve those objectives. Policy guidelines can take the form of everything from specifying procedures, job responsibilities, and performance indicators to the writing of requests for applications that ask service providers to specify how they would use grant monies to achieve the objectives of policy. Program policy guidelines are the explicit ways in which decision makers constrain the decisions of policy implementers in order to ensure that they are carrying out activities accountable to public objectives.

Although rather general in its language and layout, the concept of a decision system as demonstrated in Figure 3.1 is an important model to keep in mind when thinking about the use of policy research for public decisions. Some of the lessons are simple but profound. There have been instances in which public organizations focused a great deal of attention on developing a database (just one part of a management information system) but did not think clearly about what kinds of roles needed to be established and funded to ensure that data were adequately analyzed and communicated to policy makers. In some instances, an excellent database has been created, but the database is virtually divorced from the planning and policy decision processes at the right side of Figure 3.1. Without the crucial bridging roles and procedures—information development and information application procedures—data will remain mute because they cannot speak for themselves.

The following sections elaborate a few examples of the variety of forms a decision system may take. These examples are taken from actual public policy and indicate that the concept of a decision system is making headway in government procedures and policy administration. The explicit examples briefly described here—sunset legislation and demonstration projects—illustrate what might be called experimental policy making.

Sunset Legislation

Sunset legislation is an idea that has been used by the federal legislature and various state legislatures for several decades. Sunset legislation simply means that a particular set of programs or a particular set of expenditures will be authorized with the explicit requirement that they lapse and require reinitiation within a specified number of years. The legislature will review the policy or program at that time and determine whether it should be authorized again. The idea behind sunset legislation is that it eliminates the temptation to let existing programs go on to avoid the controversy that would be engendered by cutting them. The action that is required of legislatures is to reinitiate, not to cut. If the legislature does nothing, the program or policy will die.

From a policy research point of view, this means that the legislature will be looking for reasons and evidence supportive of the reinitiation of the legislation. Presumably, some of these reasons and some of this evidence will be provided through policy research. In some instances, sunset legislation has taken on many of the attributes of the decision system model outlined earlier. In California, for example, the Farr Davis Driver Safety Act of 1986 was implemented as a piece of sunset legislation that authorized the use of an innovative and relatively untested piece of technology as a countermeasure for persons convicted of driving under the influence of alcohol. This example of sunset legislation is explicated in greater detail in one of the cases in Part Two of this book. For our purposes here, it is important to note that the Farr Davis Driver Safety Act authorized judges to assign the use of alcohol breathalizers as a condition of probation for DUI offenders for a pilot period. After three years the legislature would have to reauthorize their use. The act also limited the use of the devices to judges in four designated counties and required that the Office of Traffic Safety (OTS) select these counties. The OTS was further required to implement a rigorous policy experiment to determine the degree to which the program had or had not been successful in reducing recidivism among those offenders assigned to the device. The legislation required that the results of this study be published and made available to the legislature prior to the sunset of the initial authorization for use.

The Driver Safety Act is an example of a piece of sunset legislation which required the production of data, the interpretation of data, and the explicit reporting of results in the form of useful information. The legislation created a review point at which this information could be directly used to inform further policy decisions about the use of alcohol breathalyzers as a DUI countermeasure in the state of California. In this type of sunset legislation scenario, policy research becomes an institutionalized part of the legislative process.

Demonstration Projects

Demonstration projects provide start-up funding for local applications of general policies formulated at more inclusive levels of government (state or federal governments). Demonstration projects are typically implemented through broadly disseminated requests for applications (RFAs) that encourage local programs to specify how they would carry out the general intent of the demonstration. Demonstrations are appropriate for policy areas in which higher levels of government have established policy priority but there is no clear consensus on what steps should be taken to reach the objective. In other words, demonstration projects are most appropriate for situations in which need and purposes are clear, but the means to achieve those purposes are not.

One of the expected outcomes of demonstration projects is lessons for improved policy. Because different local grant recipients are expected to have different specific approaches to addressing a problem, it is anticipated that the more effective and useful approaches will come to the fore. Most explicitly, these successful programs can serve as models for improvement or replication in other settings. The demonstration project then is an example of encouraging experimentation in diverse settings so that we can learn from local experience in identifying promising approaches to achieving policy objectives.

It follows that demonstration projects must incorporate funding for policy research. If local variations of the demonstration are not clearly documented and assessed, it will not be possible either to know which ones are more effective or to replicate the successful program model. Therefore, evaluation of some kind is typically a requirement of demonstration projects. This evaluation may be local or cross-site. In local evaluation, the local grant recipient is required to conduct or contract for an independent, local evaluation with reports to the local program and to the funding agency. In direct cross-site evaluations, a single evaluator typically takes a sample of programs and applies a common research design to look for commonalties in effectiveness in program approach. The case studies that follow include a number of examples of local evaluations that have been carried out under the auspices of a demonstration program.

The difficulty presented by demonstration programs is one of attaining standardized information across the dispersed sites so that adequate comparison can be made to establish those approaches which are more effective, particularly in contexts other than the program as locally implemented. Recent literature has addressed the unique requirements of demonstration studies (Springer and Phillips 1994).

As these examples indicate, policy research is increasingly being institutionalized in the public setting in contemporary public decision making. We turn next to the question of how research can make contributions at various phases and stages of the policy-making process and identify distinct roles through which policy research can be delivered.

Decisions and the Policy Sequence

As noted in Chapter 1, policy research may be requested by decision makers throughout the policy process. Although the sequence is complex, scholars of policy making have developed several models of policy-making phases. These models define different decision-environment processes and settings that evolve as a policy moves from initial identification of a problem or need through the decision to act, the implementation of action, and the assessment of results. The discussion here will follow a simple four-phase model (see Table 3.1). This model includes *planning* (determining what needs to be done), *decision and policy making* (deciding exactly how to do it and making a commitment), *implementation and maintenance* (actually carrying out the action), and *evaluation* (assessing the results).

Viewing policy sequentially implies that policies always have clear-cut decision points that define them. However, some scholars have argued that what appear to be policy decisions are, in fact, accidents or the end results of group conflict. This is in part due to the fact that national, state, and even local political systems tend to be pluralistic, meaning that key

TABLE 3.1

The Policy Sequence

1. Planning
2. Decision and policy making
3. Implementation and maintenance
4. Evaluation

policy moves are often made in disjointed, compromised increments rather than by wholly rational means. As noted earlier, the literature of the policy analysis/rational model approach to policy research overestimates the frequency with which decision makers face clear policy choices.

The sequence is also oversimplified in the sense that it is repeated at various points in the actual history of a given policy. Agencies given responsibility for implementation of a legislative mandate, for example, will go through a planning and decision-making process themselves, albeit with more constraints than in the legislature.

Nevertheless, policy researchers as a rule need to be cognizant of where in the sequence of policy their efforts are being directed. Decision makers tend to need different kinds of information at different stages of the policy sequence. Rigorous choice analysis, for example, is more likely to be appropriate at the policy decision stage than at the implementation stage, when key policy decisions have presumably already been made, and options are fewer.

Table 3.2 illustrates the relationship between the policy sequence and the types of information typically required by decision makers at each stage. This matrix is not intended to be definitive; it is probably possible to generate all five kinds of policy research information at any stage of the policy sequence; the matrix depicts the most logical and common needs—those that are particularly salient for each stage. Several patterns deserve comment. First, the prevalence of exploratory and descriptive information needs is evident. They are primary in all but the decision and policy-making phase. Even here, the assumption is that policy options and needs have been clearly defined at the planning stage, and this information underlies the estimation and choice that is the unique concern of the decision stage.

The importance of exploratory and descriptive information follows directly from the situational nature of policy research. Rather than focusing on abstract and relatively stable theory, policy research is embedded

TABLE 3.2

The Relationship Between Policy Stages and Types of Information

Policy Stage	Exploratory	Descriptive	Causal	Estimation	Choice
Planning	√	√		√	
Decision and Policy Making				√	√
Implementation and Maintenance	√				√
Evaluation	√	√	√		

in specific situations in a dynamic and diverse world. The first step in conducting a policy research study is to explore and describe the specific situation to which the analysis applies. This may be a target population at the planning stage, an agency at the implementation stage, or a program in a specific community at the evaluation stage. In any case, exploration and description are essential to setting the parameters and applicability of the study.

As indicated earlier, choice analysis—the information need most closely associated with the policy analysis process and rational model approaches—is associated with the policy decision and implementation stages of policy. These are the points at which resource allocations are made and specific activities are prescribed. Causal research problems—and the impact evaluation methods associated with them—are most dominant at the evaluation stage of policy.

A careful reading of the matrix suggests that policy researchers would be well advised to develop their skill and experience at exploratory and descriptive policy research, for it is nearly always in demand. Most of the case studies in this book involve at least some exploratory or descriptive research, and some are nearly exclusively descriptive. This is arguably a realistic representation of the prevalence and importance of exploratory and descriptive techniques to applied policy research problems.

Policy Researchers

As a rule, policy researchers do not initiate their own applied research projects. Rather they receive opportunities (or orders) to participate from client/decision makers. Therefore, regardless of the frequent vagueness of the policy sequence itself, applied policy research nearly always has a clear beginning point. The means by which policy research is initiated depends in large part on the institutional identities of and the relationship between the decision maker(s)/client(s) and the policy researcher(s).

As Chapter 1 observed, policy research is so ubiquitous in modern government that, inevitably, many kinds of individuals are responsible for it. There are, therefore, many different plausible situations wherein policy research is initiated. However, for the purposes of explaining our approach, we concentrate on two very common scenarios for the initiation of policy research projects: the in-house project and the outside consultant scenarios.

The In-House Project

In the first scenario, a decision maker—usually a manager or director of an executive agency—authorizes a policy research project to be conducted by a member or several members of his or her staff. The selected staff members may be part of a special office that has ongoing responsibility for such projects within the agency, or they may be involved in such efforts only occasionally. In either event, they will usually have relatively vast experience with the issues their superior wants investigated. As an in-house project, the approach may be relatively shielded from the view of other political stakeholders and the general public. Initiation of the project may originate in the form of a memorandum detailing the interests of the director or manager in the issue at hand, or it may be initiated by a request from a legislature or outside agency.

Advantages and Disadvantages

Staff evaluators have opportunities that consultants do not have. They typically know the agency and program context very well and require less time for orientation to the environment and research. They also have access to program information and agency data on a continuing basis.

But staff evaluators also have constraints. They may find it difficult to take an independent and critical stance in conducting their research and making recommendations. They often find themselves in the position of brokering the various objectives and interests of different managers and constituents inside an agency.

Use of Consultants

This second scenario involves the hiring of or some other form of contracting with policy researchers who are not directly associated with the agency that needs the research completed. Most commonly, this will involve a contract with a consulting firm of some kind, but it may also involve a special governmental agency or office that is charged with conducting policy research. In either event, the policy researcher team will not necessarily be particularly familiar with the agency and its specific concerns.

Initiation of such projects often (but not always) stems from some sort of legislative mandate requiring that a policy, program, or agency be evaluated. Frequently, the written legislation of new programs contains a clause mandating an outside evaluation. When that is the case, the agency charged with implementing the new program usually opts to authorize a consulting firm (or individual) to conduct the necessary research.

Sources of Outside Policy Research

A common way to locate and select a qualified consultant to conduct the research is by circulating a request for proposals (RFP). An RFP is a document specifying the scope of the desired research, the required end-products, the available funding, and other details that circumscribe the project. Subsequent to the release of the RFP, consulting firms submit competitive proposals that outline their plans (and budgets) for the requested research. The agency awards the contract to the firm that best meets the criteria outlined in the RFP. Cost may be an important criterion in determining the firm that gets the contract, but it is usually not determinative. (Appendix A contains an example of an RFP.)

The other common means of enlisting outside policy research—mandating an auditing or analysis-oriented agency from within the government itself—may entail a legislative act authorizing the agency to do the research. In this instance, the legislative body (frequently a committee or subcommittee) describes what it wants to find out via the proposed research. Further details concerning the legislature's request are often discussed in conference with representatives of the agency conducting the research.

Outside consultants themselves may be from different professions or organizational settings. The most common source of outside consultation is firms that provide research and management consultation services. At the federal level, numerous large corporations—sometimes referred to as "beltway bandits"—specialize in federal research contracts. Large auditing and accounting firms often compete for policy research contracts focusing on the implementation stage of the policy process.

Universities can be another source of external policy analysts. Universities have research institutes that compete for policy research contracts, and professors may take on smaller research contracts on their own. Some policy analysts move between academic and consulting settings throughout their careers.

Advantages and Disadvantages of Using Consultants

The advantages and disadvantages of using outside evaluators mirror those of staff evaluation. Outside evaluators may require more time to become familiar with the environment and the research, although they may develop considerable familiarity with settings in which they do repeat work. Outside evaluators may also produce less information because they are not as sensitive to the interests and constraints of decision makers. This latter criticism is most often made with respect to university-based evaluators.

Because they are outside of the standard operating procedures of the organization they work with and study, outside evaluators must take special care to establish good communication and working relations with their clients. Earlier in this chapter, many issues related to effectively communicating results that were raised. These issues take on special importance for outside evaluators.

This chapter has focused on the context in which policy analysts work. This environment strongly conditions the tasks that face the analyst. In some instances, the conduct and use of policy research is highly institutionalized. More frequently, the policy analyst must develop an understanding of the context and work closely with clients to encourage use of their information.

Chapter 4 focuses more directly on the planning, organization, and implementation of the tasks of policy analysis itself. Although analysts must be attuned to context, they also must have command of the variety of techniques and methods at their disposal to meet information needs in appropriate ways. Chapter 4 establishes a framework for making these methods decisions.

Discussion Questions

1. What is the difference between data and information, and why is that difference important to the conduct of policy research?
2. Why are "data" frequently of little use to decision makers? How can policy research make data more useful?
3. Why must the production of information be multifaceted? Think of examples of the various modes of producing information for decision makers. Which is(are) most effective, and why?
4. What is a "decision system"? Describe a government agency that you are familiar with and that has something resembling a decision system. Is it effective?
5. Are you familiar with an example of a decision system that incorporates sunset legislation or a demonstration project? Is it effective as such?
6. What are the advantages and disadvantages of the in-house and outside consultant scenarios in producing useful policy research? Which system would you prefer working in? Why?
7. Which part(s) of the policy sequence is(are) most likely to require the use of policy research information. Why?

Assignments and Activities

1. Identify a part of your state or local government that uses something resembling a decision system. Try to link its components to those listed in the diagram in Figure 3.1
2. After identifying several pieces of policy research (see Assignments, Chapter 2), identify who the policy researchers were and under what conditions the policy research was initiated. What part of the policy sequence does the research appear to be linked to?
3. Locate a copy of an RFP, RFA, or similar document that requests outside assistance for policy research. What kind of information need does it address?

CHAPTER 4

How to Design and Conduct Policy Research

A Practical Approach

If set approaches like the policy analysis and program evaluation models are not always ideally suited to the "real-world" information needs of decision makers, how should policy researchers go about their task? How can policy researchers best attune their efforts to the policy process? This chapter proposes a systematic yet flexible step-by-step approach based on our experiences with dozens of research projects. This approach is intended to be more sensitive to the varying contexts under which policy research is conducted, and therefore more practical, than are the other strategies discussed earlier. The proposed approach places explicit emphasis on the information needs of clients and the significance of the policy sequence.

This model is *not* intended to replace other strategies and techniques for conducting policy research; rather, it is intended to put them in applied perspective. Other approaches may easily be incorporated within this framework. For example, if conditions are favorable, the policy analysis process of reasoned choice may be employed as part of a larger research plan. Nor is the model intended to directly explain techniques. The model can be used to help select appropriate tools, techniques, and methods, but it does not explain exactly how to use them (nor does this text). The emphasis is instead upon developing a conceptual (yet practical) framework in which to cast research projects. However, the case studies that follow do demonstrate how various research tools can be applied in real policy research situations. The approach is illustrated in Figure 4.1, with the models' key components and their associated products. The remainder of the chapter discusses the model step by step.

FIGURE 4.1.

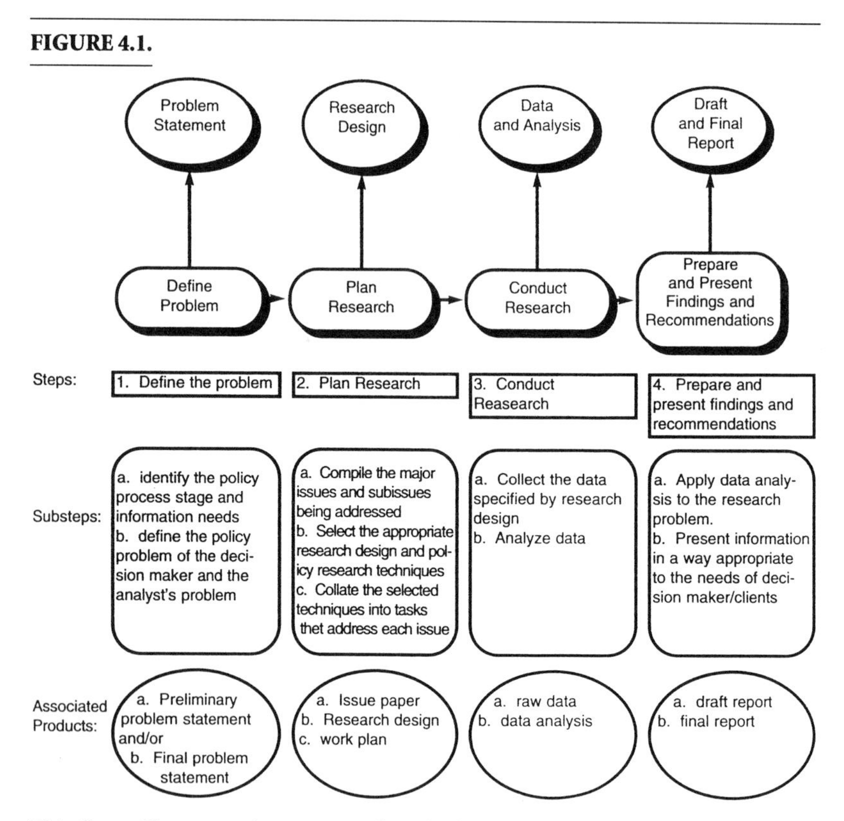

This figure illustrates the sequence by which policy research typically proceeds. Note that not every project will entail each substep and product to the same degree of detail.

Keeping Track of the Details

A successful policy research project will take many twists and turns and produce a multitude of memos and stick-on notes communicating good and bad news. To ensure that nothing gets lost in the cracks, project researchers maintain a project log, an internal document that records all of the many specific decisions and actions associated with a study, as well as notes on events and factors that affect the progress of research. Such a log may be particularly helpful when a project is long and complicated and the work of a team or teams of researcher(s) must be coordinated. The project log is an open-ended document initiated at the onset of a program and maintained to its conclusion.

Define the Problem

Once a potential or actual client has initiated the policy research process, the policy researcher becomes an active participant in the task of *problem definition.* Problem definition is the critical initial step in the research process that sets the stage for everything that follows. But as the discussion of the policy process in Chapter 3 illustrated, problems come to policy researchers in a variety of contexts, including internal memos, legislative mandates, requests for proposals, and other possible interfaces between information consumer and researcher. All of these linkages share defining characteristics: they are usually vague and open-ended. They also are often self-contradictory, overly ambitious, or poorly conceived. A poorly conceived or misconceived understanding of the issues at hand can lead only to research that misses the mark. Generally, the burden falls on the policy researcher to exact a more meaningful definition of the problem so that it will be amenable to systematic research (MacRae and Wilde 1979).

For both the client requesting the research and the policy-researching individual or team, the initial step, then, is to define the research problem. (The word *problem* is a convenient term to connote the issues or areas that concern the client, although such issues may not necessarily represent problems *per se.* One could also think in terms of defining *key questions, issues,* or *areas of interest or concern.*) Problem definition is a daunting task. One practical way to help ensure a proper understanding of the problem is to divide this step into three subcomponents: (a) identifying the policy/process/stage and information needs; (b) defining the policy problem of the decision maker/client; and (c) defining the analyst's problem.

Identify the Policy Process Stage and the Client's Information Needs

Chapter 3 contained the suggestion that an important part of conducting policy research was recognizing both the information needs of the decision maker/client and the position the problem or issue occupies in the policy sequence. Identifying the stage of the policy sequence and the type of information requested by the client will go a long way in shedding light on the actual research problem. Knowing the degree to which the problem is an exploratory, a descriptive, a causal, an estimation, or a choice issue narrows the options of the overall research strategy. However, more substantive information about the problem is also necessary at this juncture.

Define the Client's Policy Problem

At this early stage of the game, the goal is an initial, working definition of the problem at hand. Problem definition is a task that tends to require constant readjustment throughout a policy research project; quite often, the more a researcher knows about a problem, the more its definition may change. It stands to reason, therefore, that the more comprehensive and accurate the problem definition is at the onset of a project, the less time researchers will devote to backtracking later in the process. Some methods that can facilitate problem definition are those associated with exploratory research, especially unstructured interviews with knowledgeable individuals, observation, and literature reviews. Such activities can clarify the range of issues that are necessary or important to the policy problem or objective and that probably will be affected by the actions of the client.

The process of problem definition is sometimes called "scoping" the problem. Patton and Sawicki (1993:13) refer to the boundaries of analysis established during problem definition as the "policy envelope." The form of the policy envelope itself is often unclear because there are often mismatches between the factors that influence the policy problem and the factors that the client controls.

Defining the exact scope of issues may require negotiation and discussion with the client. Much of the challenge of policy research will be determining how the client's concerns can be adequately met within the limitations that inevitably circumscribe the research project.

Define the Analyst's Problem

A useful concept that speaks to the heart of the challenge of problem definition is that of the *analyst's problem.* The analyst's problem is always somewhat different from the *problem situation,* the problem as presented by the client (MacRae and Wilde 1979:17). A policy researcher must recast the problem situation into a practical, manageable, and hopefully *actionable* framework for analysis. According to MacRae and Wilde (1979:17–18), the analyst's modifications of the client's problem situation may depend on "your own values, the time and resources you have for analysis, your interaction with those affected, your eventual findings, or the positions of the persons or groups on whom you depend for putting your recommendations into action." In other words, policy researchers must be able to live with the problems they agree to research. A crucial characteristic of the analyst's problem is that it has clear links to available or collectible data and feasible research techniques.

Associated Products: The Preliminary and Final Problem Statements

At this early point in the research process, only confidential "internal" documents need be produced. The *preliminary problem statement* is a brief description of the major problems or questions to be addressed by the research, including pertinent background information. This statement is helpful in focusing efforts at the onset of a project. Although the preliminary problem statement is for internal use only and may change as understanding about the problem increases, it may later be incorporated into the research proposal or other products. It will eventually be sufficiently refined to become a more definitive product, the *problem statement.*

A good problem statement fulfills three functions:

- It expresses a specific problem in a meaningful way.
- It eliminates irrelevant issues and information.
- It focuses on critical, *actionable* aspects of the problem.

Plan the Research

Effective planning is critical to efficient use of research resources—primarily time and money—and is also necessary to ensure valid, useful results. The importance of planning cannot be overemphasized because the planning step links the task of problem definition to actual data collection and analysis efforts. A systematic approach to planning a policy research project could include the following steps:

- Compile the major issues and subissues to be addressed.
- Select appropriate research design and policy research techniques.
- Collate the appropriate policy research techniques into tasks that will adequately address the issues identified in step two of the process.

Compile the Major Issues and Subissues

Once a working draft of the problem statement has been developed, further analysis of the problem into major issues and subissues is usually necessary and helpful. Breaking a problem down into subissues ensures that research will be comprehensive enough to address the entire problem. It may also provide a means of double checking that the problem selected in this step is not excessively broad or vague. There is no one best way to go about the task of analyzing and expanding upon an initial problem statement. The following generic strategies may, however, be applicable.

- *Analysis by program component* Typically, a program or policy selected for research will include several components. Components for a job training program, for example, might be counseling, training, placement, and supervised employment. An appropriate means of framing research about such a program could include evaluation of the effectiveness of each component. The specific issues that would be researched will be somewhat different for each component.
- *Analysis by program goals* Another way of analyzing a problem is to examine its stated (or unstated) goals and objectives. Goals and objectives may cross-cut program components but may nevertheless be a more sensible way of looking at a research problem. This is particularly true when a program has clear (perhaps legislatively mandated) goals and objectives.
- *Analysis by agency participation* Many public policies and programs entail participation of and coordination with several public agencies. In such cases, separately researching the contributions of each agency may be a profitable strategy. Mental health policy, for example, frequently requires cooperation among mental health agencies, social service agencies, housing agencies, rehabilitation agencies, and others.
- *Analysis by program procedures or processes* Public programs frequently constitute a chain of sequenced events. One way of analyzing such programs is to identify each critical event and determine the key issues associated with it. For example, critical events in a work-release program at a prison might be screening of candidates for the program, selection of participants, prerelease

counseling, identification of outside sponsors, development of a release work plan, release of participants, monitoring of participants, and so on.

- *Analysis by designated research methods* Occasionally a research project will be structured by methods mandated by the client or mandating authority. For example, a public agency may commission a survey. Because the "problem" in this case is conducting the survey itself, analysis will probably begin with looking at the individual steps that must be taken to complete the survey: developing the survey sample, developing the survey instrument, pretesting the survey instrument, and so on.

Select the Research Design and Research Techniques

This is a major decision point in the policy research planning process. At this point, preliminary decisions about the overall research strategy will be made. In this context, *research design* refers to major research methods that will be used in the project. For example, the research design for a study of parking problems in a central urban area could include the following major methods:

1. An analysis of parking revenues by time of day and geographic area
2. A survey of local business owners
3. Focus-group interviews with parking enforcement personnel
4. A survey of downtown workers

Of course, additional details for each of these methods would be necessary. For example, how will revenue data be analyzed? How will businesses be selected for the survey? Will the survey be conducted over the phone or by mail? And so on.

If the task of problem definition has been properly executed, and appropriate data are available, selecting appropriate methods should be fairly straightforward. Problem definition should provide an indication of whether the problem calls for exploratory, descriptive, causal, estimation, or choice analysis. Methods will be selected from those associated with each type of research. The second major source of guidance in the selection of research methods is available existing data. For example, if an agency already collects comprehensive data that are relevant to the research problem, original data sources like surveys may be unnecessary. Hence an important part of selecting research methods is reviewing existing data sources.

Collate the Research Techniques into Tasks That Address the Issues

The objective here is to ensure that a source of information will be created for each issue and subissue developed in Step 2. The challenge is linking the appropriate means of gathering that information to each issue to ensure that the task adequately addresses the issue.

The amount of resources available for the project is a crucial consideration in this planning step. Resources may be constrained by a budget written into the contract or by organization customs or regulations. Among the major sources of expense in a typical research project are personnel, travel, equipment, printing, and overhead support costs. Additionally, some requests for proposals (RFPs) and other research requests specify the methods to be employed in a prospective project, such as cost-benefit analysis or surveys. In this case, the task of assembling research methods may address more technical details of the project. Translating the major research design components of a project into specific tasks is a critical means of ensuring that project resources match the conceptual scope of the project.

Associated Products: The Research Proposal and the Work Plan

The Research Proposal

If the policy research has been initiated by means of an RFP, the problem statement, issues paper, and work plan will be incorporated into a *research proposal.* The research proposal will be structured according to the specifications enumerated in the RFP. In other instances, policy research may be initiated through legislative mandate, through attempts to influence policy or judicial decisions, or through informal requests by legislators, administrators, or other interested parties. In these cases problem statements and research plans may remain internal and may not be articulated in a formal document such as a proposal.

The RFP process typically forces analysts to articulate issues and considerations that are important to the success of any policy research project. RFPs usually require the following kinds of information.

1. *Background* This section will typically contain the consultant's initial take on defining the research problem. Frequently, only a portion of the background information necessary to complete a research proposal will be contained in the RFP or other initiating documents. In that case, the applicant is obliged to research the issue at hand. In some cases, this "preresearch" can entail a fairly significant effort, including formal data collection efforts. The recent history of the policy issue, including institutional responsibilities (such as the agencies and key individuals involved in implementing the programs in question) are normally included in the background section of the proposal.
2. *Understanding of the Problem* RFP respondents will typically be asked to state clearly their understanding of the major research questions to be answered through the requested study. This statement of the research questions involves discussion of why these questions are important for addressing a significant policy or program issue. Problem statements may include a list of specific information objectives to be fulfilled in the project.
3. *Scope of Work* Minimally, this section includes an outline of the major research tasks and products envisioned by the policy research team. As a rule, the research and design and methods described in this section are provisional, subject to (negotiated) change as work on the project progresses. Nevertheless, completing this section of the proposal requires that the researcher envision appropriate methods despite lacking comprehensive familiarity with the research issue.
4. *Timeline* The timeline provides a set of dates for the completion of the major tasks outlined in the Scope of Work section of the proposal. Project management techniques, such as a Gantt chart, may be of use in planning more complicated projects (see, for example, Burman 1972).
5. *Budget* A policy research project budget will typically contain estimates for the following categories of expenditures: personnel, materials (including printing costs), travel expenses, equipment, and overhead expenses.

6. *Personnel* In this section the applicant lists the individuals who will actually conduct the proposed research. Usually included will be the resumes of the key staff assigned to the project, and their respective roles. The following roles may appear.

    - Principal investigator or project director: Responsible for overall direction and supervision
    - Research coordinator: Manager of the technical aspects of project
    - Research consultants: People who provide technical assistance in research design, data analysis, and report writing
    - Research assistants: People who collect and code data and assist in data analysis
    - Project secretary: Person who provides secretarial support for research (Putt and Springer 1989:366).

7. *Organizational Capabilities* In this section, the applicant describes the firm's qualifications and experience that are relevant to the project under consideration. The listing may include descriptions of organizational resources the firm will provide, such as computers and other hardware, offices, telecommunication and printing equipment, and libraries.

The Work Plan

The RFP's Scope of Work statement and Timeline can serve as the framework for the *preliminary work plan,* an internal document providing further elaboration on the specific activities that will comprise the research design. The preliminary work plan should also contain or accompany an *analysis plan,* which specifies as closely as possible exactly what will be done with any data collected. The analysis plan should tie each piece of data collection and analysis into one or more of the questions or issues identified in the applicant's statement of the research problem. Ensuring that these ties are made helps to minimize unnecessary and/or irrelevant data collection. A common problem with research plans is that they overload projects with data collection that proves either excessive or unnecessary. Clearly specifying the purpose and use of each data element can minimize this problem.

Collect and Analyze Data as Specified in the Work Plan

Data collection and analysis comprise the major part of the policy research effort. Notwithstanding the best-laid research plans, however, the products from the preceding steps in the process often require modification. Quite commonly, problem definition statements change as familiarity with the problem situation increases. Concomitantly, research methods and tasks also must be updated. For example, a project that at first blush appears to require causal analysis may require more in the way of descriptive research to augment the causal portion.

Associated Products: Raw Data for Analysis

The shape of data analysis depends on the methods employed in the project. In the case of quantitative data, the goal is to produce tables, charts, and graphs that distill the essence of whatever analysis has been conducted. More quantitative data require initial compression into summary reports that can be incorporated in the draft report. Qualitative data, drawn from sources such as interviews and field observations, require careful integration into analytic statements. In some instances, primarily qualitative data can be summarized quantitatively.

Organize and Present Information as Appropriate for the Client's Needs

Writing a policy research report is a challenging task; there is no set blueprint for the design of research reports. Just as problem definition and the research design must be created with the client's information needs as a paramount consideration, so must the final report speak to those needs. Report writing is more of an art than a science. However, several techniques can help to ensure an effective report (see, for example, Rothman 1980).

Associated Products: The Draft Report and the Final Report

Both draft reports and final reports can follow a variety of outlines. One strategy would be to organize the report following the same analytic strategy when dividing the problem into issues in Step 3. Morris, Fitz-

Gibbon, and Freeman (1987:77–89) present a generic policy research outline that may prove useful for many kinds of studies. Regardless of the outline selected, most reports also contain a title page, an executive summary, a table of contents, an introduction, conclusions and/or recommendations, and appendices (Putt and Springer 1989:376–378).

Draft reports may be distinguished as those that are circulated to the client and those that remain in-house. Putt and Springer (1989) emphasize the *necessity* of involving users in research projects. To help accomplish this, policy researchers frequently circulate draft and/or interim reports to clients: "Through maintaining linkages with users, project directors reap dividends in keeping interested parties committed to the project, thereby enhancing subsequent usage" (Putt and Springer 1989:375).

A key distinction in final reports is among those that contain recommendations and those that do not. The decision of whether to include recommendations is usually imparted by the client/decision maker, although it may be negotiated with the policy maker at the onset of the project.

Caveats on the Use of the Model

The policy research model we have described is intended as a general guide to conducting policy research in the multitude of contexts in which it occurs. However, not every project will be well served by the model. For example, academic research projects—which frequently are not client-centered—generally have much more latitude in selecting and defining research problems and information needs. So-called quick analysis problems (Patton and Sawicki 1993:158–163), limited in scope and duration, do not allow enough time to follow this model in its entirety.

Our model, like every policy research model, tends to exaggerate the extent to which policy research can be conducted in a well-planned, rational, and step-by-step fashion. As emphasized earlier, real policy research frequently involves backtracking as problem definitions and appropriate research methods change during the course of a project. Even if the model is not followed in the precise order presented here, however, most projects will need to address the same tasks and products.

This model purposely underemphasizes the role of policy research techniques and methods, on the assumption that readers will acquire methodological expertise elsewhere. The model is intended to provide a framework for putting those techniques to work. Part Two, Case Studies in Policy Research, uses examples of actual research projects to illustrate how this model compares with actual policy research practice.

Discussion Questions

1. What are the major differences between the policy research model presented in this chapter and the policy analysis approach described in Chapter 2?
2. Why will the order of the steps in the model not always be accurate for a given project?
3. What is the difference between the analyst's problem and the problem situation? What ethical dilemma might be posed by this distinction?
4. What parts of a policy research project are likely to be the most expensive?

Assignments and Activities

1. Again looking at policy research you have located (see Assignments, Chapter 2), how is the report organized?
2. Does the report present information in such a way as to be useful for its intended audience of decision makers? Explain your answer.
3. Using the RFP presented in Appendix A, propose an appropriate preliminary problem statement and issue paper. Write an appropriate research design and work plan in outline form.

PART II

Case Studies in Policy Research

Overview

Eight of the nine remaining chapters of this book are case studies of actual examples of policy research. The ninth chapter comments on these cases. The case studies reflect some of the many different forms policy research can assume, and they were selected to help illustrate the concepts explored in Part One. They include various types of information needs, different parts of the policy sequence, a variety of policy research clients and stakeholders (including different levels of government), and so on. The case studies are as follows:

- Chapter 5, The Emergency Substance Abuse Treatment and Rehabilitation Block Grant (Anti-Drug Abuse Act of 1986): Improving Government Procedures
- Chapter 6, Evaluation of the California Ignition Interlock Pilot Program: A Policy Experiment
- Chapter 7, The Extended National Youth Sports Program (ENYSP): A Formative Evaluation
- Chapter 8, Deinstitutionalization and Community Services in Virginia: A Policy Assessment
- Chapter 9, Evaluation of Welfare-to-Work Programs: The St. Louis POWER Demonstration

- Chapter 10, The Southwest Texas State High-Risk Youth Program: Policy Research and Professional Practice
- Chapter 11, The Dropout Prevention Mentor Project: Delivering Unexpected Messages Through Policy Research
- Chapter 12, Housing Sales in Urban Neighborhoods: Using Policy Research to Inform Planning

Most of these case studies are formally "evaluations" of programmatic efforts. This is partly attributable to the authors' intent to fill a gap in the literature concerning policy research that is directly relevant to state and local decision makers. Evaluation is a prominent policy research input at this level.

Nevertheless, the cases demonstrate a great variety of applications of evaluation findings at different points in the policy cycle as well as different types of information needs. Evaluation of demonstration programs, for example, have application in policy formulation; formative evaluations have application to program implementation, and so on.

Each case study follows a similar organization that serves to highlight how the policy research exemplifies concepts identified in the previous chapters. The outline follows a fairly consistent pattern that usually includes the following headings.

Introduction

The chapter title gives the title of the policy research project. The introduction gives some background and highlights the policy research concepts that the case study best exemplifies.

The Policy Problem

This subsection describes the policy context of the research. The discussion typically includes the basic background and history of the policy and/or programs that the research addresses. It helps establish why the policy research was necessary, and what it may contribute to policy decisions. Some of the case studies address very specific programs and others deal with broader policy concerns.

Initiation of Policy Research

This subsection includes discussion of who requested the research, who conducted it, and why. The case studies reflect a variety of contexts for both client and researcher. Clients include local, state, and federal government agencies as well as nonprofit organizations. Policy researchers include government agencies, consulting agencies, and individuals. Additionally, the case studies represent different *mechanisms* for initiation of policy research, including legislative mandates, requests for proposals (RFPs), and more informal means.

The Policy Research Task

This subsection includes a general, introductory discussion of the nature and scope of the policy research task implied by the request from the decision maker. This discussion includes the nature, rigor, and scope of the actual research requirement, but also includes tasks related to establishing relations with the client, clarifying study purposes, and communicating the requirements and limitations of the research task to the client.

Objectives

This subsection outlines the general purposes of the policy research; what did the policy research team need to accomplish? The decisions may include specific objectives as stated by the client, or objectives that were developed by the policy researcher. In some instances the negotiation of specific objectives is an important part of the overall policy research task.

Challenges

Each policy research task involves unique conditions, often constraints, that represent challenges for policy researchers. This section helps to clarify how the realities of the research context affect the research process, and how policy researchers must be responsive and creative in addressing these realities.

The Decision Context

A major factor distinguishing policy research from other types of research is the intention to use it directly for decision-making purposes—policy-related, programmatic, or managerial. The context of the policy research is examined in this section from the perspective of its use—the extent and nature of its potential impact on decisions.

The Institutional Context

Understanding the identity and functions of the agencies and organizations involved in providing the services that are the subject of study is a critical step toward conducting policy research. This section describes the key agencies, organizations, and individuals involved in making decisions pertinent to the case study research projects. Some studies focus on only one organization, whereas in others many organizations participate in the decisions.

The Policy Cycle

Policy research may be necessary at any point during the policy cycle explored in Part One. The case studies illustrate the significance of the context of the policy cycle; each study occurs at a different point in the cycle, with significant implications for how policy research is conducted.

Clients and Stakeholders

The case studies represent policy research that has affected a wide variety of clients and stakeholders. Different clients generally connote different kinds of information needs and research products. The case studies view these needs and products from several angles.

Research Design and Implementation

Given the policy background and decision context explored in the previous sections, this section provides a detailed overview of how policy research was actually conducted in each case. First, the information needs of the client—the driving force behind effective policy research—are explored. Then the specific research design components, including techniques and methods, are laid out and explained. Finally, some of the key findings derived from those methods are presented, including an explanation of how the methods led to the research findings.

Information Needs

Chapter 2 emphasized the significance of the information needs of decision makers in shaping policy research. Each case discusses the information needs of the various decision makers, relating them to the typology of needs discussed in that chapter. Because real research situations virtually always require a variety of types of information, the discussion in some cases identifies the relative priority of different information needs.

One of the most important decisions that policy researchers, in consultation with their clients and others, must make is how to limit the scope of policy research. Without such limits policy research can easily become overly broad, which may reduce the utility of the findings. Thus, this subsection may also contain discussion of the boundaries or "policy envelope" of each case study.

Design and Methods

Each case study includes a description of both the overall research design and the specific techniques or methods used to implement it. The designs range from those that are relatively simple, straightforward, and structured to those that involve multiple methods and complex interpretations. The discussion of design and method includes explication of the logic of the research, and the rationale for selection of data collection and analytic techniques. The discussion emphasizes tradeoffs between technical and practical considerations, and the differences between research considerations and usage considerations.

Selected Findings

Although space limitations do not permit exposition of all findings, each case study includes key, representative excerpts from the findings of each project. In most instances, the findings include tables drawn from the original policy research. Furthermore, the findings are linked to the research methods described earlier in each case study.

Communicating and Using Results

Once a policy research study is complete, the findings and interpretations must be communicated to potential users. Traditionally, this has been done through technical reports, but policy researchers interested in fostering use of their findings are turning to other modes of communication. The story of a piece of policy research is not complete until the resulting policy actions are identified.

Reporting Results

This subsection provides a description of how the research findings were organized and presented, including a discussion of how written reports were organized, as well as efforts to enhance the dissemination of the research products. Where appropriate, other means of communicating with stakeholders are discussed.

Selected Recommendations

When appropriate, several of the more significant recommendations that emerged from the research findings are presented. In other instances, other avenues of influence on the decision-making process are described.

Action

To what extent did the findings and recommendations generated by the policy research result in action by decision makers? In keeping with the theme of a broader understanding of how and when research is used, each case concludes with a discussion of the extent and nature of the influences the research had on decisions or institutions.

Lessons for Policy Research

This section links the specific experiences recounted in each case study to more general themes about how policy research should be conducted in order to best improve the decision-making process. In most instances, these lessons serve both to illustrate and to build upon some of the themes explored in Part One.

Focus on Research Methods

In each case study, a box with this title highlights some specific research method featured in the project. The discussion explores the method in greater detail than in the case study narrative and weighs some of the practical pros and cons of the method. References are provided for those who would like more information on the method.

Case Study at a Glance

Each chapter contains a second box that summarizes the case study and how it exemplifies several of the key concepts described in Part One. These summaries provide a convenient means of reviewing the principal lessons drawn from each case study.

CHAPTER 5

The Emergency Substance Abuse Treatment and Rehabilitation Block Grant (Anti-Drug Abuse Act of 1986)

Improving Government Procedures

Introduction

This case study provides an example of an exploratory research problem. The Evaluation of the Alcohol and Drug Treatment and Rehabilitation Block Grant was conducted by a consulting firm in 1989. The project explores implementation of a federal grant program on a statewide basis in California. The case study demonstrates how an open-ended problem can provide useful information and recommendations to decision makers.* It also exemplifies the research challenges inherent in exploring a large, complex, and geographically disparate program in an intergovernmental context.

The Policy Problem

In the late 1980s, drug and alcohol abuse were widely perceived as a national crisis. Much of the federal policy response to the drug problem during the Reagan and Bush administrations had been in the form of

*This case study is based largely on a report by the EMT Group, Inc. (EMT Group 1991a).

stepped-up drug interdiction and related law-enforcement efforts. However, critics of this "supply-side" effort believed that drug (and alcohol) treatment, as well as education and prevention programs, were a necessary complement to the "war on drugs." In response to this impulse for drug policy change, Congress passed the Anti-Drug Abuse Act of 1986 (for background on this issue, see, for example, Sharp 1994).

Initiation of Policy Research

The Anti-Drug Abuse Act of 1986 was intended to provide emergency funds to increase provision of alcohol and drug abuse services. A nationally created program, the Act authorized state governments to fund drug and alcohol programs by means of Alcohol and Drug Abuse Treatment and Rehabilitation (ADTR) block grants. Unlike more rigid categorical grant programs, the ADTR block grants were provided for the general purpose of increasing the state's ability to meet the need and demand for alcohol and drug abuse treatment and rehabilitation. The block grant strategy was based on the assumption that state legislatures and agencies were in the best position to determine how to spend the funds to achieve those purposes.

ADTR funds were authorized by amendments included in Title IV of the Anti-Drug Abuse Act of 1986. This title, or portion of the legislation, addressed drug and alcohol "demand reduction" efforts and included additional subtitles such as "Drug-Free Schools and Communities," "Indians and Alaska Natives," and "Miscellaneous Provisions." Enacted in October of 1986, the legislation contained a 186-page "Purpose of the Act," which is broad in scope, establishing initiatives including those: "To provide strong federal leadership in establishing effective drug abuse prevention and education programs, to expand federal support for drug abuse treatment and rehabilitation efforts, and for other purposes."

Drug and alcohol programs may generally be divided into the categories of interdiction, prevention/education, and treatment. While the overall intent of ADTR cited in the Purpose of the Act recognized the importance of prevention and education, the explicit language of the act emphasized more focused intent concerning treatment.

Thus, the major purpose of ADTR (as revealed in the act and in hearings conducted prior to its enactment) was to provide states with added financial resources to provide treatment and rehabilitation services to users of drugs and alcohol. According to the act, ADTR funds could be used for such purposes as:

1. activities to *increase the availability and outreach of programs* provided by major treatment centers and regional branches of such centers that provide services in a state in order to reach the greatest number of people.
2. activities to *expand the capacity* of abuse and drug abuse treatment and rehabilitation programs and facilities to provide services for those who have been refused treatment due to lack of facilities and or personnel.

The legislation, therefore, was intended to increase service levels in drug and alcohol treatment programs. The congressional committee report that preceded the act stated that the ADTR funds were "intended to deal with an emerging drug abuse crisis which requires the training of treatment counselors and expansion of treatment services in response to increased demand."

The federal origins of the program thus reflect a broad legislative intent. The enabling legislation does not attempt to prescribe services to be delivered, but rather to meet the *general* needs of state governments. Guidance for the use of ADTR funds is notable for its breadth and the discretion it grants to states.

In many ways, this legislation typifies the level of specificity contained in the laws creating many programs that policy researchers evaluate. The ADTR law encourages, but does not really require, that states use the funds to do a variety of things. For example, it uses language that urges states to "provide leadership," and expand treatment "to effective education and prevention." Such broad language presents a challenge to policy researchers, who must in effect narrow down the criteria by which policies are judged.

The ADTR grants brought a significant increase in federal funds for alcohol and other drug programs, but the funds arrived in an atmosphere of uncertainty. There was little time for states (and therefore counties) to plan how to best use the funds. The implicit assumptions were that a need existed for these funds and that they could be put to good use within the existing service system. The funds also were announced and perceived among recipients as one-time-only funds, although a second year of funding was eventually approved. The lack of certainty about long-term availability constrained the ways in which funds were used in many counties.

The Policy Research Task

The evaluation requirements attached to the ADTR funding reflected the broad intent and general language of the overall allocation. States were required to spend a significant amount of the budget (approximately 10 percent) to evaluate the program, but no explicit information objectives were set. In California, counties were responsible for detailed decisions concerning services in the alcohol and other drugs field, so state level officials also left the explicit definition of evaluation requirements very open. In sum, the ADTR evaluation task was very loosely defined in the request for proposals from outside contractors.

Objectives

The external evaluation team that submitted the successful bid for the ADTR project had wide discretion in defining exact research objectives, even after the award of the contract. This team had long experience working with the agency, and saw this well-founded but open research design as an opportunity to explore issues that might be important in improving the state's policy-making and policy guidance mechanisms. Accordingly, the team set the following major objectives:

- To clearly document the flow of ADTR funds from the state to the counties; from the counties to programs or providers; and from providers to specific client services.
- To use multiple methods to assess the degree to which the funds actually increased or enhanced targeted services.
- To generate information and make recommendations concerning the degree to which different mechanisms for allocating funds (for example, assessing need, selecting providers) effected the attainment of funding purposes.

Challenges

A number of factors posed challenges for policy research in this case:

- The legislative intent for the program was vague and multifaceted.
- Clear-cut goals and objectives were absent.
- There were few effective restrictions on the use of the ADTR

funds, so judging the appropriateness of their disbursement was to be problematic.

- The client's informational needs were not well specified.
- Existing data regarding ADTR were fragmented and incomplete, due to the relative autonomy of counties in the system, and were not well suited to detailed or highly precise analysis. (If the data had been more comprehensive, the state Department of Alcohol and Drug Programs [DADP] might have elected to conduct an in-house study.)
- The diversity of programs and activities authorized by ADTR meant that the research plan would have to be flexible and incorporate a variety of program goals and strategies. Although the overall tenor of the project was exploratory, for example, some descriptive and causal analysis was also appropriate. For example, one key research issue was to determine the impact of the grants on local funding priorities. Although this issue is not amenable to analysis by means of a traditional experimental research design, it does call for a causal approach.
- The extreme intergovernmental character of the program—federal, state, county, and nonprofit organizations all had considerable discretion in the program—focused attention on the interaction between governmental entities. But such issues are difficult to explore definitively. For example, how could decisions about the impact on county priorities of allocation and regulations at the state level best be determined?
- Perhaps most significant, the ADTR program did not establish precise objectives or clear criteria for success, placing the burden of these tasks on the policy research project.
- The targeting requirement in the legislation suggested that measurement of the characteristics of the persons and/or communities served would be an important part of the research, despite the lack of clarity about program goals.

The Decision Context

The ADTR grant was initiated from within a fairly complex set of institutional arrangements and processes. Many stakeholders had at least an indirect interest in the study outcome. Because of the legislative mandate for the research, there was some hope that the study results would have perceptible impact on policy in this area.

The Institutional Context

In California, counties are deeply involved in planning and implementing state-funded alcohol and other drug services. Each year, the counties submit an alcohol and drug program plan to DADP—the state Department of Alcohol and Drug Programs; the plan includes a preliminary budget and explanatory material on proposed expenditures of funds from federal, state, and local sources. The state's decisions are based fundamentally on the county plans. Ultimately, funding under the program proceeded through a multigovernmental maze, as illustrated by Figure 5.1.

Thus, county agencies bear responsibility for developing detailed decisions concerning alcohol and drug policy and expenditures. ADTR funds were administered in the context of this highly decentralized system, although the state usually made minor modifications in the county plans. The 58 California counties differ greatly in population, urbanization, and other factors that affect the need for alcohol and drug services, so need, planning, priorities, and service capabilities vary significantly among counties.

Furthermore, the statewide information system does not provide fully standardized reporting for all counties. The lack of complete, centralized, and standardized information on drug and alcohol services makes comprehensive monitoring efforts difficult.

FIGURE 5.1.

The ADTR Funding Process

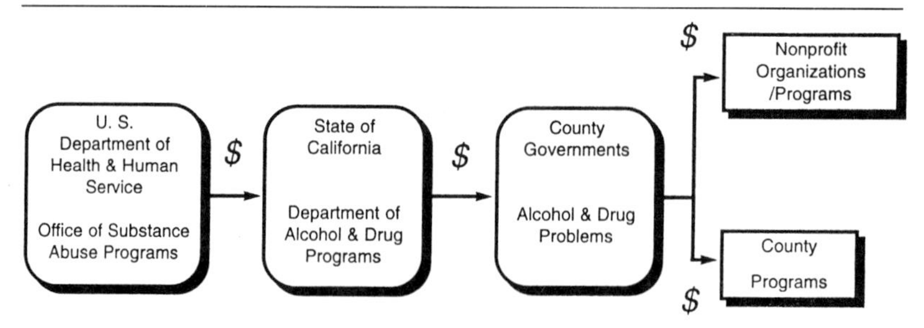

This diagram illustrates the complexity of ADTR funding, which flowed from the national government, through state and county agencies to service providers in both governmental and nonprofit agencies.

The Policy Cycle

The policy research associated with this case study was initiated by the state DADP. The research was mandated, however, by the federal government, which specified that a certain amount of the ADTR funds be dedicated to evaluation of the use of the grant in individual states. The research follows the implementation of the program across the state, although at the time of the research it was unclear to all concerned how long the grant would continue to fund the programs it created.

Effectively, the research was to be conducted during the policy implementation stage—from the perspective of the ADTR grant. The policy had already been *initiated*—the key decisions about how to use the ADTR funds were made before the evaluation began. Some of the activities, however, preceded the administration of the grant, whereas others were spurred by the grant itself. Programs in the latter category were in some cases in the initiation stages. Presumably, many of the activities were to continue past the life of the grant and others would be disbanded if the grant was discontinued.

What implications did the policy sequence have for the policy research problem? When considered as over 500 separately funded and managed programs, ADTR activity was incredibly disjointed. Clearly, programs that had existed for years could not be examined in the same manner as those created as a result of the ADTR program.

Difficulties in disentangling the effects of ADTR grants from ongoing trends also could be anticipated. Federal grants like ADTR are often intended to provide incentives for governments below the national level to create new programs. In this instance, policy researchers needed to be able to distinguish between expenditures that would have been made in the absence of the grant program and those that were the result of the grant.

Clients and Stakeholders

The client for this project was the California Department of Alcohol and Drug Programs, the agency that was the direct recipient of the federal block grant funds. Federal grant programs channel federal money to state or local governments, enabling the national government to address local problems without necessarily directly intervening. A block grant is generally a relatively large grant that is directed to a policy area—in this case, drug and alcohol abuse—with relatively few restrictions on its use.

The state of California opted to use its allocation of more than $20 million to fund *county* drug and alcohol abuse programs. In California, many state-funded programs are implemented by corresponding agencies in the 58 counties' agencies. Just as the state received broad discretion from the federal government in the use of the ADTR grant, so did the counties receive a free hand from the California state legislature. Counties were authorized to use the funds for treatment, rehabilitation, and prevention within spending guidelines that targeted funds for special populations such as racial minorities, women, the aged, the disabled, and the homeless.

The counties in turn frequently enlisted the assistance of private, nonprofit social service agencies to provide direct services to the targeted groups. Increasingly, government agencies turn to such contractor agencies to implement policies without (directly) using their own employees. Donald Kettl (1988) has labeled this growing reliance on nongovernmental agencies "government by proxy." He argues that governmental reliance on intermediaries is often problematic, although not always unsuccessful.

For policy researchers, use of outside contractors to implement programs adds another layer of stakeholders (and therefore additional complexity) to evaluating public programs. This program was (a) funded by the federal government, (b) administered by state governments, (c) managed by county governments, and frequently (d) implemented by nonprofit private agencies, or "providers." Although the client in this case is a state agency, the project invokes the interest of a multitude of policy actors.

Research Design and Implementation

Given a fair amount of leeway with which to work, the policy research team devised a project that would both provide the state DADP with answers to its mandated questions and yet also provide insight into why the grant worked the way it did, or failed to work.

Information Needs

This case is unique in that, outside of some general guidelines, the policy research was almost entirely open-ended. The Anti-Drug Abuse Act itself did not prescribe specific services or outcomes to be funded; rather it reflected a federal effort to meet the general needs of states. Therefore, the policy research team operated under conditions of maximal flexibility to define the research problem, design a research plan, and so on.

Not coincidentally, the client in this case study, the California DADP, faced an extraordinary amount of uncertainty about the ADTR program. The program represented an unexpected influx of federal revenues at a time when such revenues were generally in decline. The enabling legislation required that California account for its use of ADTR funds and also demonstrate that it had upheld the letter (if not the spirit) of the Anti-Drug Abuse Act of 1986. At the same time, the agency was encumbered with the task of allocating the funds and conducting conventional auditing responsibilities. The magnitude of the task of evaluating the ADTR program was beyond DADP day-to-day capabilities, and the services of a consulting firm were enlisted by means of the request-for-proposal (RFP) process.

Preliminary interviews with DADP staff indicated that the agency was particularly concerned with the following issues:

1. How was ADTR money being spent by county governments?
2. Were the processes of allocating funds, setting priorities, use planning, and monitoring appropriate and effective? How did they affect the use of funds?
3. Were groups targeted by ADTR receiving services?
4. Were new programs and/or new clients being funded, or were funds merely maintaining old service levels?
5. What implications did the above issues have for the implementation procedures used by DADP?

The information needs represented by these issues are quite vague and open-ended, although in some cases more pointed. Clearly, DADP was facing neither a clear-cut choice of policy alternatives (a choice problem) nor trying to determine whether ADTR-funded services were effective (a causal problem). Rather, the agency was attempting to acquire baseline information about a brand-new program, unsure whether the program was being implemented in a manner consistent with federal and state legislative priorities.

In some cases, the needed information was rather specific, such as the issue of whether targeted groups were receiving services. In other cases, broad, open-ended information was the goal, such as the issue of how ADTR processes affected implementation and funds allocations. In sum, DADP was facing an exploratory research problem that also entailed several descriptive issues.

Research Design and Methods

The concerns outlined in the preceding section necessitated a flexible, multifaceted research approach that emphasized project description while exploring for potential issues. As noted earlier, the ADTR program represented a federal, state, county, and private nonprofit partnership. Research activities were planned that corresponded to each of these strata of participants. Because so little was known about the shape and impact of the program, a good deal of original data collection was appropriate. Multiple data sources were used whenever possible to corroborate potentially unreliable information.

Research Design

Because of the primarily exploratory nature of the information needs of the client, the research design placed considerable emphasis on qualitative data, including documentary analysis, site visits and observation, and interviews. These efforts served to help put into context the quantitative information (primarily fiscal) that was collected.

The resulting research design was multimethod, and sought to integrate relevant information from events at federal, state, county, and provider levels. The strategy for the design was to maximize flexibility and openness to unanticipated findings. Given the framework of broad discretion in ADTR decision making, it was impossible to anticipate exactly what research questions would be most important. The multimethod approach was consistent with the largely exploratory information needs of DADP.

Research Methods

The specific data collection and analysis methods used in the project, categorized by level of jurisdiction they were associated with, were as follows:

1. *Federal Level*

- *Document review,* including enabling legislation (P.L. 99–57); House Report 99–792; congressional debate; U.S. Department of Health and Human Services (DHHS) Block Grant Regulations; and correspondence between DHHS and California governor's office. *These documents were used to help clarify the legislative mandate for the program and its history in the state of California.*

2. *State Level*

- *Interviews* with Department of Alcohol and Drug Programs staff. *These interviews were used to help establish the goals, objectives, and strategies of the state's staff with primary policy responsibility for the ADTR program.*
- *Documentary analysis,* including

— state's application to the U.S. Department of Health and Human Services for ADTR funds

— DADP instructions to counties clarifying use of funds and cost restrictions

— DADP Federal Fund Expenditure Plans for the three most recent fiscal years (FY 1987–1989)

These documents were an important data source that detailed exactly how federal funds were supposed to be spent.

- *Analysis of existing data,* including

— County Alcohol Program Plans (FY 1987–1988 and FY 1988–1989);

— County Drug Program Plans (FY 1987–1988 and FY 1988–1989); and

— County "Intended Use of Anti-Drug Abuse Funds" forms submitted to DADP

These data were used to compare actual spending patterns and program priorities with those suggested by the legislation and the plans of the state and counties.

3. *County Level*

- Documentary analysis of county drug and alcohol plans, related fiscal information, and other documents submitted to DADP
- Telephone survey of county alcohol and/or drug administrators concerning decision process and uses of ADTR at county agency level

These county-level data sources provided contextual information about how counties viewed the ADTR funds and which decision rules they used in allocating funds among service providers.

4. *Provider/Program Level*

- Mail-in survey of a sample of the more than 500 local programs funded by ADTR concerning the use and impact of ADTR funds

- Case studies, including site visits, of 18 programs that received ADTR funding

These data were used to help clarify and illustrate the specific kinds of activities ADTR funds were enabling. The case studies included structured interviews with provider staff and program participants, along with observation of program activities. The case studies were particularly useful in dramatizing the impact of the funds on specific communities.

Selected Findings

Consistent with the goals of primarily exploratory research, the findings for the report were broad and suggestive, rather than specific and definitive. The following sections describe some of the most significant findings in the report, and the data and analysis used to support them.

Increased Services

At the broadest level, the report found "a positive result": A greater than 10 percent increase over the number of persons served prior to the program. During a two-year period, more than 10,000 persons were estimated to have received treatment and other services that they would not have received without ADTR funds. Increases in service levels were detected in alcohol programs and in drug prevention programs.

A number of data sources collated in the report pointed to the overall conclusion that the program increased service levels. The specific statewide figures cited in this finding came from an analysis of data from CAL-DADS, the statewide drug service monitoring system. However, the CAL-DADS data were known to be incomplete and somewhat unreliable. For this reason, the report used a multiplistic "triangulation" technique by bringing together several other indicators of service levels. These included both the survey of county DADP directors and that of the service providers; both supported the conclusion that service levels had indeed increased as a result of the ADTR funds.

Appropriate Funding Procedures

The report determined that "the DADP allocation procedures, the ADTR decision and planning processes put in place by most county agencies, and the uses of ADTR funds by service providers were . . . consistent with the purposes of federal enabling legislation and the state of California."

No single method or analysis could adequately support such a broad-based finding. Moreover, criteria for evaluating these procedures and processes were not evident in the enabling legislation or other sources. Therefore, this finding sprang from a lack of conflicting evidence in the wealth of information collected in the course of the research. In other words, the exploratory research activity did not uncover any fundamental problems with the ADTR program.

Responsible Funding at the County Level

The late notification about the availability of funds combined with the perception that ADTR would provide only one-time funding, created a situation in which counties sought to responsibly fund programs that could be initiated quickly and would not produce major disruptions if funding were discontinued.

This finding was supported by both major survey efforts (of county DADP directors and providing agencies), and from analysis of the funding decisions made by counties. Interview data also supported the conclusion that the perceived short-term nature of the ADTR program had significant consequences for how funds were spent.

Experimental Programs

Some counties used ADTR to initiate or fund new, experimental programs; approximately one-fourth of the state's ADTR grant went to fund such programs. In other instances, ADTR funds were used either to enhance existing services or to prevent declines in existing services, in spite of declines in other funding sources.

Policy researchers must often develop new concepts in the course of performing their analyses of programs and policies. In the case of the ADTR program, the consultants created a typology of program types funded by ADTR funds. The typology was generated as a result of the legislature's interest in the issue of whether ADTR funds were being used to fund new programs, or merely keep older ones going. The typology was the result of an analysis of county and provider budgets and plans, as well as site visits, case studies, and interviews.

Types of Programs Funded

Analysis of patterns in the quantitative data and in the case studies identified three general models of program use of ADTR funds:

TABLE 5.1

Estimated Proportions of Experimental, Enhancement, and Maintenance Alcohol and Drug Abuse Programs Funded by the ADTR Grant.

Emphasis	Alcohol Programs	Other Drug Programs
Experimental	14%	36%
Enhancement	33	23
Maintenance	53	41

1. *Experimentation:* These programs, activities, or initiatives were new to the providers. Experimentation often meant adding a new service that was already part of the services delivered by a particular county. Experimental programs were often fully or nearly fully funded by the ADTR grant.
2. *Enhancement:* In these programs, funds were used specifically to increase the capacity of programs or to improve program quality in areas in which a provider was already delivering services.
3. *Maintenance:* This pattern was distinct from the experimentation and enhancement models in that it did not reflect an attempt to focus funding on specific activities. Maintenance funding represented an adaptation of the use of ADTR funds to the ongoing programs of the counties. In other words, funds were used to continue programs that might have been cut in the absence of ADTR funds. This was the most prevalent category among the ADTR-funded programs. More than 50 percent of the drug programs and more than 40 percent of the alcohol programs were found to fit the maintenance model (see Table 5.1). In an important and creative analysis, the evaluation team demonstrated that experimental and enhancement uses were maximized when counties used focused "request for purposal" procedures to allocate funds.

Communicating and Using Results

Because the ADTR study was mandated by state legislation, communication of results was structured into the contract between the policy research team and the state in the form of a series of written reports. However, the prospects for the use of research results were less than optimal, as state officials tended to review the evaluation as a requirement rather than as an opportunity for improvement.

Reporting Results

The final report was primarily organized around allocation patterns, utilization patterns at the state, county, and provider levels, and process information. Use of data largely conformed to the same categories: allocation patterns were derived from analysis of existing financial documents, and utilization patterns from analysis of two surveys. Process information came from two primary sources: interviews (for state-level processes) and site visits (for program-level processes). The report also contained explicit recommendations, although these were coached as "implications" based on the major findings (see the Selected Recommendations section that follows.)

Selected Recommendations

1. Noting the lack of comprehensive and accurate data for evaluating ADTR and other DADP activities, the DADP was advised to create a master planning mechanism that would involve the counties in data collection and planning within a clear statewide framework.
2. The state was advised to move away from population-based funding and toward an alternative method based more closely on need for drug and alcohol services. In this regard, a standardized system of needs assessment at the county level was also recommended.
3. DADP was advised to take steps to minimize the "maintenance" use of ADTR and other "one-time" funds, such as requiring recipients to demonstrate a use of funds consistent with programmatic intent. Well-constructed RFPs served this purpose in some study counties.
4. The report recommended that the state rethink the role of policy research itself. It advised that future attempts to evaluate state-funded, but county-implemented programs be focused on county level developments.

Action

The ADTR study was a major policy research effort that probably had few policy action consequences. The reason for this general lack of utilization lies in the origins of the study and the motivation for its implementation. As noted earlier, the study was commissioned due to a federal requirement attached to the emergency block grant allocation. The state agency had few explicit expectations concerning the information to be provided in the study, or its use. In fact, the report met the state's obligation to document the use of the federal funds, and to estimate their impact. Once this obligation was met, few of the stakeholders had much motivation to use any of the policy or procedural implications drawn from the study.

The lack of utilization also stems from the nature of the most significant implications of the study. Essentially, the study implied that if the state wanted to exercise some control over the use of funds passed through to counties and, eventually, service providers, a process that creates explicit and public statements of intention to use the funds to meet those objectives was necessary. The RFP process achieved this. Although this is an important finding for reformers or others interested in the performance of government structures and processes generally, it will not attract the attention of most administrators with responsibility for specific policy areas. Because the audience was primarily middle-level bureaucrats with responsibilities for meeting federal grant requirements—and not a governor, legislature, or reform commission—the study's failure to stir action is not surprising.

Lessons for Policy Research

One of the fascinating implications of this case study for policy researchers is the extent to which the recommendations are more penetrating than and in some cases unrelated to the findings in the report. This is not an altogether rare occurrence in the realm of policy research. Frequently, when outside policy researchers analyze a given program, they expect a certain degree of rationality—that is, a system well organized to produce certain results. But in many instances, they find programs that have been implemented in an almost accidental, unorganized fashion. The disorganization of the policy or program system becomes more important than its more substantive aspects.

In the case of ADTR, the policy research team expected to find a rational allocation process and the appropriate data systems to support it.

The research work plan was designed to conduct a straightforward analysis of funding decisions. Instead, much of their efforts consisted of collating disparate pieces of information about the ADTR process and trying to make some sense of the whole picture in what they had found. In this case, the apparent disorganization of the system eclipsed the more mundane findings of how ADTR funds had been allocated. The report concluded that where the money went was perhaps not as important as the issue of the organization of the processes that drove the system.

Discussion Questions

1. Generally, how is the policy environment of this program likely to affect the information needs of its implementers?
2. The ADTR represented only the latest in a series of drug service programs by various governments. How is the fact that other programs precede it likely to make evaluation difficult?
3. How would the minimal planning time and "one-time-only" status of the ADTR program affect decisions about planning its evaluation in California?
4. Imagine you are an executive with DADP. What would you need to know about the program?
5. What other stakeholders are likely to be concerned about the findings of the project?
6. How might the concerns of the stakeholders in this project be expected to affect its design, implementation, and dissemination?

Assignments and Activities

1. Conduct a brief literature review of materials that might be used to conduct problem definition for this case study. Summarize your findings.
2. Write a mock, one-page RFP that describes the information needs of the DADP.
3. Try to find a copy of the evaluation of the ADTR program in your state and/or county. Compare it to the one described in this chapter.

FOCUS ON RESEARCH METHODS

Interviews

In exploratory research projects like the ADTR evaluation, heavy reliance on qualitative research methods is common. In this instance, the research workplan included *interviews* with a variety of individuals from various agencies and organizations, including stakeholders. The interviews helped the policy research team understand how the ADTR grant processed *really* worked—they afforded insights into the various informal processes that affected the implementation of the grant, as well as the attitudes of policy actors closely involved with the program.

Unlike many research techniques that are conducted in an unobtrusive, distant manner, an interview is a face-to-face, interpersonal role situation (Frankfort-Nachmias and Nachmias 1996:232). Interviews may range from free-form *unstructured* (or *non-directive*) interviews—with relatively few fixed questions—to more formal *structured* (or *schedule-structured*) interviews that specify the topics and questions for each interviewee. Perhaps the most commonly used approach is that of the *semi-structured* (or *focused*) interview. The semi-structured interview combines focus on specific questions with a more free-flowing approach that enables the interviewer to explore certain topics more extensively.

Interviews are typically the linchpin of a policy research project; they can give policy researchers—particularly those without extensive personal knowledge about the program or policy in question—a much deeper understanding of the perceptions and motives of actors in the policy process, the reactions of clients, the actual implementation of planned policies, and the context in which policy is implemented. Ultimately, this enhances understanding of how and why policies work (or don't work).

However, interview data can be confusing and difficult to manage, particularly if it is spread over a large number of interviewers and interviewees. Analysis of interview data is not as straightforward a process as is, for example, statistical analysis of quantitative data. Documenting interview results for further analysis is time consuming and a weak point in many studies. Analyzing interview data effectively requires creativity and insight.

Note: For more details on how interviews may be used to improve policy research see, for example, Frankfort-Nachmias and Nachmias (1996); Gordon (1992); and Murphy (1980).

CASE STUDY AT A GLANCE

Program Title and Policy Area Emergency Substance Abuse Treatment and Rehabilitation Block Grant (Anti-Drug Abuse Act of 1986).

Program and Policy Background An intergovernmental grant program (federal to state) intended to increase services for drug and alcohol abusers consisting of Alcohol and Drug Abuse Treatment and Rehabilitation (ADTR) block grants. The ADTR grants were to be used to create new programs, increase the capacities of existing ones, and were to be targeted to increase services for specific groups.

Client and Other Primary Stakeholders The client was the California Department of Alcohol and Drug Programs. Other stakeholders included the federal government (Department of Health and Human Services); California County governments (Departments of Drug and Alcohol Programs); local service providers (county nonprofit agencies).

Information Needs The research was initiated through an RFP process by the California Department of Drug and Alcohol Programs (DADP), and was mandated by the grant legislation. Largely exploratory information needs were specified in the RFP, as well as more specific descriptive information about program expenditures.

Research Design and Methods The research was conducted with multiple methods appropriate to a largely exploratory research problem, including interviews, site visits and observations, and analysis of existing data. Two surveys, one of County DADP directors, the other of program providers at the local level, were also conducted.

Findings and Recommendations The report found that the ADTR funds did expand the availability of drug and alcohol-related services. Yet it also found that most funds went to maintaining existing services rather than creating new ones or expanding the capacity of old ones. Above and beyond that, the report advised that the systems of tracking both service needs and allocations was wholly inadequate and needed to be replaced.

(continued on next page)

(continued)

Program Jargon and Acronyms

ADTR Alcohol and Drug Abuse treatment and Rehabilitation, part of the federal Anti-Drug Abuse Act of 1986

CAL-DADS California Drug and Alcohol Data Survey—a data instrument used by counties to track drug and alcohol programs for the state

County Alcohol / Drug Plans Documents from the counties required by the state; used to describe county use of ADTR funds

DADP California Department of Drug and Alcohol Programs

provider One of over 500 separate agencies (government or nonprofit) used to deliver drug programs under the ADTR

CHAPTER 6

Evaluation of the California Ignition Interlock Pilot Program

A Policy Experiment

with Joël L. Phillips, EMT Group, Inc.

Introduction

Policy researchers occasionally have an opportunity to participate directly in the policy process by evaluating an explicitly experimental policy. This case study is the result of a pilot program or experiment mandated by the California state legislature.* However, it also involves government agencies from every level in the U.S. intergovernmental system. The experiment was to test the effectiveness of a high-tech device that, when installed in the vehicle of a convicted drunk driver, would prevent its operation by the driver if he or she had recently consumed alcohol.

The case study illustrates that even under such laboratorylike conditions, policy researchers may find it difficult to assess the impact of public programs. It further provides an example of how even a primarily experimental research design can profit by the inclusion of qualitative research techniques. As you read through the description, try to anticipate how the limitations placed on policy research can best be met by creative methodology. But also remember how the limitations may ultimately weaken the usefulness of the research findings.

---

*This case study is based largely on a report by the EMT Group, Inc. (EMT 1990).

The Policy Problem

Drunk driving is a problem with a national profile, but legislation to address it must come from states and localities. In recent years, groups like MADD (Mothers Against Drunk Driving) and others have sparked legislative efforts to reduce the presence of drinking drivers on the nation's highways. The goal of most of these efforts is to strengthen legal sanctions against convicted motorists. The program profiled here differs in that it devoted comprehensive policy research to a new objective—the installation of ignition interlock devices that seek to prevent impaired drivers from operating motor vehicles (for background on this issue, see, for example, Donelson 1988; Gusfield 1988; Jacobs 1989).

By all available indicators, California was experiencing a substantial problem with drinking drivers at the time of this study (1986). In 1982, for example, a total of nearly 350,000 arrests for DUI—driving under the influence—was made in the state, nearly 1,000 each day. In 1986, the state had more than 2,500 alcohol-related traffic fatalities. As elsewhere, in California the DUI problem is exacerbated by its chronic nature among some offenders: In 1982, approximately one in three convicted DUI offenders in California had a prior record for the offense. This high level of recidivism—DUI reconvictions—was an indicator that spurred the state to experiment with new measures.

Practical and reliable breath-test technology for vehicles is recent. In the early 1970s, the National Highway Traffic and Safety Administration (NHTSA) concluded that a variety of technological problems made breath testing impractical as a trigger for ignition interlock systems. The devices require drivers to perform a breath test before the vehicle in which they are installed can be started; if the breath sample indicates blood alcohol above a preset level, ignition is prevented. During the 1980s technological advances made the production of interlock devices feasible on a large scale.

Most states have passed laws stating that it is illegal to operate a motor vehicle if the driver's blood alcohol count (BAC) is above a specific breath alcohol limit. These laws make other proof of impairment unnecessary. Concomitantly, the NHTSA determined that both the general public and the legal system found interlock devices to be an acceptable way of attempting to prevent DUI.

Initiation of Policy Research

California became the first state to authorize the use of ignition interlock technology as a DUI countermeasure when it passed the Farr-Davis Safety Act of 1986. The Farr-Davis Act was a multifaceted law that authorized the use of ignition interlock as a demonstration (pilot) project with a finite life. Thus, the act mandated a policy *experiment* with the following provisions:

1. Ignition interlock testing would be conducted in four counties.
2. The test results would be evaluated to determine whether the devices deterred drinking and driving.
3. The implementation of the program would be evaluated.
4. A sunset provision would automatically repeal the act in 1990 unless the legislature acted to extend or delete the repeal prior to that time.

Another important aspect of the legislation is that it authorized interlock as an *optional* condition of probation for persons convicted of DUI. Thus, interlock was to be a *sentencing option* imposed at the discretion of judges in the four participating counties. In this role, judges had nearly total discretion. Each county court could use interlock as a sentencing alternative within the following guidelines:

- Any person convicted of DUI could be granted probation under the interlock system.
- The interlock device could be used only in addition to other requirements of the law; it could not be used as a substitute for participation in an alcohol education or rehabilitation program, for example.
- The courts were required to determine the ability of persons to pay for the device, and to lower the fines for DUI should the person claim to be unable to pay for the device. The courts were required to notify the California Department of Motor Vehicles (DMV), by means of an abstract of conviction or violation, that the person was required to use the device.

The Policy Research Task

The policy research task in this example was reasonably structured and limited by legislative mandate: specifically, the research was to provide an indication of how effective the ignition interlock system was as a sentencing alternative.

Objectives

The research objectives for the study were suggested by the legislation authorizing the study. The researchers were to

- identify four representative counties willing to participate in the demonstration.
- collect and analyze data to describe the process of implementation in each county.
- collect and analyze treatment and comparison data that would support conclusions about the success of the program in reducing DUI recidivism for participants.

Challenges

Evaluation research for assessing the ignition interlock pilot program had to be designed to collect and analyze information based on an ongoing program implemented by local judges and court systems. As noted earlier, the legislation was designed to preserve local court autonomy in deciding the extent to which interlock would be used as a sentencing option, and in deciding exactly which offenders would be sentenced to interlock as a condition of probation. The recognition of local court autonomy was an important precondition for gaining the cooperation of pilot counties in using the untested device as a DUI countermeasure.

From a policy research perspective, however, the operational autonomy of the program was a challenge because it imposed significant limitations on the research design and methodology. The most important limitation was nonrandom selection of individuals to be sentenced to using the interlock device—random selection is a critical characteristic of classic scientific experimental design.

Similarly, the local autonomy built into the program meant that implementation processes would differ markedly from county to county. Even if the program was shown to have an impact, that impact could be the result of different processes and procedures in the four participating counties. Moreover, each county (by design) had different demographic and socioeconomic characteristics that could be expected to have an impact on the outcome of the experiment. For example, one county, San Diego, in the southern part of the state, is large and urban, with more than 2 million residents. Sonoma is rural and suburban and has only 360,000 residents. Differences like these could have a substantial impact on the success of the program in each county.

The sheer number of agencies participating in the pilot program meant that data collection would be a cumbersome task. Among the agencies in possession of necessary data were the state DMV (driver records), the county court and probation offices (court sentencing records), and the three interlock device manufacturers (device performance data). Considerable difficulties were encountered in the task of reconciling the various data sources—none of which was reliably complete.

The Decision Context

The ignition interlock project was conducted in a context that was reasonably amenable, but also potentially threatening, to the use of policy research. On one hand, the research was legislatively mandated and addressed a fairly specific causal research question. This would auger for a receptive audience. On the other hand, a multiplicity of stakeholders with political and economic interests in the outcome of the study could muddy the waters.

The Institutional Context

The primary clients for this study were state government agencies. Despite the fact that the interlock program was legislatively sanctioned, there was not universal support for the success of the device. The state Department of Motor Vehicles (DMV), for example, sought control over the use and testing of the device. Manufacturers of the device, of course, had a vested interest in demonstrating a positive result for interlock technology. Thus, the institutional context represented a mine field for researchers—multiple interested parties with opposing positions and perspectives.

The Policy Cycle

At first glance, this project is a classic example of an evaluation phase project. The interlock program was initiated as an experiment, and the research was mandated to evaluate its impact. However, the policy sequence differs from that required for a classic experiment in several important ways.

Although the interlock program itself was a temporary, experimental pilot project, political reality dictated that it must be built on the foundation of the existing criminal justice system. Most significantly, local courts insisted on near-total autonomy and discretion in making the decision of who would receive the interlock sentence. Rather than adopting systematic criteria, or making random assignments, the judges in the four county courts made the decision for each DUI conviction based on their own judgment. Thus, the prevailing sentencing environment prevailed on the policy experiment.

Clients and Stakeholders

The *nominal* client in this case study was the California Department of Alcohol and Drug Programs (DADP). DADP was ordered to evaluate the ignition interlock program by the enabling legislation in the Farr-Davis Act. However, implementation of the act involved a cooperative effort of several federal, state, and local agencies, as well as private concerns. Therefore a variety of stakeholders had to be considered in designing and implementing the evaluation. They are discussed in the following subsections.

Federal

The National Highway Traffic Safety Administration (NHTSA) supported the evaluation portion of the project with federal funds. NHTSA also provided technical support for implementation of the interlock program itself. For example, NHTSA conducted a series of informational tests of various alcohol interlock devices to determine their accuracy and susceptibility to circumvention.

State

The California Office of Traffic Safety (OTS) was actually responsible for implementing the act, and it also initiated and directed the evaluation study. Thus, although DADP was the client of record, OTS was most heavily involved in implementing the program. OTS participated in the selection of counties that were to test the interlock device. OTS also was responsible for certifying the interlock devices, although it received assistance in this task from the NHTSA.

The California Bureau of Auto Repair (BAR) was responsible for setting the technical standards for the installation of the interlock devices. BAR's responsibilities were specified through administrative agreements with OTS. At the time of the research project, however, BAR's proposals for regulations on interlock devices had yet to undergo necessary legal review. Thus, installation of the devices was carried out by the interlock manufacturers themselves.

The California Department of Motor Vehicles (DMV) was responsible for providing the records of DUI offenders; these records were used both in the sentencing process and as data in the research project.

County

The four counties selected by OTS for inclusion in the pilot project were Sonoma, Alameda, San Diego, and Santa Clara. (The research design section below explains the choice of these particular counties.) The primary role of counties in the study was played through the court systems that were to sentence DUI offenders to the interlock device. Additionally, county probation departments monitored installation and maintenance of the interlock devices in the vehicles of DUI offenders. Probation officers and other court officials were supposed to ensure that the devices were used properly. To this end, the Farr-Davis legislation required that persons sentenced to interlock "report to the court or the probation officer at least once annually, and more frequently as the court may order, on the operation of each interlocking ignition device in their personal vehicle or vehicles."

Interlock Manufacturers

Three different manufacturers produced interlock devices that met the testing standards set by OTS. Each manufacturer's device accomplished the necessary performance objectives in different ways. For example, different combinations and profiles of temperature, pressure, or humidity were used to prevent anyone from circumventing the device. In addition to providing the interlock devices, manufacturers performed several critical functions. Chief among these was the installation and maintenance of the interlock devices. A condition of this requirement was that manufacturers report to the courts quarterly on the performance of every device they installed. As a result, the manufacturers also kept records on the history of the performance of each device.

Convicted Individuals

Individuals sentenced to use the interlock device were required to prove that they had complied with the sentence within 30 days of sentencing. They were, of course, forbidden to operate any vehicle not equipped with the device, and circumvention of the device constituted a probation violation. Those required to have the device were also required to report to the court or probation office at least once annually.

Research Design and Implementation

The policy researchers were faced with the challenge of designing a project that would both address the focused causal issues identified by the Farr-Davis legislation and provide meaningful insight into *why* the project met or failed to meet expectations.

Information Needs

In this case, the information needs of the client were specified in the enabling legislation for the pilot program. This had the general effect of circumscribing the envelope of the research project. OTS was instructed to select four "representative" counties for the project, and to do the following:

1. Examine the effectiveness and reliability of ignition interlock devices as a sentencing option
2. Review the data collected by the participating county court systems by monitoring the results of implementing the program
3. Develop uniform sentencing and probation procedures that could be applied statewide

Although these objectives are fairly vague, the legislation was relatively specific in defining the means by which the pilot program would be judged, stating that success would be determined "by comparing the recidivism rate of those persons subject to [the interlock program] and to demographically and statistically similar cases where [the interlock program] was not applied." The law specified the following criteria:

- The program would be considered "not significant" (that is, not successful) if there was a reduction of less than 10 percent in repeat offenders (recidivism) for program participants during the two years of the study.

- The program would be deemed "a success" if the recidivism rate of participants was reduced by at least 10 percent.
- The program would be deemed "extremely successful" if the reduction in the recidivism rate was more than 25 percent.

The Farr-Davis Act further directed OTS and counties participating in the pilot program to assist in the evaluation of the program by developing reporting forms for documenting and monitoring the use of the interlock device. Although the information needs specified in the legislation clearly contained the hallmarks of a causal research problem, descriptive information was also required. The legislation called for development of procedures for possible statewide implementation of the program. This task required collection and analysis of descriptive information about the character of the implementation process. Thus the project entailed elements of both causal and descriptive policy research.

Design and Methods

Design: The Quasi-Experimental Analysis of DUI Reconviction

The central research question for evaluating the impact of interlock devices on DUI reconviction was to estimate what the reconviction rate for probationers would have been if they had not been assigned the device. The research design constructed to answer this question had to provide both quantitative information (about the impact of the devices on DUI) and more qualitative information (about how the program was implemented). In the near absence of existing data, the resulting design would require a great deal of data collection.

The key strategic design choice for determining the success of the program was a *quasi-experiment,* which attempts to emulate a classic experiment in situations where conditions are not truly appropriate for an experiment. In the case of ignition interlock, a classic experiment was not feasible because a random assignment of DUI offenders into an experimental group was impossible due to local control over the sentencing decision. Quasi-experiments are typically less able to provide definitive information about the effectiveness of public programs, but they are nevertheless a valuable design option.

In addition, the research design called for a number of qualitative data collection efforts, including the use of surveys, questionnaires, interviews, and documentary analysis. Most of the qualitative data was directed toward the issue of program implementation and processes.

The quasi-experiment was fashioned by creating a matched comparison group of DUI convictions; the comparison group was used to serve the same function as a formal control group in a classic experiment. To make results from the quasi-experiment as valid as possible, researchers had to identify and select comparison cases that were similar to the interlock "experimental" probationers in ways that could affect the likelihood of repeat offenses.

Methods

Collecting the appropriate data for the experimental design was a complicated and difficult task. Figure 6.1 illustrates the process used to create the experimental and control groups for the study. In order to identify these groups, the following sequence of tasks had to be completed.

1. *Identify probationers sentenced to interlock* In reality, interlock was used as a sentencing option in only a small percentage of DUI cases in each county. The possibility existed that gaps in the legal records might exist; the validity of the quasi-experimental approach hinged in part on the fullest possible identification of the quasi-experimental group. To identify these cases, researchers consulted three separate data sources:
    a. Notification forms sent to OTS by the county courts
    b. Manufacturers' records of court notifications that a DUI offender had been sentenced to interlock
    c. Manufacturers' records of actual installations

Any of these sources could help identify an individual sentenced to interlock who was inadvertently omitted from the other two sources. This search identified 775 confirmed interlock probationers. However, manufacturers' records indicated that devices were installed in only 584 vehicles.

2. *Collect data for interlock probationers* For each offender sentenced to interlock, local court files were collected to determine the characteristics of the quasi-experimental group. This involved merg-

ing data from three sources: court records (arrest record and court actions data); DMV records (personal characteristics); and manufacturers' records (installation data).

3. *Identify a matched comparison group* Using the data collected from the interlock probationer group, researchers constructed a comparison group by selecting an offender who was matched on five key characteristics: gender, race, age, number of prior DUI convictions, and blood alcohol count (BAC) at time of arrest. These matching criteria were selected by the evaluation team in consultation with the funding agency. Most were selected because they had shown a strong correlation to recidivism in prior research. Race was selected as a variable to check for the possibility that judges applied the program differentially across racial groups. It was anticipated that this frequently raised question concerning judicial system procedures might arise in the interpretation of study results.

Researchers believed these criteria had potentially an impact on DUI reconviction rates. However, the comparison group *could* have been similar

FIGURE 6.1.

Selection of Subjects for Ignition Interlock Quasi-Experiment

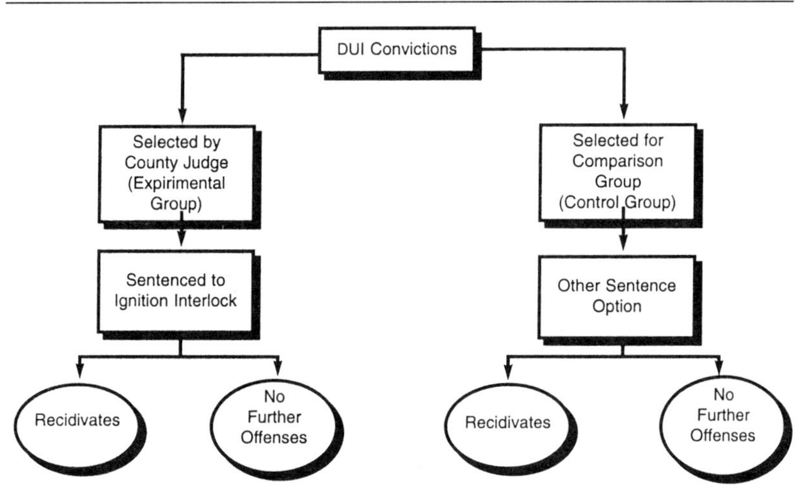

This diagram illustrates how experimental and control groups were drawn from a pool of DUI convictions. It also displays the possible outcomes that were monitered for each group.

to the interlock group in unknown, yet significant ways.

The crux of the quasi-experiment lay in comparing the reconviction rates of the interlock group with those of the matched comparison group. Methodologically, this was achieved by two means:

- A test of statistical significance of the difference between the reconviction rates of the two groups (chi square was also calculated)
- Logistic regression analysis, with reconviction serving as a dichotomous dependent variable "explained" by differences in the two groups (This technique was employed in a follow-up to the final report on the project.)

Among the most critical data needed for the study, were the driving and related court records of persons convicted of DUI in the four participating counties. These records held the outcome of each interlock sentence, as well as vital background data. Driving records for all DUI convictions were available from the state DMV. Local court files contained more detailed information about each offender, and in the crowded misdemeanor court system, identifying and tracking individual DUI offenders required a major research effort that took the following forms:

1. *Survey of municipal judges* A written survey of all municipal judges in counties participating in the study was conducted. The survey provided information about judicial awareness of the program, the use of interlock devices as a sentencing alternative, and related opinions about the program.
2. *Written questionnaires for interlock probationers* Questionnaires were filled out by a small, nonscientific sample of probationers who had been sentenced to ignition interlock. These mail-in questionnaires were distributed when respondents were having their devices maintained. They were used to provide qualitative, anecdotal insight into some of the study questions.
3. *Intensive interviews* Intensive interviews were conducted with the following groups of stakeholders: (a) judges who used the interlock-sentencing option; (b) prosecuting and defense attorneys in participating counties; (c) manufacturers' representatives; and (d) other informed persons. These interviews provided the per-

ceptions and opinions of persons most closely associated with implementation of the pilot program.

4. *Analysis of interlock logs* One potential source of existing data was available only in one participating county. Interlock devices in Santa Clara County automatically kept an electronic log that was routinely printed out at the required calibration checks. The logs indicate what happened each time an attempt was made to start an equipped vehicle. For example, if an individual who had been drinking attempted to start a vehicle, and the device prevented him or her, the event would be recorded in the electronic log. The electronic logs could be converted into data files, analyzed, and/or printed out.

In addition to these analyses, documentary analysis and literature review were undertaken. Relevant records and internal data concerning interlock were reviewed and analyzed. These documents included guidelines and procedures, forms, certification reports, interlock installation, maintenance and removal records, and service call records. The literature reviewed focused on the development of ignition interlock technology and its application elsewhere. Federal (OTHSA) reports were the most significant source of relevant literature.

Selected Findings

Effectiveness of the Interlock Device

The final report found that the interlock device produced "positive" results, but that the data did not support definitive conclusions. The report noted that the results obtained in the analysis met the legislated criteria for a "very successful" performance, but it also emphasized that the results needed to be evaluated with caution, due to limitations of the data and research methods.

Because this was the centerpiece of the policy information requested by the client, this issue was discussed in great detail. Inasmuch as recidivism (meaning DUI reconviction) was the variable of concern, an important step in analyzing the data was to define "recidivism" in operational terms. For the purposes of the study, recidivism was defined as any reconviction for DUI that appeared in the DMV system for an arrest, within one year of the time the interlock device was installed. A similar definition was used for the comparison group, whose record constituted recidivism if there was a reconviction for DUI that appeared for an arrest occurring between the time of conviction for their *last* DUI and the following year.

Table 6.1 presents the results of the quantitative analysis that provided the initial and perhaps the most straightforward answer to the question: Does ignition interlock reduce recidivism among DUI offenders? This table was a critical component of the research, since some stakeholders might base their assessment of the device on these data alone.

As Table 6.1 indicates, individuals who were sentenced to the interlock device were reconvicted at an overall rate of 13.6 percent; individuals in the comparison group were reconvicted at a (higher) rate of 16.7 percent. However, the reconviction rates for each county varied significantly. Two counties, Alameda and Santa Clara, actually experienced a higher reconviction rate for the interlock group than for the comparison group.

To determine the amount of change in recidivism due to the program, the projected recidivism rate (that is, the comparison group rate) was multiplied by the number of interlock probationers to identify a *projected number of recidivists* that would have been expected to occur without the program. Figure 6.2 displays the differences between the *projected* and *actual* reconvictions in each study county. The percentage change attributable to the program was then calculated by identifying the percentage of change from the projected number of recidivists that is represented by the actual number of recidivists. A similar number was calculated for the study groups as a whole by aggregating the county figures.

TABLE 6.1

Comparison of DUI Reconvictions for Interlock and Comparison Groups

County	Interlock Group			Comparison Group			% Change in Rates
	Number	Reconvicted	Rate	Number	Reconvicted	Rate	
Alameda	79	14	17.7%	61	5	8.2%	+133.3%
San Diego	251	28	11.2	218	40	18.4	-39.2
Sonoma	78	12	15.4	65	18	27.7	-44.4
Santa Clara	171	25	14.6	153	20	13.1	+11.9
Total	579	79	13.6	497	83	16.7	-18.3

FIGURE 6.2

Projected vs. Actual Reconvictions

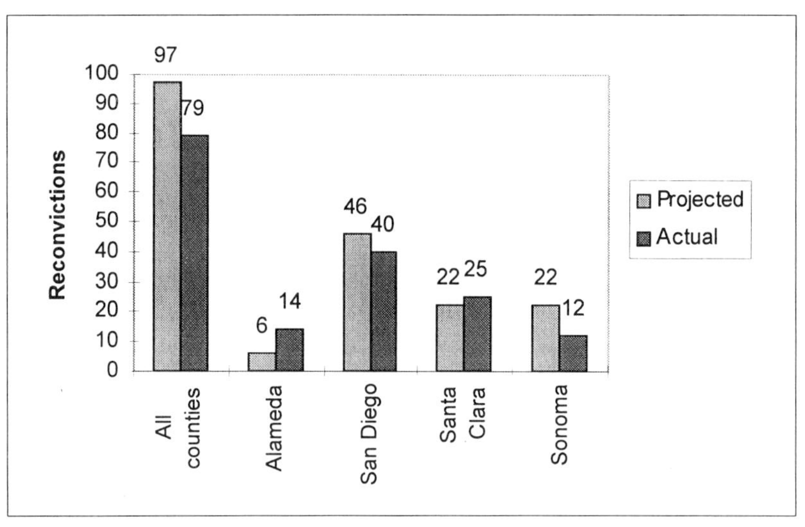

The figure shows that, overall, the projected number of reconvictions exceeded the actual number that occurred using interlock. However, actual arrests exceeded the number projected in two counties.

As the figure indicates, the results indicated an overall reduction of 18.5 percent in the projected number of reconvictions for probationers who had interlock devices installed in their cars. The figure also illustrates, however, that decreases were achieved in only two counties, San Diego and Sonoma. Indeed, in Alameda County the projected number of reconvictions increased by 133 percent, and in Santa Clara County little difference was detected. Moreover, neither the overall reduction nor the reduction observed in Sonoma met standard tests of statistical significance.

Thus, the results of the research indicated that the program had met the legislatively mandated criteria for "success" (more than a 10 percent reduction in recidivism), but it had done so at a statistically significant level in only one county. The report noted that the nonrandom method of selection incorporated in the report and the small numbers of individuals included in the analysis indicated that these results needed to be treated with caution.

The results of the study also demonstrate the frequent "slippage" in applicability of research criteria in applied settings. Because the samples of offenders and comparison cases were not "random," the application of tests of statistical significance (which assume random selection or assignment) was not technically warranted. Still, these tests are commonly accepted indicators that lend the appearance of science to a study. Part of the difficulty in communicating the results of this study was in communicating that the results may have substantive importance even though no simple indicator of scientific "significance" was met.

Implementation of the Program

To fully evaluate the interlock program it was necessary to understand how and why individual judges used it. Therefore, an extensive portion of the report provided a detailed description of how the interlock program was implemented. The report concluded that the program had been successfully implemented from the standpoint of setting standards for and certifying interlock devices. However, as a sentencing option, the program was a less than overwhelming success. Among the problems identified in the report were the following:

- Only a small number of judges consistently used the interlock sentencing option. Judicial resistance, as well as the additional burden on court personnel of monitoring the program, could prove to be major barriers to implementing the program on a statewide basis.
- One reason judges were reluctant to use the interlock sentencing option was the perception that interlock was an option for those who could afford to pay for it. The report concluded that the economic indigence provisions of the program had been "virtually ignored."
- Judges who did consistently use interlock sentencing imposed it on a variety of types of offenders, for a number of different reasons. No appropriate sentencing model emerged from the pilot study.

A combination of data from surveys, interviews, and the quasi-experiment was used to generate conclusions about the implementation of interlock. Comments taken from interviews with individual judges were used to demonstrate that the judges exercised total discretion in selecting DUI convicts for interlock:

TABLE 6.2.

Interlock Sentencing Patterns in Study Counties

County	Sentencing Pattern
Alameda	Sentencing policy was heterogeneous; it tended to target younger offenders.
San Diego	Two judges were responsible for most sentences to interlock. Interlock was frequently assigned to violators of probation from prior DUI convictions; the great majority of interlock assignees had prior DUIs.
Santa Clara	One judge was responsible for nearly all interlock sentences; most assignees were first-time offenders.
Sonoma	Courtwide sentencing policy targeted young, first offenders with high BAC.

> "I make it a personal decision. There's no set policy. It's based on the individual."
>
> (Alameda County judge)

> "Each judge sets their own policy. There is no standard."
>
> (Sonoma County judge)

Survey data demonstrated that for many judges, the cost of the interlock device, as well as other concerns, helped explain their reluctance to use the device as a sentencing option. Table 6.2 summarizes some of these data.

The survey data were complemented with additional quotes from the interviews:

> "I've seen very few offenders who could afford the interlock. Many don't even own vehicles and aren't employed."
>
> (San Diego County judge)

> "My reluctance is based on the belief that it appears to permit the wealthy to somehow avoid other more onerous conditions of probation."
>
> (San Diego County judge)

Avoidance and Circumvention of the Device

The report identified two serious problems with the installation, maintenance, and monitoring of the interlock devices.

1. Findings on the effectiveness of the interlock device were based only on the outcomes associated with individuals who actually had the device installed. The report determined that approximately one fourth of those sentenced to interlock never had the device installed—primarily because of lack of compliance with court orders.
2. The study found that the device could be successfully bypassed or circumvented.

The study therefore concluded that although the interlock device was effective in reducing DUI recidivism, it did not ensure that "determined drinking driver[s] will not get behind the wheel" (EMT, 1990). Data in support of this critical finding came from a number of sources, but primarily from a comparison of court orders for interlock installation, matched against records from both the courts and manufacturers to determine when the device was installed. The rate at which probationers failed to have the device installed varied by county, but approximately one fourth of all of those who were sentenced to use it failed to have the device installed. Although in some instances it was impossible to determine why this failure occurred, examination of the data revealed that in most cases the reason was either noncompliance (by those sentenced) or a court-ordered deletion of the installation.

Communicating and Using Results

Communication of study results proceeded primarily through structured channels as delineated by the research contract. The policy research team issued a series of interim reports that culminated with a final report when the study period ended.

Reporting Results

The final report was divided into chapters corresponding to the two major research issues: the impact of the devices on DUI reconvictions, and the implementation of the program. Additional chapters provided an analysis of how sentencing decisions were made by judges and the case management process used to install, monitor, and remove the interlock devices. These latter chapters provided important information not explicitly requested by the client agency, yet invaluable to understanding how the program worked.

Because of the critical role quantitative analysis played in this project, a detailed explanation of the quasi-experimental design was placed near the beginning of the report. In addition to describing how the experiment was conducted, this section also described in explicit terms the limitations of the findings generated by the design.

The final report contained both a summary of findings and a set of recommendations.

Selected Recommendations

The recommendations were preceded by the following caveat: "The findings of this study support a positive but nonconclusive assessment of the potential of ignition interlock as a DUI countermeasure." It also recommended that further study of the application and effectiveness of the device be conducted, noting that further recommendations had to fall within the following constraints:

- They [recommendations] could not immediately place significant additional administrative responsibilities on the court.
- They could not require significant immediate public expenditures or loss of revenues to courts.
- They should minimize reliance on individual manufacturers.

Within these parameters, the report addressed the following recommendations:

1. *Communication of information* Standardized forms should be developed and used to document interlock sentences, compliance, and results, and copies should be forwarded to all agencies involved in the process.
2. *Sentencing decisions* No recommendation was made regarding targeting specific types of DUI offenders for the devices since the "data . . . gathered through the pilot program does not allow firm conclusions concerning how to target . . . offenders."
3. *Sanctions* The following measures might be taken in response to noncompliance with the interlock sentence:

- Automatic license suspension
- Issuance of bench arrest warrants
- Withholding drivers' licenses pending installation of the device

4. *Implementation responsibilities* Lack of knowledge about the program was widespread, and OTS should be commissioned to develop and disseminate information concerning the device and its potential value as a DUI countermeasure.

Action

The evaluation report on the ignition interlock pilot project became a key element in the policy dialogue and actions concerning interlock legislation in California. Because the report findings were mixed—indicating both overall positive outcomes regarding DUI recidivism yet results that were not consistent across all counties—the cautiously stated conclusions were vulnerable to attack by both pro- and anti-interlock forces. Given the potential economic benefits to manufacturers if use of the device became widespread, and the centrality of the issue to DUI policy in the state, the qualified conclusions of the study were contested by *both* sides. One manufactuer lodged a protest with the California Office of Traffic Safety, claiming that the study was methodologically flawed; the protest suggested that the study *underestimated* the effectiveness of the device in that county. This manufacturer had supplied, installed, and maintained the devices in a county that did not show positive results. The manufacturer commissioned a professor at a local university to review the study's methods. Unfortunately for the manufacturer, however, the professor produced a report that supported the study method—the quasi-experimental design—as scientifically sound and properly implemented.

The research division of the California Department of Motor Vehicles also attacked the study but claimed the findings *overestimated* the effectiveness of the device. The DMV had not supported the interlock pilot project in the first place and had sought authority for a DMV evaluation instead. The department's major criticism of the study was that persons who had been assigned to interlock but who never had the device installed were not included in the quasi-experimental test of effects on DUI recidivism. The evaluators countered with two arguments: (a) that the study tested the effectiveness of the device and not the adjudication and the implementation process associated with it, and (b) that many of the persons who did not have the device installed may have left the state, removing them from the scope of the study anyway.

This policy dialogue was carried on by means of memoranda, meetings with the OTS and interested legislators, and several public hearings on the study and the interlock devices. Ultimately, the California legislature passed a bill extending authorization for using interlock devices as a condition of DUI probation throughout the state. The study and its generally positive result, qualified though it was, provided adequate political ammunition for those who supported the legislation. The report has also been widely circulated nationwide and cited in similar studies in other states; it has therefore probably contributed to the adoption of interlock legislation in other states.

Lessons for Policy Research

Despite being conducted under the relatively controlled conditions associated with evaluation of a policy experiment, the research described in this case study failed to yield definitive results. One weakness of using the quasi-experimental approach to formulate policy is its demanding formal structure that may break down in the field. In this case, designers of the pilot project did not foresee that insufficient numbers of drivers would be sentenced to DUI, making a statistically significant outcome relatively difficult to achieve. Political reality dictated that individual judges would retain control of the sentencing process if the project was to be implemented at all, effectively limiting the number of interlock probationers.

Nevertheless, the research associated with the experiment need not be labeled a failure. It did establish that interlock probationers were less likely than other probationers to be arrested for subsequent DUI offenses, and it identified various problematic aspects of implementation, paving the way toward further experimentation. Indeed, much of the value of the research lay in identifying the weaknesses in the way the program was run. Particularly significant in this respect were the findings of judicial reticence to use interlock devices in sentencing, and the ease with which the devices could be avoided or circumvented.

Discussion Questions

1. Assuming that a classic experiment with random selection of participants was indeed impossible, how could the impact of the program best be documented? Suggest and describe an alternative research strategy.
2. What kinds of operational difficulties do you think might be associated with collecting data in this case?
3. Why were the gender, race, blood alcohol count, and other variables of interlock offenders important to the quasi-experiment? What additional data might have been useful?
4. What problems would you foresee for the use of the research findings culled from this design?
5. How might the implications of this report differ if the qualitative data concerning program implementation had been omitted? That is, if the research had been confined to the quasi-experiment, what conclusions might have been drawn?
6. How, in your opinion, did the fact that each county's judiciary was the final sentencing authority affect the research strategy needed to evaluate the program?
7. Following the program evaluation model (see Chapter 2), what would be the ideal place in the policy sequence for a program like this?
8. What other stakeholders do you think might be considered in evaluating the interlock program?
9. Each of the stakeholder groups listed earlier plays a critical role in the implementation of the program. What implications does that have for an appropriate research design?
10. What complications arose in determining the impact of the ignition interlock program? How did the policy researchers deal with these complications?
11. What descriptive information was required to provide the legislature with useful information?

Assignments and Activities

1. Write a working draft of the research problem, including the major subissues you can identify.
2. Write a research work plan based on the preceding research design.
3. Write a memorandum explaining the strengths and weaknesses of the preceding research design. How could the research design have been strengthened?

FOCUS ON RESEARCH METHODS

The Quasi-Experiment

The central research technique upon which this project was anchored was a *quasi-experiment.* Like a classical experiment, a quasi-experiment compares outcomes between experimental and comparison (or control) groups. However, whereas quasi-experiments emulate the classic experimental design in most ways, they lack the element of random assignment to either the control or the experimental group. This feature introduces more uncertainty about the validity of results obtained from quasi-experimental designs (Langbein 1980). This uncertainty is the price that policy researchers pay for their inability to exercise the degree of control found in classic experimental design.

In this instance, the policy research team was unable to create the proper conditions for a classic experiment because the judges from each county wanted control over which offenders were selected for inclusion in the interlock program. In a classic experiment, the policy researchers would have randomly selected both those offenders who used the interlock device and offenders assigned to the control group. In practice, the policy researchers had to select a "comparison group" that resembled the nonrandom experimental group in as many ways as possible. The comparison group was created by studying confidential individual court records in a very detailed manner.

From these records, the policy research team selected a comparison group that matched each member of the experimental (interlock) group with a DUI offender of similar race, gender, number of prior convictions, and blood alcohol count, but no sentence to interlock. Each of these characteristics was selected because of a possible link with reconviction rates. By making the experimental and comparison groups equivalent with respect to these characteristics, the policy researchers sought to diminish (but not eliminate) the possibility that the groups differed in a systematic way.

Quasi-experiments are often desirable elements of policy research because of their utility in isolating causal information. However, conditions for creation of quasi-experimental designs are not always present. Pilot programs (like the ignition interlock program) are one setting for these designs. Cooperation from officials and stakeholders involved with the program or policy is also usually necessary as well. Ethical and political considerations may also hinder implementation of such a design; in the ignition interlock case, the policy research team had to work carefully to gain the confidence of court officials.

CASE STUDY AT A GLANCE

Program Title and Policy Area California Ignition Interlock Pilot Program for DUI Offenders (Farr-Davis Driver Safety Act of 1986); March, 1990.

Program and Policy Background The Farr-Davis Act authorized that ignition interlock, a new technology for preventing driving under the influence of alcohol (DUI), be tested as a sentencing alternative in four California counties. The device was installed in the vehicles of some DUI offenders, and was supposed to prevent drivers who had been drinking from starting their cars with a breath test. The act authorized the California Office of Traffic Safety to evaluate the effectiveness of the device.

Client and Other Primary Stakeholders The client was the California Department of Alcohol and Drug Programs/California Office of Traffic Safety. Other primary stakeholders included county judicial systems, manufacturers of the interlock device, and individuals convicted of DUI.

Information Needs The Act requested information both about the effectiveness of the device in preventing individuals convicted of DUI from recidivating, and about how the program was implemented. Therefore both causal and descriptive information was required.

Research Design and Methods The effectiveness of the device was tested by means of a quasi-experimental approach, using the driving records of a matched group of DUI probationers to compare with a group of interlock probationers. Additionally, interviews with judges and other persons with knowledge about the program, as well as surveys and documentary analyses, were used to provide descriptive information.

Findings and Recommendations The report found that the devices appeared to work, yet the numbers in the experiment were so limited and the effect so small that the impact of the program was not statistically significant in all counties. The report found a positive outcome for the pilot project, but it cautioned that further research on a larger scale was necessary.

Program Jargon and Acronyms

DMV California Department of Motor Vehicles
DUI Driving under the influence
Farr-Davis Safety Act of 1986 California legislation authorizing a pilot program to test the effectiveness of ignition interlock devices
ignition interlock A device designed to prevent drunk driving by making a vehicle inoperable if the driver's breath exceeds a given level of blood alcohol content
NHTSA National Highway Traffic and Safety Administration
OTS California Office of Traffic Safety

CHAPTER 7

The Extended National Youth Sports Program (ENYSP)

A Formative Evaluation

with Joël L. Phillips, EMT Associates, Inc.

Introduction

This case study is a good illustration of the policy research challenges posed by a social program with broad, long-term goals and objectives.* How can policy researchers evaluate the effectiveness of such a program in the present? In this case, policy research focused on proximate indicators of program success and effectiveness, using primarily qualitative data collection and analysis techniques.

The case also provides an example of how to organize a series of primarily qualitative case studies in a geographically disparate program. Additionally, it exemplifies a government-funded program that is directly implemented by a nonprofit organization.

The Policy Problem

As drugs and alcohol have taken a heavier and heavier toll on American society, extensive research has demonstrated that risk for alcohol and drug problems is related to multiple family, school, social, and behavioral problems that tend to occur together as a cluster of "risk factors." These

---

*This case study is based largely on a report by EMT Associates, Inc. (EMT 1991b).

risk factors are simply characteristics of youths and their living situations that tend to occur at greater frequency for those who develop problems with alcohol and other drugs. Such characteristics include poverty and living in economically depressed areas that tend to have high unemployment, inadequate housing, poor schools, inadequate health and human services, high crime, and high prevalence of illegal drug use. Many of these risk factors are associated with the disadvantaged youth targeted for participation in the Extended National Youth Sports Program (ENYSP), an extension of the National Youth Sports Program (NYSP), which is a partnership between the National Collegiate Athletic Association (NCAA) and the U.S. Department of Health and Human Services Office of Community Services (DHHS-OCS).

ENYSP was designed to be a prevention program that provides a *risk protection* for its participants. Prevention programs incorporate a variety of noncoercive strategies to increase the ability of youths to avoid abuse of alcohol and drugs (for background on prevention policies and programs for youths, see, for example, Hansen 1992; Tobler 1993; Sharp 1994:91–108). ENYSP embodies a variety of prevention strategies for its youthful participants, among them the following:

- *Education* Educational activities are straightforward attempts to provide information about the nature and dangers of drug and alcohol abuse that will enable participants to avoid them. Recent research suggests that educational activities that merely provide information are likely to be ineffective.
- *Social competence education* Education does not necessarily connote classroom instruction; contemporary approaches to drug education may include developing refusal and other skills that are said to strengthen the ability of youths to avoid drug and alcohol abuse. Social competence education can also include developing social assertiveness and leadership and improved family and peer interactions.
- *Positive alternatives* The positive-alternative strategy seeks to provide fulfilling and rewarding alternatives to the use of alcohol and other drugs. Such activities may include recreation, educational assistance, and work experiences and may focus on increasing personal accomplishment.

In practice, a typical day's activities at an ENYSP site might consist of the following:

1. Transportation of participants to the host college or university
2. Breakfast
3. Alcohol/drug-prevention activity
4. Athletic activities
5. Lunch
6. Return transportation

Such activities were typically staggered in different ways, depending on the number of participants and other site characteristics. Activities were conducted by both professional and volunteer staff, including program administrator, program director, drug education specialist, community liaison, cultural enrichment coordinator, and program aides. ENYSP guidelines indicated a desired staff-to-participant ratio of between 1:15 and 1:20.

The advent of the extended NYSP, made possible by the DHHS-OCS grant, marked a significant change for the NYSP. NYSP is a summer weekday program with a long tradition of athletic activities. The extended program would run from October to May, would be held primarily on weekends, and would focus more on drug prevention than did the regular NYSP. Forty-five programs nationally were selected to participate in this extended version of NYSP. Expectations were high: ENYSP was to provide greater continuity for NYSP in the lives of participating youth, strengthen the program's ability to retain participants from year to year, and help inaugurate a newly created role of the drug education specialist.

Initiation of the Policy Research

The ENYSP project was initiated solely by the client, the NCAA. The leadership of the ENYSP was interested in enhancing the program in such a way as to make it eligible for federal grant support; one means to help accomplish this would be an outside review. The ENYSP administrative leadership contacted a federal agency which in turn recommended EMT Associates, Inc. (a well-known policy research firm) as a potential contractor for the project. The firm assembled a proposal that sketched out the broad parameters of the project that was presented to officials from ENYSP. After extensive negotiation, EMT was awarded a contract to complete this project. In 1990, the NCAA commissioned the research team specifically to assess alcohol and drug abuse prevention activities implemented in the extended (October–May) ENYSP. The evaluation was not intended to address directly the summertime ENYSP activities. Eventually the research team went on to conduct three related evaluations; the results of one of those projects is described in this case study.

The Policy Research Task

The policy research task of evaluating the ENYSP was a daunting one: The program is large and geographically and organizationally decentralized. The objectives of the program were vague and multiple.

Objectives

The objective of the policy research team was to provide the decision-making client—the NCAA—with information it could use to improve the drug-prevention component of the ENYSP.

Challenges

Drug-prevention programs have several characteristics that make conventional program evaluation techniques difficult to apply. First, the goals of such programs are typically broad and vague, if not unspecified. Precisely what is successful prevention? What proportion of participants should be affected for the program to be considered a success? ENYSP, like most prevention programs, did not have a clear policy about what it was trying to achieve. Indeed, part of the challenge to the research was to assist ENYSP in articulating its goals.

Second, prevention is frequently directed toward future, long-term goals. One of the ostensible goals of a drug-prevention program is to keep participants away from the abuse of alcohol and other drugs on a long-term basis. Obviously, such long-term impacts cannot be verified in the present.

Third, prevention programs operate in a maelstrom of other influences on the lives of their participants. ENYSP participants were selected on the basis of their presumable exposure to negative influences, such as poverty, broken homes, and the proximity of alcohol and drugs to their daily lives. In such environments, disentangling the impact of drug prevention is problematic.

And, finally, the target of drug-prevention programs—abuse of alcohol and other drugs—is behavior that inherently cannot be directly monitored or verified. Direct indicators of ENYSP success could be expected to be difficult to derive.

Another challenge to the project was the geographic scope and local autonomy of the ENYSP sites. The extended program, the focus of the evaluation, existed in 45 different cities across the country. Each site could be expected to face a different set of circumstances, such as a different clientele for potential participants, a different local climate of drug abuse and availability, and a different relationship with its host collegiate institution.

The tradition in the NYSP was to allow a maximal amount of local program control over many aspects of the program. Decisions about hiring staff, for example, were left to local program administrators, as were decisions about program scheduling, the content of activities (including drug-prevention activities), and so forth. Although the variety encouraged by such a decentralized program was appropriate, it made the task of making generalizations about the program a difficult one. Clearly, some local ENYSP sites were going to be much more effective at delivering quality drug prevention than were others.

The Decision Context

The decision context for this policy research project was relatively straightforward, because the client was a nonprofit organization with a relatively substantial amount of discretion in shaping the program. However, the program was actually operated by many very autonomous sites, meaning that policy research information had to incorporate multiple perspectives and values about the program.

The Institutional Context

The National Youth Sports Program is, as noted earlier, a partnership of the NCAA and the DHHS-OSP. NYSP is a summer sport instruction and physical activity program intended to promote health, positive social interaction, discipline, and self-esteem. NYSP participants are underprivileged youths between the ages of 10 and 16.

At the time of the research, participating NYSPs were located in 113 cities and 41 states across the nation. Local programs are located at colleges and universities, and they build on the tradition of college athletics as a means of extending the resources of these institutions to their local communities. Over the 20-year history of the program, NYSP evolved from a primarily athletic program to one that embraced the goals of providing additional educational and experiential opportunities for its participants, including nutrition, disease prevention, vocational development, higher education, and drug education.

In 1989, Congress awarded NYSP $3 million via the Anti-Drug Abuse Act of 1988 Community Youth Activity Program. These funds were awarded on the basis of the NCAA proposal, which was selected in a competitive process administered by DHHS-OCS. The funds were authorized to enhance the drug-prevention component of the NYSP. More specifically, the funds were to be used to add drug education specialists to the staff of each of the summer NYSP sites, and to operate extended NYSP (ENYSP) activities between the months of October and May on a pilot basis at 45 sites.

The Policy Cycle

Although the federal funding that spurred the creation of ENYSP and the additional focus on drug-prevention activities arrived in 1989, NYSP in its summertime incarnation had a significant history preceding the evaluation effort. Further complicating matters, drug prevention activities were already part of the NYSP before the expansion initiated in that year. Additionally, the NCAA did not request the policy research until the new initiatives were already in place.

The implication of this sequence for research was that although the program was designed as an experimental pilot, it could not easily be evaluated by means of experimental methods. Also impractical was choice analysis, because the important features of the new program initiatives were already decided upon. These factors pointed toward a more process-oriented, descriptive policy research effort.

Clients and Stakeholders

Though funding was federal, the client for this project was the NCAA, which administered the ENYSP with the assistance of a grant from the DHHS-OCS via the Community Youth Activity Program of the Anti-

Drug Abuse Act of 1988. DHHS-OCS has oversight responsibility for the program.

The 145 colleges and universities nationwide and involved as sponsors of local ENYSP were also significant stakeholders. These institutions frequently contribute staff, funds, equipment, and use of facilities to the ENYSP activities. Many of the ENYSP staff are employed by or associated with these host schools.

NYSP participants and their parents were the final group of stakeholders.

Research Design and Implementation

Information needs

Although the NCAA monitored the activities of each ENYSP site through an auditing function, it had relatively little knowledge about how the newly inaugurated drug education initiative was being implemented, nor how well the new extended version of NYSP was faring. The research project's assessment was intended to accomplish the following major purposes:

- Documenting activities and participation in the ENYSP, with a particular focus on alcohol and drug-prevention activities
- Providing a detailed description of the organization, staffing, planning, and implementation in a representative sample of ENYSPs, and focusing on prevention activities and their coordination with the ENYSP in each site
- Assessing the consistency of the ENYSP prevention activities, especially with respect to what is known about effective prevention elsewhere
- Identifying the strengths and limitations of the extended ENYSP prevention program and providing the client with specific lessons and recommendations for improvement of their prevention activities in the future
- Assessing the effectiveness of ENYSP prevention activities in reducing the likelihood of alcohol and drug abuse among participants

Given this broad-based request for information, the research problem was primarily exploratory. However, elements of both descriptive and causal research were also requested. In sum, the situation demanded a clear description of how drug prevention was being implemented, an evaluation or assessment of that aspect of ENYSP, and an indication of whether ENYSP prevention activities "worked."

Existing data relevant to the policy research effort were very limited, partially because the program operated with a high degree of local autonomy. The records maintained by the central NYSP administration focused primarily on fiscal accountability and auditing information. Little was known—and less recorded—about how individual sites went about pursuing drug prevention. The extended program was a recent creation, precluding a wealth of data. These circumstances suggested that an extensive amount of data collection would be part of the research project.

Design and Methods

Design

Pursuant to the exploratory and descriptive information needs described by the client, the research conducted for this case was broad and in large part qualitative. At the center of the design was extensive fieldwork in the form of case study-site visits to a selection of ENYSP sites, along with direct observation of prevention-related activities at these sites. A second major data source was a survey sent to key staff members at each ENYSP site. This survey enabled programwide generalizations to be made, while the case studies would provide the necessary details about how ENYSP worked in a variety of settings. A third major data component involved a series of surveys of ENYSP participants that resembled a quasi-experiment. The survey was an attempt to determine whether ENYSP drug-prevention activities had any discernible impact on the knowledge, attitudes, or behavior of its youthful participants.

The overall strategy behind this design was to provide both detailed site-level information about the ENYSP processes and procedures, and complementary programwide information from the mail-in surveys. Data about the direct impact of the program, if any, would come from the surveys administered to participants before and after the extended ENYSP program year. These data could be analyzed in light of findings about the programs collected from the case studies and observation at each site. Thus much of the data collected from these three major sources would be overlapping, allowing findings from one data source to be cross-checked with that from another.

Methods

Many of the methods used in the study were intended to provide descriptive information about ENYSP *processes.* This process information was to provide *proximate indicators* of program success. For example, much of the case study and on-site observation activities were to be directed toward documenting such processes as staff selection, planning of drug-prevention activities, selection and development of drug prevention curricula, and so on.

The specific research methods used in the study were case studies and site visits, on-site observations, and program surveys.

CASE STUDY/SITE VISITS To provide outside perspective and to guide the activities of field research assistants, research associates visited each study site at least once. Each site visit included the following sorts of activities:

- Semi-structured interviews with ENYSP auxiliary staff, including drug education specialists, activity directors, enrichment coordinators, and community liaisons
- Observation of ENYSP activities, including athletic instruction and other activities; drug and alcohol education; and other enrichment activities
- Discussion and other collaborative work with on-site research assistants
- Observation of site environments and catchment areas

Additionally, at some sites, focus group interviews with small groups of ENYSP participants, parents, and community figures were conducted, tape-recorded, and transcribed for subsequent review.

ON-SITE OBSERVATION On-site observation of prevention and other activities was conducted by field research assistants. In all, more than 90 individual drug and alcohol enrichment sessions were observed and documented by on-site assistants. Additionally, the site visits by research associates enabled corroborative observation of on-site activity as well as coordination and oversight of the efforts of research assistants. The data collection effort consisted of the following specific tasks and activities:

1. *Selection of ENYSP study sites* This process required balancing known characteristics of ENYSP sites and their respective localities to produce a representative group of programs. The strategy was to select a group of sites that represented the geographic, demographic, institutional, and fiscal variation among ENYSP sites. Although the 13 sites ultimately selected did not comprise a truly representative scientific sample, they did represent a good deal of the variety ENYSP embraces.
2. *Selection and training of EMT research assistants for each site* Typically, research assistants were independent consultants or graduate students who resided near host campuses of ENYSPs. Training for participation in the study took place at a national ENYSP conference.
3. *Interviews with key ENYSP staff* To enhance the understanding of each site's prevention effort, research assistants conducted structured interviews with ENYSP staff, particularly drug education specialists. These interviews touched on drug and alcohol enrichment curricula, prevention philosophy, and other relevant topics.
4. *Observation of specific prevention and other ENYSP activities* Using instruments specially designed for this purpose, the on-site research assistants carefully documented, in 10-minute segments, each drug and alcohol enrichment session. Other activities, such as athletic instruction and games, field trips, and meals were also documented, though typically in less detail than the drug and alcohol enrichment activities. Documentation of these observations consisted of carefully describing the following aspects of each session:

- The *type of activity* conducted by ENYSP staff (such as lectures, discussions, video presentations, and so forth)
- The *reaction* of ENYSP participants (such as attentiveness and distraction)
- The *quality* of interaction between ENYSP staff and participants
- The *content* or *focus* of the specific activity (such as decision-making skills, information about drugs and alcohol)

5. *Evaluation of ENYSP activities* After the conclusion of each observed session or activity, the EMT research assistants were instructed to carefully evaluate the activities they had documented. Each activity was evaluated on a 5-point scale (unsatisfactory to excellent) along the dimensions shown in Table 7.1.

TABLE 7.1

Breakdown of Activities for Evaluation on a Scale of 1(Unsatisfactory) to 5 (Excellent).

Course Content
- Clarity of activity objectives
- Appropriateness of activity to objectives
- Reaction of youth participants
- Effectiveness of communication

Instructor Effectiveness
- Knowledge of topic
- Clarity
- Receptivity to questions
- Enthusiasm
- Organization
- Overall teaching ability

Environment and Structure
- Distractions, if any
- Disruption by participants
- Physical comforts

Overall Rating
- Composite rating of session

6. *Coding and analysis of observation documentation* The collected observations and evaluations of ENYSP activities by each site's research assistant were assembled and encoded to create a database that contained summary information for each session. In sum, the information about 93 sessions was encoded, providing a quantitative perspective on the ENYSP prevention effort. These data were subsequently analyzed from both an aggregate, quasi-national standpoint and a site-specific basis. Additionally, the on-site observation data were reviewed for the purposes of gleaning anecdotal information about specific activities and their outcomes.

PROGRAM SURVEYS A set of five surveys was mailed or delivered to each program site. Each survey tapped the background characteristics, experience, and other qualifications of its respondents, as well as perspectives on drug-prevention issues. These surveys were as follows:

- *Project manager/activity director survey* This survey requested project managers or activity directors from each site to describe their perspective on a number of prevention-related issues, including: (1) risk factors facing program participants, (2) criteria for selecting drug education specialists, (3) importance of various drug education topics, (4) preferred drug education activities, and (5) related program procedures and organizational information.
- *Drug education specialist survey* Drug education specialists at each site were asked to comment on a variety of prevention-related issues, including: (1) importance of various pedagogical skills, (2) planning of drug education activities, (3) use of packaged curricula, (4) time spent in various activities, and (5) other specific questions pertaining to drug education philosophy.
- *Enrichment coordinator survey* Enrichment coordinators at each program site were asked to respond to survey items similar to those given to other program staff. Additionally, they were asked to describe community resources used in ENYSP enrichment activities.
- *Staff survey* ENYSP staff, such as instructors and aides, were asked several questions about their views related to the program's drug prevention.
- *Resource specialist survey* Resource specialists—individuals from outside the ENYSP who have contributed to enrichment activities—were asked to comment on the program. Resource specialists include such community figures as law-enforcement officers, school officials, health-care workers, and other individuals with expertise in prevention. Included in the resource specialist survey were questions about coordination with ENYSP staff and activities.

As is frequently the case in ambitious, complex evaluation research designs, several problems arose during the execution of the above tasks. To an uncertain, but definite, degree, these problems made the findings less conclusive and/or less able to be generalized to all ENYSP sites. However, in nearly every instance, the study employed multiple data sources, which tended to strengthen overall validity. The most significant caveats were the following:

1. *Lack of a scientific sample of sites* As stated previously, the group of sites selected for intensive study did not comprise a random, scientific sample. For that reason, aggregate results based on data drawn from these sites could not necessarily reflect in any reliable

way on the entire ENYSP. The sampling of sites did, however, reflect the variety of ENYSP sites.

2. *Subjective documentation and evaluation of prevention activities* Although the instruments for recording and critically evaluating ENYSP sessions at study sites were carefully designed for this purpose of the study, the validity of the observations depended finally on the ability of individual research assistants to make impartial and accurate judgments. To an unknown extent, however, such judgments were subject to idiosyncratic flaws. For example, it was possible for an assistant to be inadvertently coopted into the perspective of the ENYSP staff and thus be less likely to record truly critical observations about specific sessions. Unfortunately, this "halo effect" of the program on the observers could not be accurately gauged, but the possibility that it occurred meant that observations were not uniformly reliable.
3. *Lack of comprehensive data for all sites* For a variety of unforeseeable reasons, data collection efforts were not complete at every site. In one instance, for example, a research assistant resigned his post in the middle of the study. At several other sites, research assistants either failed to attend or failed to properly document one or more of the relevant prevention-related sessions.
4. *Inability to document certain prevention activities and processes* The bulk of ENYSP programming is not, in fact, directed toward drug prevention. To the contrary, only about 7 or 8 hours of drug and alcohol enrichment is required of individual sites over an entire program year. Yet the sum of all ENYSP activities and social processes—such as athletic instruction and activities, role modeling, nutrition, cultural enrichment, and bonding—are undoubtedly related to the effectiveness of ENYSP as a prevention tool. Nevertheless, the quality and impact of much of these nonexplicit prevention "co-factors" were not well documented in the evaluation research design.

Therefore, although the focus of this study was necessarily on the more or less recognizable prevention-specific efforts, the predominant impact of ENYSP could well have been a more holistic one. In other words, just about every ENYSP activity could be viewed as a prevention activity. Yet the policy research necessarily focused on the drug and alcohol enrichment component, perhaps because it was the most practical approach to the information needs of the client. Moreover, this component represented the most manipulable aspect of ENYSP; prevention activities could most easily be adjusted and adapted. The major thrust of ENYSP—interaction between youths and adults—could less readily be modified, but it was arguably the most important.

Selected Findings

On the whole, the study found ENYSP to be an appropriate and potentially effective prevention program. However, the research effort was concentrated on identifying areas in which the program could be improved.

Model of Prevention Process

In a program as geographically diverse and with such a high degree of local autonomy, valid generalizations are difficult. Much of the report addressed specific issues that did not necessarily apply to the program as a whole. One contribution of the ENYSP study that did address the entire ENYSP effort was drawing attention to how complicated the path to effective prevention is. The report stated that weaknesses anywhere along the chain of activities could decrease the effectiveness of the program's prevention effort.

First, the unique setting of prevention resources and drug and alcohol risk factors and problems framed each site's program. Programs with ready access to comparatively more resources had an advantage, just as those situated in particularly troubled areas faced longer odds. Second, the ENYSP staff at each site—their qualifications, abilities, and dedication—were of critical importance in making the program work. Third, each NYSP site had to be able to envision its prevention goals and objectives, and subsequently seek to achieve those goals with a specific prevention strategy. Fourth, the specific activities that comprise the implementation of this strategy required planning. Fifth, prevention-related activities had to be appropriate and conducted so as to capture the attention of participants. Finally, ENYSP participants had to attend these activities regularly in order to receive an adequately intensive amount of drug and alcohol education.

As is typically the case with descriptive, formative research, insight into the processes that underlie the ENYSP prevention model came from multiple data sources. Perhaps the greatest such contribution, however, came from visits to ENYSP sites across the nation. The collective experience of the research associates provided a wealth of primarily qualitative data about how the program worked. These insights were transcribed into field reports, which were subsequently read and reread in an effort to look for common patterns of program processes and outcomes. The program process model was generated in large part in this manner.

Given the complexity of this chain, and the tenuousness of several of its important links, it is not surprising that the report found that not all ENYSP sites were optimally effective in their prevention efforts. Focusing on the chain of critical processes described above, the report identified the most common lapses in the prevention process identified by the data collection effort.

Inconsistent Attendance Rates

The study found that participation rates at some sites were inconsistent and occasionally disappointing. The significance of this finding is obvious: Effective prevention is impossible without consistent attendance among participants. Among the most significant causes for lagging attendance was irregular scheduling patterns for the program at some sites. At other sites, the program faced stiff competition from other organized youth activities or inadequate transportation for would-be participants. Attendance rates were monitored by the sites' research assistants, and during site visits by research associates. Causes for attendance variation were identified primarily through interviews with staff during site visits.

Limited Experience of Prevention Staff

The report laid heavy emphasis on the qualifications and experience of the staff charged with leading the prevention effort, the drug education specialist position. It indicated that some staff lacked extensive experience or professional qualifications to plan and implement effective prevention activities. A primary reason for inadequately qualified staffing was the recruiting process, which at many sites was done on an informal, in-house basis rather than through an extensive outside search process. The report found that some of the drug education specialists, despite their enthusiasm and devotion to their role, sometimes used methods and messages counterproductive to known good prevention practice.

The qualifications of drug education specialist(s) (DES) were gleaned from the survey administered to them at all program sites. The survey enabled calculation of such summary information as average DES experience with NYSP, education, and other pertinent information. Insight into the importance of the recruiting process came primarily from observation of drug education specialists in action during site visits. The report used direct quotes from the survey questions to illustrate different patterns of drug education specialist recruitment.

Inadequate Planning and Sense of Purpose

The report found that a lapse that affected many ENYSP sites was a lack of sense of a specific purpose for prevention activities and a concomitant lack of planning effort. Such difficulties are common among prevention programs, due in part to the lack of reliably effective prevention techniques.

Communicating and Using Results

Reporting Results

The final report was issued in two separate parts. One part focused on program processes, whereas the other contained the analysis of the before-and-after participant surveys and focused on program outcomes. The first part was organized both by program element (such as staffing or curricula) and by issues identified by questions. For example, one chapter of the report was titled Drug Education Staffing and Roles. Four of the six issue-questions addressed in the chapter were the following:

- How appropriate are the qualifications, backgrounds, and experience of ENYSP drug education specialists?
- Are drug education specialists recruited in optimally effective ways?
- How are ENYSP drug and alcohol education activities planned?
- How appropriate is the use of outside resources in ENYSP drug education?

The first part of the report also contained a summary chapter that reviewed the major findings of the study and presented specific recommendations. The second part of the report, which was based on the pre- and post-program survey administered to ENYSP participants, placed more emphasis on quantitative data and analysis.

Selected Recommendations

Recommendations were formulated to address each key finding. Among them were the following:

- Mindful of the important role played at each site by drug education specialists, the report recommended that each site actively search its respective community for applicants with professional backgrounds in drug prevention *and* experience working with high-risk youths. The report further recommended that drug specialists be offered intensive training in prevention-related topics.
- Because prevention activities observed in individual sites tended to vary from practices known to be more effective, ENYSP sites were encouraged to avoid straight information-giving lectures in favor of more interactive and/or participatory models.
- ENYSP sites were encouraged to develop policies that would reward and increase attendance and to inventory the specific drug and alcohol risks that affected their respective communities.

Action

The ENYSP evaluation provided a wealth of findings with both formative and summative implications. The use of this policy research provides good examples of the ways in which research findings may shape programs without explicit recommendations that change policy in relatively dramatic ways. The report indicated that a significant weakness of the ENYSP lay in the approaches to prevention taken by well-meaning local staff without extensive training in effective prevention techniques. Furthermore, the report was accompanied by a handbook on planning effective prevention and curricula that were explicitly responsive to the misconceptions common in local programs. These resources provided guidance on planning more effective prevention approaches. The study also alerted the director of ENYSP to the importance of guidance and monitoring of local prevention program content, and to the crucial importance of specific local staff, such as the instructional coordinator. All of this changed the way in which the central and local staff viewed the prevention component of their program, and presumably influenced their future actions in this area of the program.

A secondary outcome of the ENYSP research has had a lasting effect on the other prevention programs across the nation. The ENYSP evaluation supported the development of the Individual Protective Factors Index (IPFI), and supported the administration of this survey instrument to over 4,000 youths who participated in the study. The IPFI has become a leading standardized instrument for evaluation of a variety of youth interventions concerning substance abuse, school dropout, violence, or other youth problems. Subscales from the IPFI have been incorporated into a major national study of high-risk youth interventions being conducted by the Center for Substance Abuse Prevention. Thus, this research by-product of the ENYSP study made an ongoing contribution to development of programmatic and policy knowledge in the area of youth policy. Policy research can result in both immediate, practical benefits as well as long-term, more diffuse benefits for larger policy arenas.

Lessons for Policy Research

This project is a good example of how multiple methods with a primarily descriptive character can be integrated to provide useful information for decision makers. Whereas a traditional evaluation research approach might have sought to focus solely on whether the ENYSP activities had any measurable impact on their target populations, the EMT approach centered instead on finding useful information that could lead to improvements in the program. Because the client had relatively direct control over the program domain, these changes were practical and ultimately implemented. Thus, despite the fact that the direct "impact" of the program could not be well-documented (which may be an impossible task), focusing on process and immediate outcome indicators enabled the development of useful information.

Discussion Questions

1. What kinds of policy information would an agency providing prevention services typically need, in your opinion?
2. What are some of the inherent difficulties that policy researchers face when evaluating prevention programs?
3. Why were simple choice and/or causal analyses impractical in this situation?
4. What kinds of "process information" would be useful in this situation?
5. The client in this case study is a national nonprofit organization. What effects could this be expected to have on the conduct of policy research?
6. How might the fact that this project was not the specific result of a legislative mandate affect the type of information it addresses?
7. Why are qualitative methods so important to the policy research problem posed by ENYSP?
8. What sorts of overlap in the data collected by the three major data sources (case studies and site visits, on-site observations, and program surveys) would you expect to find? Is that overlap beneficial to the project? Why or why not?

Assignments and Activities

1. Conduct a brief literature review on the effectiveness of drug-prevention programs. What implications do your findings have for conducting policy research about the effectiveness and/or quality of specific programs in this field?
2. Locate a journal article or other source of a formal evaluation of a drug-prevention program. Contrast its methods, findings, and usefulness with the ENYSP study.

FOCUS ON RESEARCH METHODS

Site Visits and Case Studies

The ENYSP project relied heavily on a purposive sample of *site visits and case studies* to campuses where the program was in place. Although several national quantitative data gathering efforts were also used (such as surveys), the policy research team used the site visits to help learn in detail how the program operated, particularly in terms of processes. In policy research, a *site visit* may connote a number of activities undertaken at the location where a program actually occurs. A *case study,* which may or may not include a site visit, focuses a variety of research activities on a single program site.

In the case of the ENYSP study, policy researchers conducted case studies of a sample of ENYSP sites that included site visits to those sites. Among the research activities that occurred at each site were observation of program activities and processes, interviews and focus group interviews with ENYSP staff, participants, and other stakeholders, and discussions with on-site research assistants. Data from the case studies, which were conducted by several research associates, were assembled and analyzed on a large matrix that enabled cross-site comparisons.

Some scholars of policy research discount the value of conducting case study research because it lacks the rigor associated with more structured and quantitative approaches (see, for example, Frankfort-Nachmias and Nachmias 1996:147). However, with regard to descriptive information needs such as those entailed in the ENYSP study, the rich process and contextual insights generated by actually seeing a program in action may be indispensable and irreplaceable by other methods.

Furthermore, using a site visit or case study approach need not vitiate the validity or usefulness of policy research. Robert Yin and others have developed systematic approaches to conducting case studies that maximize both rigor and usefulness (see Yin and Heald 1975; Yin 1985; Lucas 1974).

Another consideration with respect to site visits is cost. The costs associated with the site visits in the ENYSP project were a significant part of the project budget; for that reason, only a purposive sample of sites (as opposed to a larger, randomly selected one) was visited. However, costs may be much lower with a less geographically dispersed target of inquiry.

CASE STUDY AT A GLANCE

Program Title and Policy Area Evaluation of the Extended National Youth Sports Program (ENYSP), 1991.

Program and Policy Background The ENYSP provided structured athletic activity coupled with cultural and drug-prevention education for economically disadvantaged youths. The program was implemented through sites scattered among college campuses across the nation. The NCAA received federal grant funds to increase the drug-education component of the program.

Client and Other Primary Stakeholders The client was the National Collegiate Athletic Association (NCAA). Other primary stakeholders included individual ENYSP sites, the participants, and their parents.

Information Needs Due in part to the nascent character of the program, the client had broad-based, descriptive information needs consistent with formative evaluation. Causal analysis was practically impossible.

Research Design and Methods Although extensive quantitative research was conducted in the form of surveys of program staff and participants, the pivotal research activity was a series of case study visits to a purposive sample of campuses where the program was under way.

Findings and Recommendations The project found that although the ENYSP program was apparently well designed and beneficial to participants, certain procedures were off the mark with respect to known qualities of effective drug-prevention programs. The final report recommended a series of specific, incremental adjustments in the implementation of the ENYSP.

Program Jargon and Acronyms

DHHS-OCS Office of Community Services, U.S. Department of Health and Human Services

drug education specialist ENYSP staff with responsibility for developing drug-prevention activities at each site

(continued on next page)

(continued on next page)

ENYSP Extended National Youth Sports Program
NCAA National Collegiate Athletic Association
risk factor According to drug-prevention theory, a characteristic of youths and their living situations that tends to occur at greater frequency for those who develop problems with alcohol and other drugs

CHAPTER 8

Deinstitutionalization and Community Services in Virginia

A Policy Assessment

Introduction

Across the United States, many states and communities have faced problems—real or perceived—associated with deinstitutionalization (see, for example, Bardach 1977). "Deinstitutionalization" refers to the process by which the primary treatment responsibility for the mentally disabled is transferred from mental health hospitals—often operated by state governments—to service providers in community-based settings. Deinstitutionalization is a complicated policy that encompasses the efforts of many agencies and programs. This case study relates one state's efforts to increase its knowledge and understanding for policy action in this arena through primarily exploratory policy research.* The research represents a panoply of research methods, including quantitative descriptive techniques and more qualitative and less-structured data collection efforts. The case is thus a good example of using multiple data collection methods. The case also illustrates how effective policy research can be in instigating action by decision makers.

The Policy Problem

Deinstitutionalization first became popular in the United States in the late 1960s, when mental health care professionals reached a working con-

*This case study is based largely on a report issued by the Virginia Joint Legislative Audit and Review Commission (JLARC 1985a).

sensus that care could occur most effectively and efficiently within the context of normal home and community ties. Deinstitutionalization became statewide policy in Virginia as early as 1968, when the state's general assembly (the lower house of the state legislature) authorized local governments to establish "community service boards," locally based agencies that delivered mental health services to clients discharged from state mental health facilities.

Deinstitutionalization became increasingly controversial in Virginia (as well as in other states) during the 1980s, when some criticized the practice as often consisting of little more than dumping the chronically mentally ill onto city streets (JLARC 1985a).

Initiation of Policy Research

As a result of growing concerns across the states about the fate of the mentally ill, as well as a general uncertainty about the details of how deinstitutionalization was working, the Virginia state legislature authorized the creation of the Commission on Deinstitutionalization to study related policies in the state. The legislature authorized the state's Joint Legislative Audit and Review Commission (JLARC) to provide "technical assistance" to the newly created commission (JLARC 1985a).

JLARC is a state agency that serves the state legislature by providing policy research in response to requests from legislators. JLARC had earned the reputation of being a tough but objective watchdog agency that the legislature listened to carefully. Although JLARC consists of state delegates (representatives from the lower legislative house) and state senators, in practice JLARC staff members are primarily responsible for actually planning and implementing the relevant policy research. Thus, this case study exemplifies policy research conducted within a government, but by an agency from outside the confines of the agency with the lead responsibility for the policy under study (in this case, the state's Department of Mental Health and Mental Retardation).

The Policy Research Task

JLARC staff were confronted by a daunting task: to provide the Virginia state legislature with information that could be used to help improve the entire state's primary means of mental health service delivery, including the local level.

Objectives

The general objectives of the study included the following:

- To help clarify the policy and programmatic issues associated with the policy of deinstitutionalization in the state of Virginia
- To provide baseline information about the mental health service delivery system
- To provide some indication of how well the then-current policy was working, particularly in terms of the adequacy of existing services and the procedures associated with them

(More specific objectives were also pursued in response to queries from the decision-making client, the legislature of Virginia. See the Information Needs section in this chapter.)

Challenges

The study presented a significant challenge to JLARC staff due to its potentially vast scope and complexity. Thus, this case represents an excellent example of how policy research must be shaped in order to adequately address the concerns of clients and stakeholders without exceeding available resources. When the scope is potentially as great as that encountered in this case study, policy researchers must find ways to make the project more manageable—yet in ways that will not compromise the objectives of the research.

In addition to the potential size of the study, the subject matter was also inordinately complex. The policy of deinstitutionalization entailed the cooperation of many state agencies as well as nearly every local government in the state. Further challenges existed in the lack of existing information about deinstitutionalization policies. Because the mental health service system was so decentralized—and perhaps also because of the novelty of the policy—JLARC staff could not tap existing databases for its study.

Finally, the study, which was conducted at the behest of a legislative body with fixed time horizons, had to be completed in a very short amount of time, approximately one year. Whereas some policy research projects can be conducted at a relatively leisurely pace with flexible deadlines, the deinstitutionalization study had to be finished quickly. The case study thus helps to exemplify how the political process places significant constraints on the conduct of policy research.

The Decision Context

The decision context for this study could hardly have been murkier or more complicated. Consider the following circumstances:

- Many policy actors—both clients and stakeholders—were involved in the delivery of services associated with deinstitutionalization.
- The policy of deinstitutionalization lacked firm legislative and programmatic parameters, having evolved over the course of several decades with relatively little strategic focus; thus, the position of the study in the policy cycle was not straightforward. It was focused primarily on providing information for planning and decision making for future policy direction. To do this, however, information on existing program effectiveness and implementation would go along with information on needs and demands.
- The information needs of the client—the state legislature of Virginia—similarly lacked specificity and focus.

The Institutional Context

Deinstitutionalization, as implemented in many states, entails a complex network of policy actors with a variety of responsibilities. The formal part of this network in Virginia included the state's Department of Mental Health and Mental Retardation (DMHMR) and the 40 local mental health agencies, known as community service boards (CSBs). DMHMR was the primary funding source for services associated with deinstitutionalization, and also provided technical support to the CSBs and monitored the quality of local programs. The provision of actual services to deinstitutionalized clients was the responsibility of the CSBs.

However, deinstitutionalization also connoted a less formal network of state and local agencies that provided a range of necessary support services to discharged individuals, including financial support, housing, and job training. Although these are not mental health services, such services contribute to the success or failure of deinstitutionalized individuals.

The agencies involved with the delivery of services to the deinstitutionalized clients are discussed in the following subsections.

Department of Mental Health and Mental Retardation

DMHMR was responsible for planning, coordinating, and providing mental health programs in Virginia. Most important to the process of deinstitutionalization, DMHMR operated the state's 15 inpatient treatment facilities (primarily hospitals), providing both intensive acute treatment and long-term care for the mentally ill.

The department's central office also played an important role in the community mental health system that served deinstitutionalized clients: ensuring that core services were available to those who needed them by planning, developing, and coordinating policies and programs for communities. A separate Office of CSB Liaison was specifically charged with the responsibility of coordinating the department's programs with those of local agencies. This office developed grants and performance contracts for CSBs and monitored CSB activities to identify potential problem areas.

Community Service Boards

The primary responsibility for actually delivering services to discharged clients from state facilities lay with the CSBs. Such services were offered either directly by CSB staff, or through contracts with private service providers. CSBs consisted of a board of directors and an executive director, as well as professional staff (such as psychologists, counselors, and nurses).

Thus CSBs played the central role in the deinstitutionalization process: They served as the primary intake point for clients entering the state mental health system and as the locus of the community-based care that is central to the concept of deinstitutionalization. By state law, the CSBs were required to provide client prescreening (that is, determining whether clients were ready to live in the community and which services they would require) as well as predischarge planning (that is, planning their exit from intensive care facilities into the community).

Because CSBs were established by autonomous localities, each had a different organization and a different set of programs, policies, and operating procedures. Whereas DMHMR had supervisory responsibility for local programs, the CSBs were also funded by local and federal funds: they had a great deal of discretion with regard to the services they offered. Their only legal mandate from the state was to provide emergency services.

Support Service Agencies

A less formally integrated network of state agencies provided important services to the clients released to the community. These services were provided to low-income clients, and because deinstitutionalized individuals are typically unemployed and with limited incomes, many of them qualify for support services.

Among the agencies that provided such services in Virginia were the Department of Social Services (DSS), which provided income supplements to clients in the form of an auxiliary grants program financed in part by the federal government, and the Department of Rehabilitative Services (DRS), which in many instances provided therapy and/or training to the deinstitutionalized.

The DSS role was the most significant to the study. The auxiliary grants were a significant source of funding for housing the mentally disabled. Additionally, the DSS had an important role in licensing board and care facilities known in Virginia as "homes for adults." Homes for adults are residential facilities for dependent individuals (such as the elderly or mentally disabled), usually operated by private individuals. In Virginia, they housed a large number of former residents of state mental institutions.

The Policy Cycle

As explained earlier, the policy of deinstitutionalization had been initiated in the state of Virginia nearly 15 years prior to the study under discussion here. However, initial scoping activity conducted by JLARC staff revealed that the policy was not a clearly delineated one. Deinstitutionalization, it seemed, was more of a policy concept than a specific series of legislation and/or procedures and regulations. Indeed, the issue of the apparent lack of a coherent deinstitutionalization policy had sparked the need for a similar JLARC study in 1979 only five years prior to this one (JLARC 1979). The 1979 study concluded that although deinstitutionalization had created progress in reducing the population of state mental institutions, considerable gaps existed among the provisions for taking clients who were discharged from such institutions. For example, clients were sometimes released into communities without prior warning or consultation with local mental health officials. Accordingly, the state's mental health service delivery system was fragmented, uncoordinated, and lacking central policy direction.

Thus the position of deinstitutionalization in the policy cycle was ambiguous. From the standpoint of time, the policy had been in place for some time and was clearly ripe for evaluation. Nevertheless, a clear policy had yet to be articulated, and perhaps that was the impetus for the policy research—the need to help further specify the appropriate parameters for deinstitutionalization.

Clients and Stakeholders

As the preceding discussion has demonstrated, deinstitutionalization-related policy in Virginia affected or involved a wide range of groups, agencies, and individuals. The primary client for the project, of course, was the Commission on Deinstitutionalization (and the state legislature it represented), but in a sense nearly every agency involved in the delivery of mental health services associated with deinstitutionalization was also a client. (That is often the case when policy research is conducted for legislative bodies.)

If not actual clients, the several state agencies that provided support services for people with mental disabilities were clearly stakeholders with a direct interest in the findings and recommendations of the JLARC study. (These agencies included the Department of Social Services and the Department of Rehabilitative Services.)

Additionally, several clientele groups associated with deinstitutionalization policy were also quite interested in the results of the study, including the state's representatives of the Alliance for the Mentally Ill and other groups and individuals (including parents of mentally ill clients) with an interest in the policy.

Finally, a number of local agencies beyond the CSBs provided services to discharged clients or were otherwise affected by the policy of deinstitutionalization. Entities such as local jails, courts, and hospitals frequently served as points of intake to the mental health service delivery system for dysfunctional clients in the community. Additionally, nongovernmental agencies such as the Salvation Army and shelters for the homeless also provided services and were thus interested parties.

Research Design and Implementation

The research design that emerged from this policy and decision-making context was necessarily both of broad scope and relatively unfocused. Due in part to the fact that the primary client—the Virginia state legislature—was relatively unclear about its information requirements, the study had a distinctly exploratory nature.

Information Needs

Clearly, the legislature was generally concerned about the overall effectiveness of the state's mental health delivery system, but "effectiveness" can imply many things and many possible research foci. Indeed, this study is an example of how a relatively open information request gives the policy researcher some discretion about what to do and how to do it.

Implicitly, however, the legislature placed several specific information requests in addition to its concern about the overall effectiveness of the system. For example, part of the impetus for the study was the visibility of so-called street people on city streets throughout the state. At public hearings conducted by the Commission on Deinstitutionalization, participants frequently voiced concerns that discharged clients were possibly falling through the cracks of the system. To what extent, if any, were these apparently homeless individuals the product of inadequacies in the state's mental health service system? This question pointed the JLARC policy researchers toward a more specific, descriptive information problem.

Some members of the legislature had also voiced concerns about the perceived and/or documented adequacy of adult homes. How appropriate were these privately operated residential facilities as housing placements for clients discharged from state mental health facilities? This question also placed a relatively more focused, descriptive question before the policy research team.

The study, therefore, helps to illustrate how the information needs of decision makers can be plural—in this instance, both exploratory and descriptive. What is also interesting is the extent to which the request from the legislature apparently avoided possible forays into questions that involved matters of either choice or causality. That is to say, no mention was made of investigating the actual effectiveness of deinstitutionalization policy vis-à-vis other policy options—which would have been a policy choice problem. Nor did the information request seek to determine the actual effectiveness of discharging clients from state institutions, a request that would have pushed toward a more causal research problem.

Thus, as is often the case with intragovernmental policy research,

JLARC was given a relatively wide scope with which to approach the policy of deinstitutionalization. The legislative resolution that called for the study merely called on JLARC to "provide technical assistance to the commission (on deinstitutionalization)" (JLARC, 1985a). JLARC, in turn, directed its staff to conduct a follow-up of a similar JLARC-authored study that had been completed in 1979. However, JLARC staff were also requested to conduct research in other areas "salient to deinstitutionalization policies." (JLARC, 1985a). Inasmuch as deinstitutionalization policies touched on many other programs and agencies, the parameters of the study were potentially quite broad indeed. It is not unusual for policy researchers to have a broad mandate that allows them significant discretion in deciding what policy makers will hear.

However, the study did not extend to a variety of tangential areas. For example, deinstitutionalization policies also apply to the areas of mental retardation and substance abuse. For the most part, the study avoided these areas. Additionally, the study avoided collecting data about the *effectiveness* of deinstitutionalization; that is, it did not seek to determine whether placing chronically mentally ill individuals in the community was making them or society better off. The resource and time constraints of the study kept it more focused.

Design and Methods

Given this quite open-ended mandate for policy information, JLARC responded with a research design that employed a variety of data-collection methods appropriate for a primarily exploratory research problem. The overall emphasis of these efforts was on providing baseline, descriptive information about how the state's mental health system was performing, with an emphasis on the outcomes associated with the chronically mentally ill.

Design

The research design placed a relatively heavy emphasis on the collection of unstructured "qualitative" information to support several more quantitative data-collection efforts. In order to be practical and manageable, the research design omitted any more rigorous techniques, such as experiments, sophisticated data analysis, or cost-benefit analysis. Quite probably, such methods would have yielded inappropriately narrow information of limited utility to decision makers in this context. The approach that was used, however, was quite appropriate given (a) the primarily exploratory information needs of the client and (b) the lack of preexisting baseline information about the policy system. Thus, this case provides a good illustration of how policy researchers must occasionally pick and choose among a wide variety of options among research methods to try to meet the information needs of their client/decision maker.

Methods

Specific data collection activities are described in the following subsections.

TRACKING A SAMPLE OF DEINSTITUTIONALIZED CLIENTS A key means of establishing baseline information about the performance of the mental health system was tracking the status of a sample of deinstitutionalized individuals from their origin in the state mental health facilities to their placement (if any) in communities around the state. The tracking task actually entailed three separate data collection activities:

1. Drawing a random sample of 350 clients who were discharged from mental health facilities during a one-month period
2. Requesting information from state hospital staff for each client, including admission status and discharge status, client management procedures, and service needs upon discharge
3. Completion of a follow-up questionnaire from the staff of each community service board to which clients in the sample were discharged, including the status of the discharged client, services delivered, and housing and financial status.

This three-step data collection effort enabled JLARC staff to assess the overall ability of state and community agencies to keep track of and to properly serve the chronically mentally ill.

SURVEY OF COMMUNITY SERVICE BOARD DIRECTORS Given the important role played by community service boards (CSBs) in delivering services to discharged clients, a comprehensive survey was submitted to each of the 40 CSB directors. The survey was intended to provide baseline information about the adequacy of community programs and services, as well as issues associated with the funding, costs, and adequacy of community service efforts.

CASE STUDY SITE VISITS To provide more in-depth, qualitative information about the mental health service delivery system, detailed case studies were completed at a purposive sample of 5 CSB sites. Additional, less intensive site visits were made to 10 additional CSB sites around the state. Case study sites were selected to reflect a variety of criteria, including geographic diversity, funding levels, program reputation, and proximity to state mental health facilities. Site visit activities included review of program documents (including client records), interviews with CSB and other program staff, observation of CSB facilities and programs, and visits to selected client housing sites.

INTERVIEWS WITH MENTAL HEALTH SYSTEM PROFESSIONALS To help provide additional depth and accuracy to the more systematic data collection efforts, JLARC staff interviewed a wide range of professionals directly or indirectly involved with providing services to clients with mental disabilities, as follows:

- Administrators from the state DMHMR, including program, fiscal, and support staff
- Directors and other staff from the state's major mental health facilities
- Administrators and various program personnel from the state DSS
- Staff from a variety of other state agencies, including the Virginia Housing Development Authority, the Department of Rehabilitative Services, and the Department of Housing and Community Development

REVIEW OF AGENCY RECORDS AND FISCAL DATA Existing data from agencies responsible for providing services to people with mental disabilities were reviewed and analyzed, including reimbursement and other fiscal data from the state DMHMR. These data were used to help identify the cost of various treatment and placement alternatives for discharged clients.

SITE VISITS TO HOMES FOR ADULTS To examine the availability and quality of placements in adult homes (board and care facilities), JLARC staff visited a purposive sample of 21 homes for adults. (A purposive sample is a nonrandom sample that is selected on the basis of the usefulness of each observation to the goals of the research.) A "critical case" strategy was used to select homes for study, such that the homes selected were those considered to be both the best and the worst in each area. This strategy enabled the range of quality and appropriateness of placements to be documented. During these site visits, JLARC staff interviewed operators of the home for adults, observed the facilities, and reviewed documents for residents with mental illnesses.

Selected Findings

The broad net of data collection efforts yielded an extensive collection of significant findings that addressed the full range of the state's mental health service delivery system. Consistent with the multiple methods employed by the study, most of the findings stemmed from more than one data source, with some exceptions. The key findings are described in the following subsections.

Profile of Discharged Clients

The most structured data collection method employed by the study was tracking the sample of discharged clients. Some of the findings from that effort are displayed in Table 8.1. From the standpoint of the objectives of the study, this profile was useful in conveying the service needs of the typical discharged client: most clients in the profile were young, single, unemployed, and required both supervision and medication to survive in the community. Most were not capable of functioning independently of the efforts of community service boards. This finding implied that the availability and adequacy of CSB services was critical to the overall success of the state system.

Adequacy of Client Management Procedures

"Client management" refers to the procedures and services related to keeping track of discharged clients and ensuring that they received appropriate and adequate services. Through the variety of data collection techniques employed by the JLARC policy researchers, a diagram that mapped the client management process similar to that in Figure 8.1 was created. The diagram illustrated the potential weak or "leakage" points in the system.

The study found that although client management practices appeared to have been improved, several patterns of inconsistent or incomplete procedures persisted throughout the mental health system. For ex-

TABLE 8.1

Profile of Discharged Clients (*n*=350)

Average age	35 years	
Gender	Male	58%
	Female	42%
Employment status	Unemployed	85%
	Employed	15%
Marital status	Unmarried	83%
	Married	17%
Mental health status at time of discharge	Improved, not recovered	82%
	Unimproved, not recovered	7%
	Other	11%
Prior hospitalizations during previous two years	No prior hospitalizations	28%
	One prior hospitalization	33%
	Two prior hospitalizations	39%
Ability to live independently	Requiring daily supervision	79%
	Remainder needed no supervision	
Need for psychotropic medication	Needing psychotropic medication(s)	79%
	Remainder needed no medication(s)	

ample, clients referred to mental health hospitals by local courts frequently failed to receive prescreening that might have prevented inappropriate admissions and/or improved coordination of services following discharge. Predischarge planning, although routinely completed by hospital staff and CSBs, was found to lack comprehensiveness and coordination between hospitals and CSBs. Some clients were being discharged while on "temporary leave" from state facilities, making proper predischarge planning impossible.

Note that whereas the quantitative data collection techniques helped establish how often some of these problems occurred, learning about how and why they could exist was established primarily through interviews and observation. Thus, the two general approaches complemented and supported each other in this study.

Adequacy of Community Services for Discharged Clients

The study established that community services for discharged clients were woefully inadequate. Data from the profile of discharged clients, for example, demonstrated that half the sample received only medication monitoring, meaning that other needs (such as housing and job training) may have gone unmet. The study described the following service gaps:

FIGURE 8.1

Deinstitutionalization Process

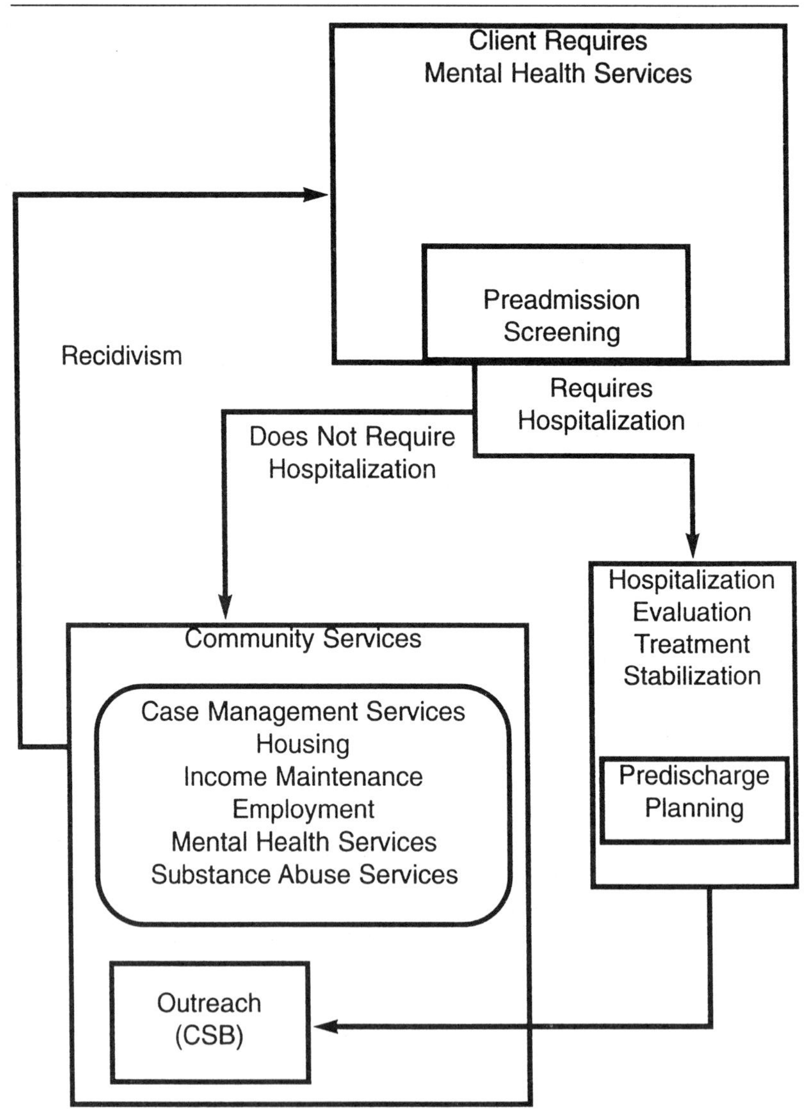

The diagram illustrates the flow of clients from diagnosis and to and from admission to hospitals and community-based services.

- *Absolute service gaps* Communities fail to provide an important service. For example, an absolute service gap would occur when a CSB offered no day support programs for its clients.
- *Program gap* Community lacks a specific program in a general program area. For example, a CSB could offer housing for certain types of clients but lack a housing program for chronic clients.
- *Capacity gap* Community offers a program that does not adequately serve all clients who need it.

This sort of taxonomy is frequently a by-product of policy research. Policy researchers often have to devise new terms and conceptual frameworks to help make sense of complicated policy arenas with limited existing conceptual tools.

Based on information from a number of data collection methods, the study found that the state's community service system contained a significant number of each type of service gap. Inadequacies were found throughout the "continuum of care" represented by inpatient, day support, outpatient, residential, and other service options. The study placed particular emphasis on the lack of housing for discharged clients because without adequate housing, clients could not make progress in dealing with their disabilities. The study established that the responsibility for housing clients was scattered among a number of state and local agencies, resulting in a lack of coordination and funding for adequate housing.

Table 8.2 presents data showing housing patterns for people with mental disabilities in Virginia in 1985. The second column is an estimate based on the survey of CSB directors. The third column is based on a profile of discharged clients. This comparison was used to help document some of the housing shortfall. Note that the data tend to reflect similar housing patterns, although one was generated from the summation of survey data and the other from the more rigorous follow-up study. The fact that the two indicators yielded approximately similar results bolstered the validity (and credibility) of both, thus providing a good illustration of the utility of using multiple measures to triangulate accurate policy information. Triangulation consists of increasing the accuracy of a measure by means of the use of multiple indicators.

Problems with Homes for Adults

The study found that homes for adults were an "unplanned component" of the state's deinstitutionalization policy. Although these homes should have

TABLE 8.2

Where People with Mental Disabilities Lived in Virginia in 1985

Setting	Statewide Estimate	Sample of Discharges
Family	45.9%	50.0%
Own dwelling	14.1	12.0
Homes for adults	13.5	4.1
CSB housing programs	3.3	3.8
Nursing home	1.6	0.6
Boarding home or hotel	9.6	1.7
Private home	1.8	1.5
No stable residence	2.1	1.2
Jail	N/A	5.7
Hospital	N/A	4.8
Other	2.1	8.2
Residence unknown	6.0	6.4
Total (*n*)	13,822*	343**

* Based on survey of CSB directors
** Based on profile compiled from follow-up study of discharged clients

been able to properly administer medications, provide adequate activities and programs, supervise potentially destructive behaviors, and enable access to CSB services, the existing laws and regulations did not serve to ensure that these conditions were satisfied. Although the report provided various sorts of documentation to establish the frequent inadequacies of homes for adults, vignettes drawn from the site visits, such as the following, were particularly effective in conveying the nature of the problem:

> The (policy research) staff entered a(n) . . . adult home during the lunch hour. The home was dark, dirty, and in apparent need of repair. Bed linen appeared to be filthy and residents were wandering about unattended. Only one staff person was on hand. The individual was busy preparing lunch, while also attending to other duties around the home. Although he had not received training or related experience in caring for the mentally ill, the individual boasted that the home accepted the worst cases, clients that other homes would not accept.

Having established that recordkeeping, staffing, and linkages to CSB services were inadequate in many adult homes, the report concluded that, as then regulated, the homes were frequently inappropriate and/or inadequate placements for discharged clients.

Other Findings

The study also reported findings about a variety of other subjects and included important statements about the overall accountability in the system for both finances and service provision. For the most part, these findings were based on the more qualitative data sources, such as reviews of current legislation and regulations, and interviews with knowledgeable officials ("key informants") in the mental health system. With respect to accountability for providing services, for example, the study noted,

> Currently the State operates or supports three overlapping systems which serve many of the same clients. State hospital services are provided by the Department of Mental Health and Mental Retardation. Community services are provided by 40 community services boards and funded largely through State and local general fund revenues. Finally, residential services are provided by adult homes which are supported in part by grants and monitored by the State Department of Social Services. The links in authority between these entities are often unclear, contradictory, or inoperable. As a result, accountability is diminished. Moreover, the operation of overlapping systems is financially inefficient. The outcome of this situation is the limited effectiveness of State policies and programs. Because accountability for services is unclear, many clients do not receive the services they require. The overlapping systems, coupled with a lack of accountability, make it difficult to identify and address problems in the delivery system. (p. 65)

Had the study relied exclusively on quantitative data-collection efforts, such a statement would have been difficult to establish. The use of multiple types of data helped contribute to a study that could address real policy and programmatic issues.

Communicating and Using Results

The JLARC study exemplifies a key difference between policy research generated by outside government agencies and policy research produced by consultants or done in house. The JLARC findings and recommendations about deinstitutionalization were announced at public hearings that were closely covered by state news media. Local newspapers (in the state capital of Richmond) featured the findings as well. The hearings were sponsored by the state legislature's Commission on Deinstitutionalization, guaranteeing a high public profile.

Reporting Results

The primary means for reporting the study results was a written report. The report was organized according to the various substantive program areas included in deinstitutionalization policy, and it contained the following chapters:

1. *Client Management* (included discussion of how clients are passed from one part of the mental health system to another—primarily from state hospitals to community service programs)
2. *Community Services* (focused on adequacy of services available in communities across the state)
3. *Housing Services* (highlighted findings about housing shortages and inadequacy of adult homes)
4. *Service and Fiscal Accountability* (synthesized policy-system–level implications of various findings and additional information about authority within the mental health service delivery system)

Recommendations were offered both in an introductory chapter that served as an executive summary and in appropriate contexts throughout the report.

Consistent with JLARC policy, the report also contained responses from state agencies concerning the findings and recommendations, which had been circulated prior to the report's release in draft form. The policy of inviting comment from policy stakeholders may help to ensure both accuracy and "buy-in"—a sense of shared ownership—from those who may help to maximize utilization of policy research.

Selected Recommendations

Recommendations were offered regarding each program area addressed by the report. The more significant recommendations, also organized by substantive categories, were the following:

1. *Client Management* To ensure coordination among CSBs and state hospitals, the report suggested that the legislature require that all "candidates for hospitalization" (that is, clients referred to state mental facilities) be screened by a local community services board. It also recommended that DMHMR develop a uniform predischarge planning and assessment instrument to ensure comprehensive planning for each client's return to the community.
2. *Community Services* The report recommended that the state legislature "give funding priority to the development and expansion of community services for the chronically mentally ill" (JLARC 1985b, p. 3). It also urged that the DMHMR be directed to assess the needs for services in each of the 40 community service board areas. More specifically, the report recommended that CSBs be funded to provide more inpatient care. (Increasing inpatient care would reduce the number of clients referred to state facilities.)
3. *Housing Services* The report recommended immediate increases in resources directed toward housing and residential services across the state. It also urged that a coordinator of residential services be named to (1) help develop residential services; (2) integrate the programmatic needs of people with mental disabilities with the supply of housing stock; and (3) disseminate technical information concerning cost-effective residential programs to CSBs. The report also recommended that all homes for adults be required to "maintain a minimal amount of trained staff and to provide adequate aftercare for the deinstitutionalized."
4. *Service and Fiscal Accountability* The report recommended that the state legislature "express its intent" (clarify the state's policy) regarding the role of state hospitals. It suggested that the state reserve hospitals solely for the use of those with severe disabilities and low-incidence disabilities that could not readily be addressed in a community setting.

Action

Response to the JLARC report and recommendations was relatively swift and significant. The state legislature acted to approve most of the specific procedural improvements suggested in the report. It also approved significant increases in funds directed toward services and housing for people with mental disabilities.

Lessons for Policy Research

This case study serves to exemplify that the context of policy research plays an important role in shaping the design and implementation of policy research and the response to it. In this case study of a policy research agency, the staff of the state of Virginia's Joint Legislative Audit and Review Commission conducted an expansive piece of exploratory research that identified many significant problems in a state's mental health services delivery system. Among the policy research lessons exemplified in this case were the following:

- *Scoping is important* With limited resources, the JLARC deinstitutionalization study proceeded from a broad legislative mandate to provide "technical assessment" to a relatively well-focused research design. The JLARC study identified and delivered valuable information in areas that addressed the information needs of the legislature. Scoping was accomplished by means of a series of research activities—primarily site visits and interviews—that helped to refine problem definition.
- *Multiple methods can be very effective* Although the JLARC study was primarily exploratory, it made effective use of multiple data collection methods to ensure more reliable information. The research design called for structured, quantitative data collection efforts—most notably a tracking effort that traced mental health clients from hospitals to communities—as well as more qualitative and relatively unstructured methods, such as site visits and interviews. Data from these sources were effectively interwoven to produce more valid (and hence more convincing) policy-relevant information.
- *Policy research can be more effective in a vacuum* Among the factors that helped to make the JLARC study particularly effective was the relative lack of information available in this policy arena. Decision makers (the state legislature) as well as stakeholders (especially the state DMHMR) were operating without baseline information about how the state mental health service delivery service system was operating. By supplying baseline data, JLARC was able to gain credibility and the undivided attention of decision makers.
- *Public agencies can be more effective at disseminating results* Because it was a public agency working for a high-profile public client (the state legislature), JLARC's findings were widely publi-

cized by the news media and watched closely by decision makers. Additionally, JLARC (as a matter of routine policy) worked to build support for the study by circulating drafts of findings and conclusions to stakeholders.

Discussion Questions

1. Both the client and the policy research team in this case were government agencies. How did this affect the policy research, in your opinion?
2. How did the policy research team narrow the focus of the project from its broader beginnings? In other words, how was the *problem situation* transformed into the *analyst's problem*?
3. The project report recommended more funds for mental programs. Yet the study did not conduct any cost-benefit or cost-effectiveness analysis. How is this possible?
4. Why were the various forms of qualitative research techniques critical to the success of the study?
5. Why was the vignette on p. 170 so effective in communicating the findings of the study? Is such an approach appropriate for policy research? Why or why not?

Assignments and Activities

1. Conduct a brief literature search of the effectiveness of mental health programs. Would your findings be of any use to a policy research project like this one?
2. Try to find a piece of policy research for your state that corresponds to the Virginia study. What differences and similarities do you see?
3. Imagine you are a legislator in your state. Write a request for proposal that would accurately describe your information needs vis-à-vis the state's mental health policy system.
4. Write a critique of the methods and findings of the study discussed in this chapter.

FOCUS ON RESEARCH METHODS

Tracking Client Outcomes

When examining programs and policies with complex processes such as mental health services, tracking a sample of clients is a useful way of quantifying program outcomes. The Virginia deinstitutionalization study included such an effort; the JLARC policy researchers tracked the progress of a sample of 300 clients who moved from state mental health hospitals to community service providers. The study was used both to help make generalizations about the ability of the state's mental health system to keep track of deinstitutionalized clients and to see whether clients received adequate services once remanded to the community.

Tracking individuals within such a complex system of care (including 6 state hospitals and 40 community service areas) was a daunting task. First, the policy researchers had to receive permission to look at the confidential mental health records of individuals hospitalized for mental disorders. Next, they had to create a data collection form that would enable them to extract pertinent information from hospital records—records that were not created with policy research in mind. Concomitantly, a data collection form for the community care providers had to be prepared, one that could deal appropriately with the many possible outcomes associated with the system. For example, one possible complication was that a client discharged from a hospital in one area might wind up moving to a community in a different area. The tracking study had to document all possibilities.

Unlike many of the methods discussed in this book, tracking studies are not a widely discussed research method with an established literature giving appropriate steps. In the case of the Virginia deinstitutionalization study, the policy researchers improvised, fitting the tracking study to the conditions and information needs dictated by the situation at hand.

CASE STUDY AT A GLANCE

Program Title and Policy Area Deinstitutionalization and Community Services in Virginia.

Program and Policy Background Because of concerns about the effectiveness of the state's mental health service delivery system, the Virginia state legislature commissioned a study of deinstitutionalization—the process whereby clients of state mental hospitals are transferred to community-based treatment settings.

Client and Other Primary Stakeholders The study was requested by the Virginia state legislature. Other primary stakeholders were various state agencies—including the Department of Mental Health and Mental Retardation, the Department of Social Services, and the Department of Rehabilitative Services—and clients of state and community mental health treatment facilities and programs.

Information Needs The legislature had both broad, descriptive information needs—such as the number of clients being served by various programs—and more specific, causal information needs, such as the number of clients who were being lost by the deinstitutionalization process.

Research Design and Methods A combination of broad-based, exploratory research methods—such as loosely structured case study site visits and interviews—along with more focused, quantitative methods, such as a follow-up study of a scientific sample of deinstitutionalized mentally ill clients.

Findings and Recommendations The study found a general lack of accountability for individual clients among the various agencies that participated in the delivery of mental health and related services. It also determined that such services were underfunded, adding to the various service deficiencies that were identified. The report recommended increased funding for mental health services and tighter, more inclusive regulations for the management of mental health clients.

(continued on next page)

(continued)

Program Jargon and Acronyms

client management procedures and services related to keeping track of clients with mental disorders and ensuring that they receive appropriate services

CSB Community Service Board—a local agency with responsibility for providing service to clients with mental disorders; 40 CSBs existed in Virginia at the time of the study

deinstitutionalization The process by which the primary treatment responsibility for people with mental disabilities is transferred from mental health hospitals—often operated by state governments—to service providers in community-based settings

DMHMR Virginia Department of Mental Health and Mental Retardation

DSS Virginia Department of Social Services

JLARC Virginia Joint Legislative Audit and Review Commission

predischarge planning The process of ensuring that clients with mental disorders receive appropriate services when released to community treatment

predischarge screening The process of ensuring that clients in mental hospitals are appropriate candidates for community treatment

CHAPTER 9

Evaluation of Welfare-to-Work Programs

The St. Louis POWER Demonstration

With Liz Sale, M.A., EMT Associates, Inc.

Introduction

In August 1996, President Clinton signed the Personal Responsibility and Work Opportunity Reconciliation Act of 1996, more commonly known as the Welfare Reform Act of 1996. The act calls for drastic reductions in national spending in the areas of Aid to Families with Dependent Children (AFDC), Medicaid, and food stamps, and it dramatically shifts responsibility for the administration of these programs from the national government to state governments. While this act symbolizes the most dramatic policy shift in the area of social welfare in recent history, the national mood was beginning to shift away from welfare as an entitlement program and toward welfare as a privilege in the 1980s. Congress had already passed the Family Support Act of 1988, which mandated that states establish programs to move welfare recipients into the work force through job training, educational assistance, and transitional child care, transportation, and medical benefits.

State and local policy responses to the Family Support Act varied greatly, with several states initiating more punitive programs, such as Project Leap in Ohio, that reduced the checks of welfare recipients who did not take part in educational assistance programs. Other states have introduced programs relying on voluntary client participation. Programs also varied greatly in the range of services offered to welfare clients, from job training to educational assistance and a host of other support services.

The Policy Problem

In 1990, the Department of Human Services in St. Louis County, Missouri, developed and implemented a welfare-to-work program demonstration that took a holistic approach to service delivery for welfare recipients. The focus of the program was reflected in its name, POWER, an acronym derived from People Off Welfare, Employed and Respected. The POWER program actually went further than the 1988 Family Support Act by asserting that successful transition from welfare to the work force cannot be achieved without personal development and peer support. This premise for the program was derived from policy research that established a multilevel social system perspective on the problem of moving welfare recipients to the work force. More traditional "workfare" programs typically address job readiness and job training without providing personal and environmental support services. Thus, POWER was initiated as a demonstration that would provide lessons for establishing effective welfare-to-work programs in St. Louis, and hopefully elsewhere.

POWER program staff designers felt that many welfare recipients would fail to participate effectively in such programs—let alone achieve employment objectives—because of unaddressed problems in their personal lives and in their environment. The core of the holistic concept was to develop a program that would meet a range of needs that created barriers not only to employment but also to making effective use of services leading to employability. The program strategy was based on the expectation that addressing these multiple barriers would increase the program's success in helping participants attain jobs.

POWER staff delivered few direct services. In most instances, they acted as facilitators, referring welfare recipients to services provided by other agencies. To implement the theory that transition from welfare to the work force must include personal development and environmental support, POWER used a three-pronged approach:

- *Personal development services* were delivered by instructors and counselors with extensive job-training experience but no formal counseling background. These services were designed to help participants identify barriers in their lifestyles and situations that prevented them from moving off welfare and to take positive action to overcome these barriers. The services were delivered directly by POWER staff, both in a two-week orientation and through continued case management.

- *Environmental support services* were intended to provide ongoing resources to address the financial, logistical, and situational barriers that impinged on the ability of participants to benefit from program services. Specifically, they included a child-care allowance, a transportation allowance, and access to transitional Medicaid eligibility through existing programs. These services were arranged through POWER.
- *Education, employment, and training services* were delivered by means of Adult Basic Education classes, vocational training classes, an on-the-job training program, and job-search workshops. POWER facilitated selection, access, and effective participation in these services through links with multiple general education diploma (GED) and job-training programs.

Thus, the policy problem addressed by POWER was profound. At the local level, the problem related to the desire of local job-training officials to improve their services to a high-need group of clients. At the national level, the program had implications for successful implementation of the sweeping welfare reforms being developed at the time of the POWER demonstration.

Initiation of Policy Research

The initiation of evaluation activities for POWER was unusual because of the close involvement of the program delivery staff. The program concept arose from the experience of staff members involved in job-training programs who had been discouraged by their lack of success in serving mothers who were trying to end their AFDC dependence. These staff members could see that their efforts were overwhelmed by the many other problems the mothers had to address in order to participate in job training. For most, these barriers proved insurmountable. This issue gained urgency for staff because the initiation of the Missouri FUTURES program, the state's welfare-to-work initiative, promised to send more AFDC recipients their way.

Thus, service deliverers and administrators in the job-training division sought funding for a demonstration that would test their ideas about a program they believed might motivate participants and allow them to take full advantage of job-training services. The future program director and county administrators sought funding opportunities and eventually wrote a proposal to the Missouri Department of Elementary and Secondary Education, which administers job-training funds in the state. As part of the funding award, it was agreed that the demonstration would be fully evaluated by an independent, outside contractor.

The evaluation itself was initiated through a competitive bidding process. The county issued a request for proposals (RFP) and received several proposals. The two top-rated applicants were invited for interviews before a final selection was made. Again, the future program director was involved in this process, and the selection of a contractor had strong implications for the future of the evaluation. Specifically, the two finalists had proposed very different approaches to the evaluation. One proposed a traditional outcome evaluation based on preprogram and postprogram questionnaires with long batteries of items aimed at assessing intended attitudinal and behavioral outcomes. This approach would have focused on assessing simply whether the program had achieved its formally stated objectives at some "postprogram" state. This approach was consistent with the traditional textbook evaluation model.

The second proposal explicitly stated reasons why a simple outcome study would not address many of the policy and program issues that the demonstration would pose. This proposal explained how detailed process information would help fine-tune program implementation, how process understanding would explain *why* the program experienced success and shortcomings, and how an integrated process-and-outcome study would contribute to local policy development with respect to the coming wave of national welfare reform. The second proposal also identified ways in which the evaluator would regularly feed evaluation findings back to program staff so that they could make appropriate program improvements. The staff who made the funding recommendation found this second approach particularly appealing. The involvement of program staff in the selection process, and the explicitness of the evaluator's intention to provide formative feedback, ultimately had a positive effect on the use of evaluation results.

The Policy Research Task

This study provides an example of how policy research can be used as a tool to evaluate and improve individual program components and processes, rather than only to document whether a program, as a whole, had the intended outcomes or impact. Traditional outcome-oriented evaluation activities might have focused too narrowly upon "success" measures, such as length of employment, or wages earned. The task here was to develop a comprehensive means of evaluating a holistic approach to achieving a welfare-to-work transition.

Objectives

The objectives of the evaluation were defined in the proposal and clarified in the final interview and early contract negotiations; they were as follows:

- To describe and document the services provided to clients through POWER
- To assess client reactions to the services and provide feedback to the program
- To identify important immediate, medium-term, and ultimate outcomes, and to collect client data on their attainment
- To assess the reasons for success and failure in attaining outcomes at each stage
- To make recommendations for program and policy improvement

The fact that the client clearly understood the objectives prevented misunderstandings later in the study.

Challenges

Traditional approaches to evaluating welfare-to-work programs typically seek to measure only program outcomes, such as determining whether clients become employed and at what wages. The POWER program represented a different approach, and therefore required a creative policy research strategy. Thus, the policy research team had to devise a research plan that could tap into the multidimensional, holistic approach while simultaneously tracking and assessing traditional outcome measures. Meeting this challenge required a more formative, case study approach rather than a traditional experimental or quasi-experimental research design.

The need for a multifaceted transitional process had implications for the policy research task. For many participants, the transition process was expected to be long and difficult. To meet the final objective of stable employment, many transitional objectives would need to be accomplished. Thus, individual participants could conceivably make significant progress toward employment as a result of their involvement in POWER, even though they did not actually attain stable employment. The goals of the program were much more extensive than merely the end goal of employment.

Program success, therefore, had to be measured in terms of the program's ability to help participants achieve interim goals on the way to sustained employment. Such measures could also be indicative of the program's ability to provide support adequate enough to prevent personal or social problems from halting progress. From a research point of view, documenting and assessing the transition process was a challenge because it meant data had to be collected systematically at several points in the participants' progress through the program.

The Decision Context

POWER was a demonstration project with funding of limited duration. For the project to succeed, policy research was necessary to describe and assess the effectiveness of the program to decision makers at several levels. Service delivery staff wanted input for guiding and improving their work with clients; county administrators wanted information that would help them decide how much support they should give the program; and state (and even federal) policy makers would be interested in information that would help design more effective welfare-to-work programs. Thus, the evaluation findings had potential impact on decisions at several levels.

The Institutional Context

POWER was administered by St. Louis County's Department of Human Resources, and more specifically, by the Division of Employment and Training within that department. St. Louis County itself does not have an evaluation division, and many of the personnel involved with the design and implementation of the POWER program had little experience in evaluation or knowledge of its purposes. In addition, the Division of Employment and Training staff had experience in training unemployed persons for the work force through job readiness and job-training programs, but they had no experience addressing the particular needs of AFDC recipients, many of whom had never worked and who had practical and personal needs (including child care and transportation) that the county had not had to address in the past. This posed particular challenges for program implementation and made the need for process, in addition to outcome, evaluation all the more important.

Another relevant institutional factor was the degree of cooperation required between the different entities within St. Louis County to implement this holistic program approach and, concurrently, to evaluate the effectiveness of this approach. POWER's core two-week personal development program services were held in one building with three program staff. After the two-week period, participants were supposed to enter one of three additional programs: a GED program at several different locations throughout the county; a job-training program at a job-training center; or a job-readiness training program at another location. Evaluation activities therefore had to occur at several different sites, and understanding the degree of cooperation between POWER staff and other staff affiliated with the program's success was crucial.

Although the POWER staff was involved in evaluation activities and committed to using results to improve their program, staff in the ancillary organizations that provided training and support services to POWER clients had no such prior commitment. If the evaluation produced important recommendations for clients, they may or may not have felt a need to follow up on them.

The Policy Cycle

The POWER study is an example of policy research that was consciously designed to have implications throughout the policy cycle. Indeed, this aspect of the policy research team's response to the competitive RFP was part of the reason for the award. Whereas the research was called an evaluation, it was clearly more than a traditional outcome study. The focus on process meant that the study directly addressed the implementation stage. The demonstration aspect of the project anticipated that it could provide information relevant to policy formulation and planning.

Clients and Stakeholders

In this case, the most important group of stakeholders was the POWER program staff. The program concept had really been developed by a few local staff members in the St. Louis Department of Human Resources, and these people were very attentive and involved with working with the policy research team. The program director, her direct supervisors, and the two POWER caseworkers were all intensely interested in the results of the study, both for concrete suggestions for program improvement and for more general policy direction within the department's job-training programs.

Another group of stakeholders was the other government agencies that delivered services to POWER clients. The Missouri Department of Elementary and Secondary Education, for example, provided funding for the demonstration and had an interest in the report for their own program development purposes. The four GED programs (all in local school districts) and the job-training referrals for POWER clients (publicly supported nonprofit organizations) were concerned about assessment of their services. A final group of stakeholders were the POWER clients themselves.

Research Design and Implementation

Information Needs

POWER embodied a novel approach to welfare services, one that embraced multiple program goals, and the information needs of POWER staff therefore extended beyond tightly focused causal information needs. In addition to information about whether program participants succeeded at finding jobs and other goals, POWER staff needed to know how and to what extent the *process* of transition from welfare to work functioned. Thus the program needed descriptive information that could be used to assess individual program components, and not merely causal information documenting whether the program, as a whole, was successful in achieving ultimate objectives.

One common problem with welfare-to-work programs is their tendency to focus (often inadvertently) on clients who are most likely to succeed in meeting the program's goal. This can be achieved, for example, by selecting clients who are the most employable and are likely to get jobs anyway, or by focusing program resources only on such clients. This pattern is known as "creaming." One important goal of the policy research was to determine whether the POWER participants were in any way atypical of welfare clients in the area. This exemplifies a descriptive research information need. The research was designed primarily to describe the progress of clients through a logically organized series of steps.

Design and Methods

Design

As noted earlier, the evaluation team for this study proposed a design that departed from simple premeasurement, postmeasurement, and comparison group logic. The fundamental design depended on specifying the "expected" movement of clients through multiple program steps, specifying intended outcomes for each step, and measuring the degree to which clients attained these multiple, sequenced outcomes. Knowledge of which outcomes were achieved and which were not would support inferences about how and why the program worked or did not work.

Methods

As part of the demonstration project design, policy research was conducted over a two-year period and was designed to move from a more formative emphasis on implementation to a more summative focus on program outcomes. The policy research used a multiple-method data collection, an appropriate approach to collect information about a program with multiple objectives. Information about program outcomes was gathered from three principle sources:

- *Case tracking* Information about all 173 program clients was gathered from the inception of the program. Case tracking included existing information gathered from case records and was supplemented with information from POWER staff regarding client status. This case-tracking data collection was the central feature of the POWER research design. Many program evaluations rely almost entirely on self-reported information gathered from clients through questionnaires or interviews. The nature and quality of the implementation are thus inferred from client perceptions. The strategy used for the POWER evaluation focused on close documentation of the program and the progress of clients through its sequential components. The primary data sources were program attendance records and case-tracking forms developed collaboratively by the evaluation team and program staff.

- *Client interviews* Attempts were made to interview by phone all clients who participated in the program. Interviews included questions regarding the status of the client in the POWER program and their satisfaction with various aspects of their lives. (Clients were sent a letter from POWER staff informing them that they would be interviewed by a member of the policy research team.) About half of the clients were eventually interviewed. Additionally, several clients were interviewed on a more intensive, face-to-face basis to gather more in-depth information about program processes.
- *Staff and referral interviews* The POWER program managers and caseworkers were interviewed in depth early in the evaluation and again at the completion of the project. Staff members were asked about program goals, intervention strategies, and implementation issues. Evaluators also worked very closely with staff in developing complete tracking data for each client. Because most of the actual educational and job-training services were delivered by external agencies, the evaluation design also included in-depth interviews with the staff in the GED and job-training provider organizations. These interviews included a general overview of the goals, strategies, and track record of the program, and they were focused on the appropriateness of the services for the specific POWER target population.

Selected Findings

The POWER evaluation generated a large volume of information. The tracking format produced detailed information in the movement of clients through the program, and the survey and interview information provided rich detail about the status of clients at each stage of program progress. The volume of data, and the need to synthesize findings from different data sources, required substantial analytic skill and effort. Multimethod research can be very revealing, but it requires hard work and skill to produce its potential benefits. Select findings from the full study are discussed in the following subsections.

TABLE 9.1

Comparison of POWER Participants to St. Louis County's AFDC Population

Characteristic	POWER candidates	County AFDC population
34 years old or younger	73%	89%
Female	97	100
African American	75	88
Single-parent household	98	95
3 or fewer children	91	92
	n- 206	*n*- 8,028

Client Profile

With respect to the issue of client "creaming" mentioned earlier, comparisons of POWER participants to the general AFDC population in the area indicated that the POWER program did not select an unrepresentative clientele. Table 9.1 compares POWER participants to the St. Louis County welfare population in terms of their age, gender, race, marital status, and number of children. In summary, the table indicates that the POWER population was very similar to the AFDC population in St. Louis County. They did tend to be a little older and were less likely to be African American. Additional profile data revealed that a large majority of the POWER clients faced multiple barriers to employment, including low educational levels. Creaming was not evident from the standpoint of potential barriers to employment.

Transitional Dropout and Success Rates

The findings provided information on the progress of POWER clients through the program, and they estimated the degree to which participants were able to reach transitional goals and to attain and maintain employment. The flowchart in Figure 9.1 summarizes this information in visual form. This type of flowchart is a common product of policy research—it assembles information from disparate sources into a digestible format that summarizes many program outcomes simultaneously.

As the figure indicates, around three-fourths of all POWER participants who completed the personal development class started another

FIGURE 9.1

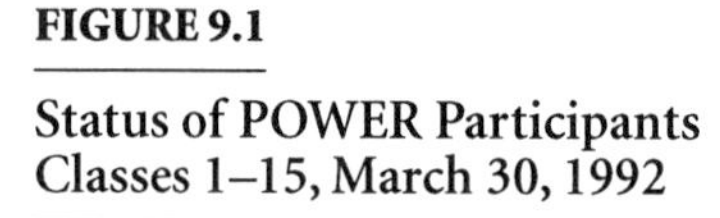

Status of POWER Participants
Classes 1–15, March 30, 1992

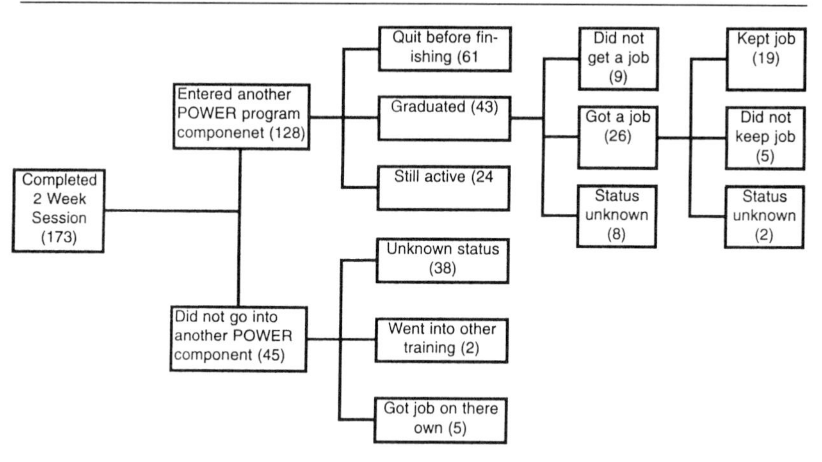

component to the program, and around one-fourth graduated from the next component (either a GED program or a vocational education program). Approximately 15 percent found employment, and 11 percent were still employed nearly two years into the program's history.

The data in Figure 9.1 could be used to pinpoint those phases in the program that gave clients difficulty—phases they did not complete. Table 9.2 displays the transitional drop-out rate that indicates the percentage of participants that did *not* complete a particular step in the program (such as, those who did not enter any of the educational- or job-training options offered by POWER after completing the first stage). The table also presents a transitional success rate, which includes those participants who *did* complete the transition; the overall success rate is the percentage of the total 173 participants who completed the 2-week class and reached each successive level.

The transitional drop-out and success rates enabled policy researchers to identify those points in the transitional welfare-to-work process that are most problematic for participants. The rates clearly indicate that the greatest percentage of drop-outs occur during the educational and job-training segments of the sequence. Thus, the research helped to establish that the program's overall success rate could best be improved by focusing on the problem of effective participation in the education and training-services programs.

This finding was of great importance for developing useful study findings. Specifically, it gave the process findings on the GED and job-training components of the program special importance. If programs like POWER were to succeed, it is essential to understand *why* clients were dropping out at these points.

This link between intermediate outcomes and process findings was fruitful. The GED programs to which POWER clients were referred did not target students with the background that typified POWER referrals. The programs used computer-based instruction that assumed high motivation and self-learning skills. POWER clients often felt overwhelmed and unsupported in this environment—and accordingly left the program.

For job training, the issues were somewhat different. The remote location of the training center and the limited child-care and transportation allowances meant that the logistics of participation for many POWER clients were difficult, contributing to program drop-out rates. These findings had clear implications for improving program success.

Who Drops Out?

The evaluation data set included information on client circumstances and background that could be used to describe who was successful in completing program components—transitional objectives. This analysis provided evidence consistent with the process findings reported earlier.

Table 9.3 presents findings on the percentage of clients who com-

TABLE 9.2

Summary of POWER Participants, Progress through Stages of the Program (*n*=173)

Completed a two-week class and....	Transitional Drop-out Rate	Transitional Success Rate	Overall Success Rate
Progressed to another program component	26%	74%	74%
Completed at least one program component after two-week class	58.7	41.3	24.9
Achieved employment	25.7	74.3	15.0
Maintained employment	20.8	79.2	11.0

TABLE 9.3

POWER Participants' Perceptions of Program Impact

Area of Life	Big Difference	Some Difference	No Difference	Not Applicable
Feeling good about self	54.7%	33.3%	9.3%	2.7%
Setting achievable goals	54.7	34.6	8.0	2.7
Developing better job skills	48.0	25.3	21.3	5.4
Making new friends	40.0	36.0	20.0	4.0
Taking control of their lives	37.3	38.7	21.3	2.7
Getting a job they liked	28.0	20.0	26.7	25.3

pleted a training or education component beyond the two-week orientation. The results indicate that clients with younger children and more children are much less likely to succeed, confirming the importance of problems related to child care. Similarly, the negative effects of low academic achievements are clear. Even though the POWER program did not cream at entrance, the configuration of program services did not adequately meet the needs of many welfare mothers with low educational attainment and with young children.

Self-Reported Effects

As described earlier, the POWER program concept included objectives other than attainment of employment or completion of specific training; the personal development class and other personalized components of the program were designed to bring about attitudinal and behavioral changes that could prepare participants to take advantage of future opportunities.

Survey data were used to help document the program's effectiveness in this area. One of the basic objectives emphasized in the POWER program was self-esteem—the degree to which participants felt good about themselves and recognized their own worth and self-respect. The attainment of such goals (other than employment) was an important objective of POWER participation. Table 9.4 provides an indication of how survey results were used to measure the extent to which POWER benefited participants in at least some way.

One implication of this analysis is that the POWER program's phased and multifaceted approach to aiding the long process of transition produces at least some perceived benefit for the majority of participants. Furthermore, the most widely reported effects were associated with the objectives of the initial two-week program. Programs that focus only on education or training probably do not achieve this broad, positive contribution because they do little to address the basic transitional needs of clients. Some may actually damage self-esteem and other basic attitudinal requisites by creating a situation in which those with greater needs are more likely to fail. Only policy research with a commensurably broad focus could have captured the various ways in which the program succeeded (or in some cases, failed) to meet the larger needs of clients in the POWER program.

TABLE 9.4

Program Successes by Client Characteristics, as Reported in Survey of Clients

	Percentage Who Succeeded	Percentage Who Did Not Succeed
Age (years)		
18–21	32%	68%
22–25	49%	51%
26–29	50%	50%
30–34	33%	67%
35–39	44%	56%
40+	0%	100%
Children		
1	47%	53%
2	43%	57%
3	33%	67%
Preschool Children		
Yes	39%	61%
No	55%	45%
High School Diploma		
Yes	49%	51%
No	28%	73%
Reading Ability		
Less than 8th grade	29%	71%
8th grade or higher	47%	53%

Communicating and Using Results

The involvement of program and agency personnel in the award, design, and implementation of the evaluation created a positive context for communicating study findings and recommendations. The evaluation team was actively involved with the program staff and did not hesitate to make recommendations for program improvements.

Reporting Results

The POWER program provides an excellent example of the effective use of evaluation information, for several reasons:

- The program staff and departmental supervisors had a personal interest and role in the development of the program and in the selection of an evaluator. They *wanted* to use the program to learn more about how to help clients make a successful transition from welfare to work.
- The winning evaluation proposal stated a clear intention to deliver useful information and described how this information would be produced through a case study approach that combined process and outcome results. The program staff knew what they would be getting and that it would fit their information needs.
- The evaluation team established a strong and cooperative working relationship with program personnel. They regularly scheduled planning meetings with staff, developed evaluation materials in consultation with staff, and regularly observed program activities. There were no surprises in evaluation data or analysis.
- Reports were prepared to convey findings and recommendations in clear, nontechnical language. A timely interim report emphasized ways to improve program services. All reports were reinforced with oral presentations, using overhead projections and handouts.

Selected Recommendations

Because the POWER evaluation was as much a process evaluation as an outcome evaluation, recommendations were fed back to POWER staff in quarterly memos, a one-year interim report, and a final report after the conclusion of the two-year evaluation period.

The evaluation study demonstrated that the program was serving its target population, that it had been successful in addressing participants' self-concept and building self-esteem, and that that for those who had obtained employment, there had been a slight increase in post-POWER program hourly wages. While approximately 20 percent of POWER participants actually acquired a job during the study period, many more participants achieved other important transitional objectives, such as finishing an educational or job-training component. Indeed, self-reports would indicate that more than 90 percent of the respondents achieved some transitional objective through their participation in POWER. Furthermore, the relatively low quality of the jobs acquired by POWER participants indicates that getting a job is typically part of an even longer transition to stable employment with a future.

Although the program was successful in engaging clients in the transition process, it was less successful in effecting sustained involvement in active transition activities for a significant number of participants. Evaluation recommendations focused on this important finding.

Ideally, the POWER program would facilitate transition by being housed at one central location with the intensive personal development phase of the program extending over a six-month to one-year period. However, given resource constraints, the report made the following recommendations:

1. On-site GED instruction with limited class sizes to maximize interaction between teachers and participants
2. Better referral procedures to available community resources to minimize individualized attention to personal issues beyond the expertise of POWER staff
3. Mandatory attendance at support group meetings to enhance attendance
4. Lengthening the two-week personal development phase to three or four weeks to enhance social skill building, including conflict resolution and decision-making skills
5. Systematic documentation of client personal backgrounds and support systems to help guide program development

More problematic, the report emphasized the need for training programs that would be more accessible and appropriate for this population and that would lead to careers with a future. These training services were outside of the immediate control of POWER. Enhanced support for transportation and child care were also identified as significant needs.

Action

POWER staff were quite receptive to the evaluation recommendations and implemented some of them immediately, resulting in improved program implementation. The most important action was the initiation of on-site GED training with an emphasis on the needs of POWER clients. Staff also modified their counseling approach, and adjusted the two-week course to focus more on specific problems and skills clients will need to progress successfully through the program. Evaluation played a key role in assisting program staff to focus on addressing the general issues of personal and social development, and to leave more complex, psychological issues to referral agencies better equipped to address them. Second, evaluation also assisted program staff in recognizing that, whereas community resources may be scarce or inadequate in many cases, program success would depend on forming strong linkages with community referral agencies that are equipped to address the issues facing this population.

Lessons for Policy Research

The evaluation of the POWER program demonstrates that useful recommendations regarding program issues can have a significant impact on program implementation, and that using a case study approach to process and outcome evaluation can help determine where program implementation is successful and where it needs to be enhanced. Although the study did not use a classic scientific experimental design, it did provide convincing and practical information on program effectiveness because descriptive findings were closely linked to program logic and intent.

The POWER demonstration policy research provides a good example of an evaluation design and implementation that avoided the problems credited by many evaluations that adhere too closely to rigid formal models of summative, outcome evaluation. An evaluation that addressed POWER outcomes without the kind of process analysis described here would have missed the issues of inappropriate support services that would have remained hidden within the program's black box.

Discussion Questions

1. How did the national welfare policy agenda affect the initiation of this project?
2. For what reasons was the contract awarded to the policy research team? What implications does this have for generating useful policy research?
3. How was utilization built into the research design of this project?
4. How was the research design consciously designed to be relevant to the entire policy cycle?
5. Why wasn't a classic experimental design used for this study?

Assignments/Activities

1. Identify a welfare-to-work program in your area (or state). Write a brief proposal to evaluate it that builds on the lessons from this case study.
2. Briefly describe a design for an experimental approach to evaluating the POWER program. Would it be practical? Why or why not?

FOCUS ON RESEARCH METHODS

Pilot Projects and Policy Research

One of the most appropriate uses of policy research is in the context of a *pilot* (or demonstration) project. These projects are generally small-scale experimental (and therefore temporary) programs or projects intended to test the effectiveness of a particular policy strategy. If the pilot program succeeds, it may be replicated on a larger scale elsewhere. Although all levels of government use pilot projects, the efforts of the federal government are perhaps the most widespread. Federal agencies frequently use pilot or demonstration projects to encourage state or local governments to try new approaches to implementing federally funded policy initiatives.

Policy research is frequently legislatively mandated to evaluate the success of the pilot or demonstration program or project. Because of their experimental nature, pilot projects are frequently amenable to experimental or quasi-experimental research designs. Conditions relevant to the project can be measured before and after implementation of a pilot program, for example; or experimental and control groups of program participants can be created and monitored over the course of the project.

In the POWER demonstration project case, however, an experimental or a quasi-experimental design was not feasible. It would have been politically disastrous to randomly select some welfare clients for inclusion in the program while excluding others. Similarly, a nonrandom comparison group (similar to that used in the Ignition Interlock study in Chapter 6) was not available, since all eligible clients participated in the program. Instead, as a compromise approach, a tracking methodology (see Research Methods, Chapter 8) was used to measure the impact of the program on the participants. Unfortunately, this sort of before-and-after-with-no-control-group design cannot distinguish between impacts from the program and those from external sources. Because of that weakness, it was particularly important to use complementary qualitative methods to ensure an understanding of how and why the program worked and did not work.

CASE STUDY AT A GLANCE

Program Title and Policy Area POWER Program (People Off Welfare, Employed and Respected)

Program and Policy Background The Department of Social Services in St. Louis County (Missouri) developed and implemented a welfare-to-work demonstration program that provided a range of services to welfare recipients. The theory behind the program was that only if clients are provided ancillary services—such as transportation and child care—would they succeed at leaving welfare for permanent employment.

Client and Other Primary Stakeholders The client for the project was the Department of Human Services, which had obtained from the state of Missouri project funding that required an independent evaluation. In addition to the staff of the department, stakeholders included other agencies (such as training programs) that delivered services to program participants, and the participants themselves.

Information Needs Because POWER embodied a novel approach to welfare, one that embraced multiple program goals, the information needs of POWER staff extended beyond tightly focused causal information needs. In addition to information about whether program participants succeeded at finding jobs and other goals, POWER staff needed to know how and to what extent the *process* of transition from welfare to work functioned.

Research Design and Methods The research was centered on a quantitative outcome analysis of the progress of clients toward employment based on case-tracking data. However, qualitative data sources, such as interviews with POWER staff and clients, provided insights into the reasons behind client outcomes.

Findings and Recommendations The study found that the clients selected for the program were not unrepresentative of all welfare clients in the county, helping to validate the other findings about the program. The analysis of client-tracking data helped to pinpoint that most dropouts left the program during the educational and job-training segments. Thus, the research established that the program's overall success rate could best be improved by focusing on these segments.

(continued on next page)

(continued)

Program Jargon and Acronyms

AFDC Aid to Families with Dependent Children—a discontinued federally funded welfare program that was administered locally and whose clients were the target of the POWER program

POWER People Off Welfare, Employed and Respected

U.S. Family Support Act of 1988 Legislation that required states to establish programs to move welfare recipients into the work force

welfare-to-work program An innovative program designed to move welfare recipients from public assistance programs to self-sustaining employment

CHAPTER 10

The Southwest Texas State High-Risk Youth Program

Policy Research and Professional Practice

Introduction

Public health policy in the United States has increasingly focused on preventing disease and health-threatening behaviors, rather than relying on a traditional medical model based on treatment of chronic or acute illness. The Center for Substance Abuse Prevention (CSAP) in the U.S. Public Health Service has been a leading agency in fostering development of prevention policies at the federal, state, and local levels. This agency's efforts have been increasingly influenced by social science research demonstrating the importance of social surroundings in family, school, and community in influencing health-related behaviors (Kumpfort and Turner 1990). Within CSAP's primary focus on alcohol, tobacco, and other drug use, the agency has particularly emphasized the influences on the adolescent years when such problems become manifest. Accordingly, CSAP has funded and studied local projects that attempt to strengthen positive influences on adolescent behavior in the family, school, and community.

This case study describes policy research for one local project funded by CSAP.* This project, administered through Southwest Texas State University in San Marcos, Texas, sought to strengthen high-risk families in the local community through family education and training imple-

*This case study is based on a report prepared by EMT Associates, Inc., and funded through the Center for Substance Abuse Prevention.

mented in the home. The study is an example of outcome evaluation of a federally funded local program. This case illustrates that a policy evaluation can have implications much broader than the particular program under study; this study produced findings that CSAP disseminated to other programs.

The Policy Problem

The abuse of alcohol and other drugs is a serious policy problem with profound economic and social implications for society. In the mid-1980s, the federal government responded to the social costs by launching a variety of policy initiatives under the general rubric of the "war on drugs." Antidrug legislation created the Center for Substance Abuse Prevention (CSAP) to disburse funds and develop programs that would reduce the demand for tobacco, alcohol, and drugs. Demonstration projects designed to test the effects of particular strategies have been a major part of CSAP's work in carrying out this mandate. These projects were documented through evaluation research that was also funded by the agency.

The Southwest Texas State University High-Risk Youth Demonstration Program (SWTHRY) was a CSAP-funded demonstration that used materials developed for in-home family training by Cottage Programs International (1988), a family services organization. These materials were designed to improve family functioning through a series of nonthreatening educational and skills-building sessions. While the program was developed as a primary prevention effort related to alcohol and other drugs, it did not explicitly address issues of alcohol, tobacco, and other drug knowledge or use. Rather, the sessions focused directly on promoting healthy functioning of the family unit.

The SWTHRY family intervention targets families with children ages 8 to 14, but does not exclude older or younger siblings. Program sessions focus on positive improvements to family functioning in seven basic areas: fun, decision, pride, values, feelings, communication, and confidence. The program is not based on the idea that there is something "wrong" in the participating families that the program will "fix," but rather that it will help family members work on positive ways in which all families can improve. The initial exercises also help families to conceptualize their own ideal, the ways in which they would like their family to grow stronger. This concrete, self-directing, positive approach is consistent with sound primary prevention practice.

SWTHRY accepted the Cottage Industries program's explicit theoretical base as stated in its manual. Cottage Industries identifies cohesion and adaptability as positive attributes of families that are strong and supportive environments for children. *Cohesion* is the degree to which family members feel accepted and supported as part of the family unit, and it is closely related to the emotional side of family life. Its relation to important themes in prevention, such as the need for social bonding, self-esteem, and feelings of belonging and identity is clear. *Adaptability* means that families work together to face challenges, make decisions, and adapt to the changing environment around them. This concept is closely related to family theories that stress the importance of more open and participative family units that teach children tolerance, responsibility, and respect. The relation of adaptability to important themes in prevention such as self-efficacy, responsibility, cooperation, and assertiveness is clear. Thus, the program is consistent with important and central themes in the prevention literature, particularly the encouragement of recognized resiliency factors through family environment.

The focus on improving resiliency or protective factors for youth was the explicit link between the program's work with families, and the expected impact on alcohol, tobacco, and other drug use by youth in the participating families. The idea is that certain skills and attitudes help young people to undertake positive behaviors and to avoid socially or personally destructive behaviors. These protective factors are enhanced by positive family environments. Existing research makes it clear that the family has a pivotal role in providing protective environmental influences (Richardson, Neiger, Jensen, and Kumpfer, 1990).

Thus, the SWTHRY family intervention was based on the explicit expectation that the risk that a young person will use alcohol, tobacco, or other drugs is partly attributable to lack of family cohesion and adaptability. Therefore, the intervention was designed to work with family groups to improve family cohesion and adaptability, with the expectation that this change in family environment will improve the resiliency of youth in the family, and reduce their risk of using drugs. Figure 10.1 depicts this simple program model.

Initiation of the Policy Research

CSAP is the major federal agency responsible for funding drug-prevention efforts throughout the nation. CSAP awards fund both as block grants to states and as direct discretionary funding of demonstration

FIGURE 10.1

Expected Effects of SWTHRY Intervention

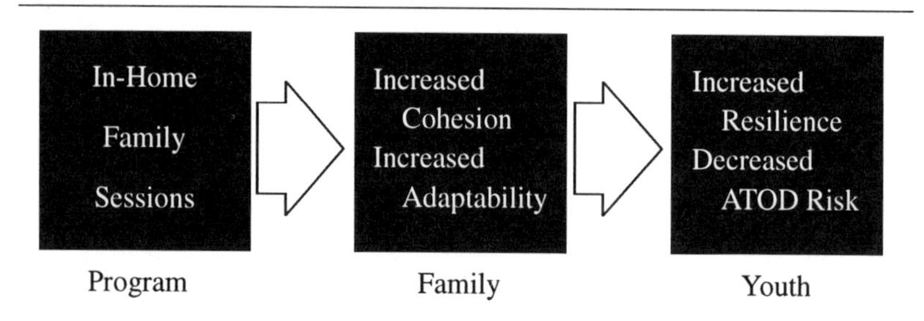

projects. The most enduring of CSAP's discretionary funding programs has been the High-Risk Youth Demonstration Program, which has provided support for more than 400 local programs serving youth who meet broad criteria for being at risk for substance abuse. The program funds projects for between three and five years, depending on funding availability, and it has always included a requirement that from 10 to 20 percent of the local program budget be expended for local evaluation. Any program receiving CSAP funding must have an evaluation plan approved by the agency and an independent evaluator who will carry out the activities within this plan. As projects that intend to produce lessons for improving prevention policy, evaluation of the demonstration projects is important. The research reported here was carried out by a local evaluator for the Southwest Texas State High-Risk Youth Demonstration Project. The evaluator was paid approximately $20,000 per year for the duration of the project and was selected by the local program managers.

The Policy Research Task

CSAP requires that local evaluation plans provide for both process evaluation and outcome evaluation. *Process evaluation* provides feedback on implementation of the project to both the local program and the federal project officer. Early in the project, the SWTHRY evaluation team placed a heavy emphasis on documenting the delivery of services, the problems that staff encountered in delivering services, and the reaction of participants.

Outcome evaluation provides evidence of the degree to which the project was effective in producing the desired impacts on program participants. The agency encourages strong outcome-oriented designs that follow the traditional experimental model. In fact, implementation of these kinds of scientific designs often encounters problems in local field settings. As discussed below, the SWTHRY evaluators had to adapt their design to meet the outcome evaluation requirements set by the funding agency (CSAP).

Objectives

The objectives of the evaluation study were consistent with the overall guidelines provided by CSAP—the agency funding the project. Specifically, the evaluation team monitored the implementation of the program and assessed the degree to which the program was able to meet its objectives for targeting families and providing the intended services to them. Feedback was provided to the program concerning the degree to which it was meeting its service objectives and the ways in which these services might be improved. These process considerations were the focus of the evaluation for its first two years.

The second set of evaluation objectives related to a rigorous assessment of the degree to which the program produced intended outcomes. As will be discussed in detail later in this chapter, these outcomes included changes in family environments and in the resiliency of adolescent family members, as well as impacts on substance use. In the last two years, the evaluation focused on producing data that would measure and support conclusions concerning program effectiveness in producing intended outcomes.

Challenges

The evaluation team encountered several challenges in meeting these objectives. The first set of challenges was related to the management of the program itself. A change in program directors in the third year significantly altered the relationship between the evaluation team and the program. Prior to that time, the evaluation team had a collaborative and cooperative association with the project director and the principal investigator for the entire project. With the change in personnel, the evaluation team was not able to reestablish this kind of cooperative relationship. For the first several months, the team had to respond to direct challenges. The new director questioned the value of evaluation information and sought to reduce the evaluation budget. Through a time-consuming process of explaining the CSAP requirements for evaluation and the ways in which the evaluation had directed program decisions in the past, the team was able to establish a reasonable working relationship with the new manager. However, input from the evaluation was not eagerly sought, nor was it used as much as it had been prior to the personnel change.

A second major challenge to the implementation of the research tasks was inherent in the project environment. The family intervention sought to serve families who resided in one of two major public housing projects within the city of San Marcos, Texas. The city itself was of moderate size, with a population of approximately 35,000; the number of families available for program participation was limited. Attempts to establish a comparison group of families to carry out the quasi-experimental design proposed for the evaluation proved to be impossible. Eventually, the evaluators acceded to the desire of program staff to convert comparison families to program participants, and the evaluation design was modified accordingly.

The loss of a comparison group because of the program's need to serve more clients is a good example of the kind of ethical and implementation dilemmas that applied policy researchers often face. The underlying purpose of prevention policy is to improve individual and community quality of life, and SWTHRY had funding that would have gone unused if more families were not served. Staff may have been alienated, with negative repercussions for the study, if evaluators had insisted that formal research requirements take precedence over serving families. The comparison method would have been weak anyway, given the program experience to that point. It was also true, however, that the major purpose of the demonstration funding, and the obligation of the evaluators, was to produce scientifically credible lessons to improve policy. In the end, the evaluators decided to cooperate with staff and to use alternative research approaches to produce a credible study.

The Decision Context

The overall context of the Southwest Texas evaluation was complex. The evaluation was a required component of a federal grant to a local university. In this context, the evaluator really served three masters:

1. Evaluators had to work closely with the project management

and staff because successful implementation of a field study such as this depends upon a cooperative relationship with the program.

2. Evaluators had to meet contractual obligations and carry out a business arrangement with the Contract Office of Southwest Texas State University.
3. Evaluators were operating within the approved evaluation design and the guidelines provided by CSAP, the federal funding office.

This structure had implications for project implementation and use. For example, the evaluator had to balance the local program desire for immediate process feedback with CSAP's desire for more rigorous outcome evaluation to support longer-term policy making.

The Institutional Context

The evaluation team had to be responsive to two distinct institutional contexts—the local context of a small program heavily influenced by the particular staff that was incumbent, and the more formally structured environment of CSAP, the funding agency. Within the institutional context, the target for process-evaluation decisions was the program management itself. Prior to the change of program managers noted earlier, the principal investigator for the project was highly interested in using evaluation information in shaping the program and exercised a great deal of discretion in directing the implementation of the project itself. With a strong leader, the local program was in a position to make effective use of lessons produced by the evaluation. In the second half of the project, the decision context changed considerably because the project manager was more interested in responding to political constituencies in the community than in using the evaluation input.

The second major consideration within the institutional context was the production of useful reports for CSAP. Evaluation team members took seriously their responsibilities as evaluators of demonstration projects, and they adopted a focus that attempted to produce lessons that would be useful for the setting of policy beyond the confines of the San Marcos project itself. (These concerns will be evident in the later discussion of evaluation findings.)

The Policy Cycle

The project demonstrates the ways in which policy research can link different stages of the policy cycle. From one point of view, this study was an evaluation of a program after it had been put in place. In the demonstration project context, however, the lessons generated from this program were explicitly expected to contribute to the refinement of new policy initiatives that would be generated by CSAP.

Client and Stakeholders

The evaluation team had to be attentive to the stakeholders and potentially attentive audiences. They included, but were not limited to, the following:

- *Program Management and Staff* The evaluation had direct relevance for the program staff and management. Not only did it reflect directly on their design and implementation of program services, it also provided a potential source of information for making management decisions. Indeed, the results of interim reports were used to seek and procure funding for family intervention from a Texas State agency after the CSAP funding ceased.
- *CSAP* CSAP was a clear stakeholder because the evaluation was focusing on one of its major funding initiatives. Furthermore, the evaluation would provide input to one of the agency's major functions—dissemination of information on promising strategies for demand-reduction policies in the area of substance abuse.
- *Prevention Professionals* Another stakeholder group with reference to the Southwest Texas study was the professional field of prevention. Youth workers and others working in fields related to preventing social and health problems will benefit from knowledge concerning the effectiveness of the great variety of interventions that are possible in this field. Interventions targeted at the family are theoretically appealing, but problems of implementation and access have limited the number of family programs that have actually been implemented. This study and its results will be of interest to this growing professional field.
- *Families* Eligible and participating families were also clearly relevant stakeholders in the program. Both implementation issues,

which affect satisfaction and convenience in program participation, and the effectiveness of the program are central issues for families.

Research Design and Implementation

The research design and implementation for SWTHRY evolved during the five-year grant period. In real-world field conditions, flexibility and adaptation are often essential to reaching study objectives. Whereas the full evaluation included a significant focus on process-related conclusions, the discussion here focuses on the outcome-related aspects of the research design.

Information Needs

This evaluation met a number of information needs for the various stakeholders. First, it provided exploratory and descriptive information concerning the project's design and implementation. In fact, a program of this type is planned in relatively simple terms, and the actual day-to-day implementation gives the program much of its content. The process of describing the program is one that requires exploratory research based on the actual activities of the program as they were carried out by the local facilitators.

The evaluation was also designed to meet causal information needs. As in outcome-oriented evaluations, a key question must be answered: *How can one be sure that the program activities produced the observed changes and outcome conditions?* This is a quintessential causal question, and causal information needs were central to the study design.

Design and Methods

Design

The design of the Southwest Texas evaluation began as a conventional, nonequivalent, comparison group design—that is, the initial intention was to administer a preprogram set of questions during the first few sessions of the family intervention for participants in the program, and to administer the same questionnaire to a sample of similar families who did not participate. Members of participating families would complete the same set of questions at the end of their involvement with the program, and the comparison families would complete these questions at a similar time.

As noted above, the design was changed by circumstances that became evident during the implementation of the evaluation. Specifically, attempts to recruit and maintain participation of a comparison group were nonproductive. Given this implementation difficulty, the research design was reoriented toward a preprogram and postprogram study without a comparison group. Even with this failure of the quasi-experimental design, the evaluators used clear hypotheses and strong measurement to compensate and produce a study with highly credible findings. The evaluation is a good example of how policy researchers were able to juggle their tools to adapt to a fluid and unpredictable research context.

Methods

The following discussion summarizes sampling and measurement considerations that were central to the revised method.

STUDY SAMPLE The sample for the evaluation was two-stage. The family sample included all participating members—adults and children 8 years of age and older—of the 52 families who completed the family program in the fourth and fifth years of the CSAP grant. As Table 10.1 indicates, 152 family members completed the preprogram questionnaire, and a total of 128 completed the postprogram questionnaire. Of these, 119 completed both questionnaires. There are a variety of reasons for nonmatches between preprogram and postprogram test participants, including family members being absent from one session or the other, individual family members leaving the program, or family members joining the program in progress.

Table 10.1 also displays the number of young people who completed questionnaires. Participating children below grade 5 were not asked to complete the youth questionnaire because past experience with the measures indicated that scale reliability deteriorates below that age (Springer and Phillips 1995). A total of 54 young people completed the pretest, and 45 completed the posttest. Of these, 39 completed *both* the preprogram and postprogram questionnaires.

The instrumentation for the SWTHRY family program was structured in two tiers to target the two sectors of the sample. At the family level, the instrumentation had to measure family cohesion and adaptabil-

TABLE 10.1

Number of Family Members and Youths Completing Preprogram, Postprogram, and Matched Questionnaires

Participants	Preprogram	Postprogram	Matched *(Both Preprogram and Postprogram)*
Family members	152	128	119
Youth (5th–12th grades)	54	45	39

ity in a way that was appropriate for this low-income, largely Hispanic population. For youth, it had to provide age-appropriate and culturally sensitive measures of adolescent resiliency and of attitudes toward alcohol, tobacco, and other drugs and the use of those substances. Through review of program objectives, curriculum, and practice, and through discussion with program staff, researchers identified the Individual Protective Factors Index (IPFI) (Springer and Phillips 1995) as an appropriate measure for youth. However, no single existing measure was found to be appropriate to the objectives, practices, and population for the family portion. Accordingly, evaluators and program staff agreed on a procedure for developing appropriate family measures. Outcome measures are discussed in greater detail later in this chapter.

FAMILY ENVIRONMENT QUESTIONNAIRE The Family Environment Questionnaire was assembled originally for the SWTHRY evaluation. It is a composite of items adapted from a variety of other instruments. As noted earlier, this approach was used to attempt to include items that would be relevant for the SWTHRY target population. Both the focused nature of the program target population and the resource constraints meant that the pilot testing and item revision necessary to establishing tested measures prior to administering the questionnaire was not feasible. In this situation, the following procedure was followed for developing measures of family cohesion and adaptability.

A pool of 65 questions was adapted or developed based on the family environment literature. From these items, 38 were selected to show face validity for measuring cohesion, and 27 were selected to reflect adaptability. These items constituted the family-level preprogram and postprogram questions. In analyzing the family questionnaire, separate confirmatory factor analyses were conducted for the cohesion and adaptability items. As expected, a dominant first factor (linear dimension) emerged in each group. To eliminate less reliable items and establish strong measures of cohesion and reliability, only those items with a strong relation to the factor were retained in composite measures. This procedure yielded measures that exhibit reliability and face validity for the purposes of establishing family-level effects appropriate to the objectives, practices, and population in this study. The generalizability of findings to other programs is suggested by emphasizing a pool of measurement items commonly used in the literature.

THE INDIVIDUAL PROTECTIVE FACTORS INDEX (IPFI) The Individual Protective Factors Index (IPFI) is an existing questionnaire used in many studies of youth programs. The reliability and validity of the IPFI have been established through use in diverse study settings (Springer and Phillips 1995). It was adopted for this study because the conceptual fit was strong, and the instrument has been used extensively in high-risk populations. The IPFI is a product of extensive conceptual development and empirical testing, including norming and validation studies on 2,416 high-risk youth in 14 sites nationwide (Springer and Phillips 1992). It was designed to provide a single measure that captures the various protective factors that have been identified as contributing to individual resiliency in children at risk (Benard 1991), and measures three major domains in which different researchers have identified protective factors—social bonding, personal competence, and social competence. Although individual programs may focus on one or the other of these conceptual areas, many programs blend efforts to strengthen youth in all three areas. The following discussion identifies the more specific protective factors found in each domain.

- *Social bonding* This domain in the IPFI concerns positive affect and commitment to basic social institutions such as school, family, and community. Social bonding measures the degree to which young people feel satisfactory involvement and motivation for accomplishments and effort in various social institutions appropriate for their age group. This domain reflects one prominent school of explanation for resiliency, that positive ties to social institutions give the individual an investment in them and in prosocial behavior. The IPFI contains three dimensions within this domain: *prosocial norms,* positive affect toward the community, including positive orientations toward others and acceptance of basic "rules of the game"; *school bonding,* acceptance of school as a meaningful environment and motivation to do well; and *family bonding,* positive affect and acceptance of family as an important environment. The family bonding dimension is particularly important for evaluating the SWTHRY family intervention. The items included in this measure reflect positive aspects, such as enjoyment in interacting with the family and pride and positive identification with the family.

- *Personal competence* Elements in this domain are common to the prevention literature and focus on one's sense of individual identity. These measures relate to the personal development of young people and the development of their own self-image and outlook. The ability to function effectively as a decision-making person in control of one's future is a common underlying theme. The IPFI contains four dimensions within this domain: *self-concept,* a positive self-image in general terms—"feeling good" about one's self; *self-control,* the ability to control impulses, particularly antisocial impulses such as anger or violence; *self-efficacy,* the sense that life can have purpose and that one's actions can effectively achieve those purposes; and *positive outlook,* the general belief that life can have a positive outcome and that it is attainable.
- *Social competence* According to Benard's (1991) review of resiliency literature, social competence is a commonly identified attribute of resilient children. Although the exact definition of social competence varies among researchers, the common theme is the ability to be responsive, caring, and flexible in social situations. This domain has to do with skills and orientations that contribute to social adjustment and the feeling of acceptance in social situations. The individual who has these qualities will elicit positive responses and reinforcement, with positive personal results. The IPFI contains three dimensions within this domain: *assertiveness,* the ability to stand up for one's self in social situations in reasonable ways; *confidence,* the social dimension of self-esteem—the belief that one is liked and likable and that one will be accepted in a variety of social situations; and *cooperation,* the desire to contribute to social groups to which one belongs, including the family.
- *Accepting or rejecting attitudes* The IPFI also contains nine items that directly measure the degree to which respondents had "ac-

cepting" (such as, curious or positive) or "rejecting" attitudes about using alcohol or other drugs, and six items that measure self-reported use of tobacco, alcohol, and other drugs. Although not an internal part of the "protective factors" index, these measures are important for assessing the degree to which SWTHRY's focus on family and resiliency affects behavior toward alcohol, tobacco, and other drugs. For purposes of evaluating SWTHRY, the authors included a measure of family supervision (4 items) that focuses on family practice in monitoring the behavior of children and in establishing clear expectations, and a measure of family interaction (4 items) that focuses on the amount of regular positive interaction that takes place in the family.

Selected Findings

In SWTHRY, as in other CSAP-funded High-Risk Youth Demonstration Projects, reduced use of alcohol, tobacco, and other drugs and reductions in associated problems are inherently intended "ultimate outcomes" (Mohr 1988). To reiterate, the program concept hypothesized that program participation would improve family cohesion and adaptability; that these changes in the family environment would include behavior changes (such as supervision and interaction) that would strengthen resiliency in adolescent family members; and that increased resiliency would reduce substance use and other negative behaviors in the young family members. The program offers a strong opportunity for examining the relation between strengthened family, resiliency, and substance use because the intervention itself does not specifically address the use of alcohol, tobacco, and other drugs. The focus is on increasing resiliency through the family, with the expectation that this increase will affect attitudes toward such substances and their use.

The following sections present the findings on family environment first, then the findings on a subsample of adolescent family members. The careful construction of the measurement plan to include two dimensions of family environment, and multiple dimensions of resiliency, enriched the analysis because it allowed the use of process information on program services to be incorporated into the pattern of hypothesized results. That is, because it is known that service delivery focused on activities related to cohesion, greater positive effects should have been observed in the cohesion measure. Similarly, those dimensions of resiliency most clearly targeted in the program activities should have shown the strongest effects. These pattern hypotheses strengthened confidence that observed changes were not attributable to generalized threats to validity such as testing effects or program-testing interaction. In that sense, the complex measurement plan helped to make up for the loss of the comparison group.

Family Effects

The family environment questionnaire administered to the full sample of participating family members provided a basis for assessing the impact of the SWTHRY program on family cohesion and adaptability. Table 10.2 summarizes this analysis. The analysis focused on change between preprogram and postprogram testing, so it used the matched sample that includes only those respondents who completed both the preprogram and postprogram questionnaires. Changes in individual scores measure the size and direction of difference between preprogram and postprogram test scores for individual respondents. All comparisons are for average (mean) scores on the composite indices. Indices were standardized to vary between 1 and 4, the range for individual items in the questionnaire. Even though the study sample is essentially a census of all participants completing the program in a defined period, statistical tests of inference were reported as a benchmark for interpretation.

The findings confirm the hypothesis that program participation produced a positive change in perceptions of family cohesion. Change scores for members of the matched sample were positive and highly significant (tested against the null condition of no change using a one-tailed test). The results also support the pattern hypothesis that participation in the program as implemented would have a greater impact on cohesion than on adaptability. Though the adaptability scores for the matched sample

TABLE 10.2

Preprogram and Postprogram Scores on Family Cohesion and Adaptability (Matched Sample Only, *n*-119)

Dimension	Preprogram Mean Score	Postprogram Mean Score	Change	Statistically Significant?
Cohesion	2.96	3.12	0.16	yes
Adaptability	1.97	3.04	0.07	no

showed positive gains, they did not achieve statistical significance by conventional standards.

In sum, results of this analysis are consistent with a positive program impact on at least one of the targeted dimensions of family environment. There were large and highly statistically significant positive changes in scores on the measure of cohesion, and smaller positive changes on the adaptability dimension. This finding is consistent with other data and interpretations in this evaluation of SWTHRY. Families preferred to work on cohesion-related sessions and exercises in the program even though they had significant problems in the adaptability area. Facilitators placed much more emphasis on cohesion objectives, probably reflecting the difficulty of adaptability goals and the sensitive nature of the issues involved in addressing adaptability goals. It follows that program impacts were concentrated in the cohesion dimension.

Resiliency Effects

As discussed above, the literature suggests that family environment is an important locus for producing resiliency in children. The discussion of IPFI measures of resiliency dimensions earlier in this chapter indicates clear relations between many of the objectives of the SWTHRY in-home sessions and specific resiliency dimensions. Sessions on resolving family conflict that target positive management of anger and effective means of nonviolent negotiation are relevant to self-control. Sessions on communication address assertiveness. Exercises aimed at sharing housework address cooperation. Sessions addressing adaptability clearly relate to the self-efficacy dimension. However, the strong tendency for families to focus on activities related to cohesion supports a hypothesis that the family-bonding dimension should exhibit the strongest effects.

Table 10.3 presents the analysis of change for the IPFI resiliency dimensions, measures of family behavior as perceived by the young people, and measures of attitudes and behavior toward alcohol, tobacco, and other drugs.

The findings presented in Table 10.3 support two major conclusions. First, participation in the SWTHRY family intervention did have a positive impact on family bonding among adolescent family members. The observed changes in family bonding between the two questionnaires are large and statistically significant. Indeed, the family bonding measure was the only measure to demonstrate any statistically significant change between preprogram and postprogram testing. This adds strong support to

TABLE 10.3

Change on IPFI Dimensions from Preprogram to Postprogram (Matched Sample Only, *n*-39)

Dimension	Preprogram Mean Score	Postprogram Mean Score	Change	Statistically Significant?
Total IPFI	3.19	3.23	0.04	no
School Bonding	3.50	3.47	-0.03	no
Family Bonding	2.90	3.12	0.22	yes
Prosocial Norms	3.39	3.34	–0.05	no
Self-Concept	3.13	3.24	0.11	no
Self-Control	2.65	2.76	0.11	no
Self-Efficacy	3.45	3.42	–0.03	no
Positive Outlook	3.09	3.17	0.08	no
Assertiveness	2.97	3.08	0.11	no
Confidence	3.24	3.24	0.00	no
Cooperation	3.38	3.37	–0.01	no
Family Supervision	1.69	1.71	0.02	no
Family Interaction	2.60	2.74	0.14	no
Use, Acceptance, and Intentions Toward Alcohol, Tobacco, and Other Drugs	3.40	3.32	–0.08	no
Self-Reported Use of Alcohol, Tobacco, and Other Drugs	2.88	2.85	–0.03	no

a conclusion that the program did impact family cohesion and that this increased cohesion included adolescents. However, the lack of significant positive change in other measures suggests that the impact of the program was limited.

Most dimensions of resiliency and measures of family supervision and interaction as experienced by the adolescents moved in a positive direction, as did family supervision and interaction. The measures related to alcohol, tobacco, and other drugs generally showed a negative trend, which would be expected with maturation in this age group. One of the greatest limitations of this study was the difficulty of interpreting results for the dimensions that did not show significant positive change. Although it is clear that the family intervention had much stronger effects on family bonding than on other measures in the table, it is not clear that the program had no positive impacts in these other areas. The secular trend in resiliency measures (Springer and Phillips 1995) and in substance use measures for the adolescent years is negative (less resiliency, more use). Without a comparison group, it is difficult to assess whether participation in SWTHRY may have modified this maturational trend.

Beyond these general conclusions, it was possible to speculate about program impacts on specific resiliency measures. The data showed relatively large positive effects on assertiveness and self-control, for example. This could reflect the concrete lessons concerning conflict resolution and communications that are found in SWTHRY exercises.

From the perspective of the project's funding agency and of preventing the use of alcohol, tobacco, and other drugs, the findings on the SWTHRY program were equivocal. Family environment has been targeted as an area of social ecology that needs greater attention if effective substance prevention is to be achieved. The SWTHRY program demonstrated that increases in family cohesion among high-risk families and their adolescent members can be achieved, but these gains were apparently not accompanied by commensurate impacts on attitudes toward or use of alcohol, tobacco, or other drugs. This finding is consistent with other evaluation results concerning family and adolescent attitudes and use. Family supervision has been cited by other analysts as an important correlate of substance use—suggesting that monitoring of behavior and setting clear parameters for behavior are important aspects of the family environment with respect to the use of alcohol, tobacco, and other drugs among these young people. However, *this aspect of family environment was not explicitly targeted in the SWTHRY intervention.* While setting boundaries and the methods for effectively doing this were part of the Cottage Programs curriculum aimed at adaptability, these parts of the program were often avoided by families and facilitators. In other words, the aspects of family functioning that were most strongly affected by the program were not strongly related to self-reported use among the adolescents.

Communicating and Using Results

The SWTHRY project presented a complex environment for the dissemination of results. The national funding agency had aspirations to produce scientific findings that would have a significant impact on knowledge and practice in prevention. The discussion of outcome findings in this chapter reflects the concern with design, measurement, and statistical issues that are crucial to this audience. Local program staff, however, are much more concerned with common-sense solutions to the specific issues they face in their program. Communication to this audience must be grounded in the detail of the program and its context, not in general issues about the effectiveness of program strategies.

Reporting Results

As noted in earlier parts of this case, communication of results varied between the process-evaluation phase and the outcome-evaluation phase. During the early years of the multiyear evaluation, the evaluator was in frequent informal contact with the project manager and provided information from the evaluation for a variety of management purposes. Formal reports contributed to this process by clearly articulating program design and assumptions and by identifying barriers to implementation. Actual use of evaluation findings, however, depended much more on the evaluator's participation in program management meetings and discussions with the project director.

In the final two years of the study, communication was limited largely to formal written reports. The impact of the outcome findings reported here will be realized largely through dissemination to the profession through journal articles, conference presentations, and CSAP publications. The evaluation reports for the program were identified as one of 37 programs within the High Risk Youth Demonstration Project that CSAP was considering as sources of scientifically valid findings on prevention effects. Findings for the study are also appearing in scientific and professional journals (Springer, Wright, and McCall 1997).

Selected Recommendations

Findings for the SWTHRY evaluation demonstrated that program staff successfully adapted an in-home family curriculum for use among high-risk families. After some modification based on early experience, the intervention was attractive to families and had a low drop-out rate. The SWTHRY intervention targeted family cohesiveness in practice, and it did have a positive impact on this aspect of family functioning. However, the impact did not diffuse to less clearly targeted areas, such as school bonding, or other resiliency factors. Reinforcing programming in other areas that target other aspects of risk and resiliency may be necessary to bring about more comprehensive change.

Finally, the SWTHRY evaluation has implications for the implementation of prevention programs in high-risk settings. Although the recruitment of community members as facilitators brought advantages in access and acceptance by participants, the facilitators did not exert much influence in guiding families to address their areas of greatest need. Both families and facilitators gravitated to the less-challenging areas related to cohesion. More training and guidance of facilitators recruited from the community would have been appropriate.

In summary, the SWTHRY demonstration did achieve its goal of generating recommendations for improved policy and practice in the field of prevention. The SWTHRY experience demonstrated the feasibility of in-home interventions for families who are at risk but who are willing to work together to strengthen family functioning. However, it supported a recommendation that careful training of community-based workers is crucial if interventions are to touch the important but sensitive aspects of family life.

The SWTHRY evaluation also demonstrates that these programs can bring about targeted change in family environments. However, the limited impacts of the program also provide a basis for important lessons concerning the importance of comprehensiveness and the limits of an affective focus in prevention practice. Thus, the study supports a recommendation that prevention practices be comprehensive and incorporate activities that specifically address a broad range of risk and resiliency.

Action

The outcome-based recommendations identified earlier have broad implications for the professional field of prevention. The very scope of the recommendations makes it difficult to know if they produced specific action. It is clear that the study caught the attention of CSAP and may influence its dissemination of demonstration findings. The study may also be read in journals by prevention program designers and implementers, thereby influencing the way they approach their work.

Lessons for Policy Research

The SWTHRY evaluation demonstrates the importance of flexibility and adaptability in applying research methods in actual field conditions. The initial evaluation design called for a formal approach to outcome evaluation through quasi-experimental design. The realities of recruiting families in high-risk environments made this design impossible within the resources available for the study. The evaluators adapted to this unforeseen barrier by using program theory to specify hypotheses and by using multiple measures to test hypothesized patterns of results. Rather than wasting the data that were collected in the study, this method's flexibility allowed a credible research result.

Discussion Questions

1. Why were scales an appropriate means to help test the effectiveness of the SWTHRY program?
2. How did the policy research team balance the information needs of its immediate client (CSAP) with those of the SWTHRY program staff?
3. What effect did changes in the SWTHRY program staff have on the research project? What implications does this have for policy research?
4. How and why was the project design changed from its inception?
5. Given that the research design did not include a true experiment, how were the findings vulnerable to criticism concerning validity?

Assignments and Activities

1. Propose a scale that could be used to measure the success of a program you are familiar with. What other means could be used to measure program effectiveness?
2. Write a memo that explains the significance of the report findings for the future management of the SWTHRY program.

FOCUS ON RESEARCH METHODS

Using Scales to Measure Policy Outcomes

The ability to interpret the SWTHRY study results ultimately rested on having valid and reliable measures of different dimensions of resiliency in youth. This aspect of the study highlights the critical role of measurement in policy research. Decision makers are interested in real-world conditions, and researchers must develop ways to measure those conditions accurately. Typically, this measurement process is not simple.

For the SWTHRY study, the measurement problem focused on the attitudes and orientations of young people. Program staff members felt they could strengthen certain attitudes and orientations that would in turn make young people more resilient in the face of risk. This type of attitude measurement is tricky, and it requires a testing and development process to produce questions that *consistently* measure the attitudes of interest. Because the attitudes are complex, good measures must be based on a number of specific questions, not just one.

Developing accurate measures of complex ideas goes beyond the technical and resource capabilities of most policy research. Accordingly, policy researchers look for existing measures that have been demonstrated to produce valid and reliable results in older studies. Even then it is important to check the reliability of these questions in each study population by using measures such as Chronbach's alpha coefficient. This alpha coefficient indicates which items in a multi-item scale are intercorrelated, providing one means of ensuring reliability.

For the SWTHRY evaluation project, the policy research team used the Individual Protective Factors Index (IPFI) to measure resiliency. This questionnaire measured concepts relevant to SWTHRY and had previously established validity and reliability.

CASE STUDY AT A GLANCE

Program Title and Policy Area Southwest Texas State University High-Risk Youth (SWTHRY) Program

Program and Policy Background The federal government has sought to foster development of effective drug prevention programs by offering grants to agencies that can design and implement them. The High-Risk Youth Program was designed to prevent substance abuse by strengthening families through education and training implemented in the home.

Client and Other Primary Stakeholders The client was the program management and staff from the University of Southwest Texas, which had obtained the federal grant to implement the High-Risk Youth Program. Other potential stakeholders included CSAP, the federal funding agency for the grant, the community served by the program (San Marcos, Texas), and prevention professionals across the country who could learn from the lessons provided by the research.

Information Needs The client required exploratory and descriptive information (both qualitative and quantitative) concerning the project's design and implementation. Additionally, outcome-oriented causal information was necessary, in part to meet federal funding requirements.

Research Design and Methods Due to problems associated with creating a comparison group for a quasi-experimental design, the research design was changed to a simple preproject, postproject study without a comparison group. Families who participated in the project were surveyed before and after the onset of the program.

Findings and Recommendations The results of the study confirmed the hypothesis that program participation produced positive changes in participants' perceptions of family cohesion and thus could potentially lead to lower risk of drug abuse. Other domains related to prevention were apparently unaffected by the program.

Program Jargon and Acronyms

assertiveness Ability to stand up for one's self in social situations in reasonable ways; a protective factor measured by the IPFI

(continued on next page)

CASE STUDY AT A GLANCE

confidence Belief that one is liked and likable and that one will be accepted in a variety of social situations; a protective factor measured by the IPFI

cooperation Desire to contribute to social groups to which one belongs, such as the family; a protective factor measured by the IPFI

CSAP The Center for Substance Abuse Prevention in the U.S. Public Health Service

family bonding Positive feeling toward and acceptance of family as an important environment

Family Environment Questionnaire Survey instrument designed for the SWTHRY evaluation; used to measure family characteristics

IPFI Individual Protective Factors Index—standard survey instrument used to measure characteristics that promote protection from drug abuse among individuals; measures the presence of such factors as prosocial norms, school bonding, and family bonding

outcome evaluation Policy research (especially in CSAP-funded projects) that provides evidence of the degree to which a program or policy is effective in producing desired impacts among program participants

personal competence An individual's sense of individual identity; one of three domains measured by the IPFI

positive outlook General belief that life can have a positive outcome that is attainable; a protective factor measured by the IPFI

process evaluation Policy research (especially in CSAP-funded projects) that provides feedback on the implementation of a program or project to both the local program and the federal project officer

prosocial norms Positive feelings toward the community, including positive orientations toward others and acceptance of basic social rules; a protective factor measured by the IPFI

school bonding Acceptance of school as a meaningful environment and motivation to do well academically; a protective factor measured by the IPFI

self-concept Positive self-image in general terms; a protective factor measured by the IPFI

self-control Ability to control impulses, particularly antisocial impulses; a protective factor measured by the IPFI

self-efficacy Sense that life can have purpose and that one's actions can effectively achieve those purposes; a protective factor measured by the IPFI

social bonding Positive feelings about commitment to basic social institutions such as school, family, and community; one of three domains measured by the IPFI

social competence Ability to be responsive, caring, and flexible in social situations; one of three domains measured by the IPFI

SWTHRY Southwest Texas State University High-Risk Youth Demonstration Project

CHAPTER 11

The Dropout Prevention Mentor Project

Delivering Unexpected Messages Through Policy Research

With Liz Sale, M.A., EMT Associates, Inc.

Introduction

Policy researchers sometimes have to deliver messages that clients or stakeholders do not want to hear. This case study summarizes an evaluation of a local program in which the client had a major investment, as well as high expectations of a positive evaluation outcome.* In this circumstance, getting the client to listen to and act on findings of program deficiencies was a real challenge. The case also demonstrates the importance of integrating the findings of process evaluation and outcome evaluation in policy research. Process findings concerning implementation problems provided a clear explanation for why outcomes had not been as strong as expected, allowing the program director to maintain her faith in the mentoring strategy that lay at the base of the program. The integration of process and outcome findings provided both information on the strengths of the program and guidance on how to improve it.

---

*This chapter is based on a report prepared by the Public Policy Research Center, University of Missouri-St. Louis and the Center for Application of Behavioral Science, St. Louis University, for the St. Louis Public School District.

The Policy Problem

The St. Louis Public School District's Dropout Prevention Program was initially funded in the fall of 1992. A grant of $271,397 by the U.S. Department of Education, under its School Dropout Demonstration Assistance Program, was for a three-year project to explore the efficacy of a mentoring approach of encouraging students to stay in school. The Dropout Prevention Program was to build upon an already successful mentoring model developed by the district, and it incorporated elements of effective mentoring approaches implemented in other school districts.

School dropout is a serious problem in the St. Louis Public School district and in many school districts throughout the country. In St. Louis, dropout rates in some schools approach 50 percent by the twelfth grade. The lack of a high school diploma exacerbates the economic barriers facing many of the district's youth, and contributes to the syndrome of economic and social problems that characterize numerous city neighborhoods. The mentoring demonstration was proposed by the Office of Federal Programs within the district as a way of countering dropout before it gets established. The program began with elementary youth and was designed to provide continuing services through middle and high schools. The demonstration targeted schools that experienced high dropout rates or that fed schools with high dropout rates. The program included two elementary schools, two middle schools, and two high schools.

The primary services of the Dropout Prevention Program were provided by home-school-community liaisons and mentors. Six home-school-community liaisons—one in each of the schools selected for services—monitored attendance; communicated with parents, teachers, and school administrators; assigned mentors to appropriate students; and provided assistance to students during or after school as needed. Liaisons were near–full-time employees located in the schools.

Mentors were volunteers from the community who agreed to be matched with individual youths from one of the program schools. The goal for the program was to have mentors assigned to approximately 1,200 students participating in the program. Mentors were recruited from public agencies, businesses, universities, and other organizations in St. Louis. They were asked to make at least one personal contact with their student each month, at least one contact a week by telephone or mail, and to meet with the student's parents at least twice each year. In addition, mentors were asked to monitor school attendance and performance and to intervene where appropriate.

Finally, the program was to provide citywide awareness of the dropout problem in the city through three awareness and promotional fliers per year. Information gathered during the course of the program would be used to develop a model for other dropout prevention programs in the future.

The evaluation data reported here were gathered in the program's second year, after it had one year to get established and in time to provide some input to program formation in the final year. By the second year, the program had made significant progress toward its implementation goals—specifically, increased recruitment and involvement by mentors, improved retention of home-school-community liaisons, and expanded services to additional students. The number of students served by the program was expanded from approximately 400 in the first year to 800 in the second. At the end of the year, about 530 mentors had been formally recruited, trained, and assigned. The program also had hired a project specialist to assist the liaisons with resources and ideas, and two program specialists assigned to recruit and retain mentors.

Although one home-school-community liaison resigned in the spring and was succeeded by another, the remaining five were with the program throughout the year. Mentor recruitment met greater success in the second year, though it was still not sufficient to provide a match for each child in the program classrooms. Furthermore, every mentor who signed up did not necessarily provide significant mentoring activity. As indicated below, these issues were addressed in the process-evaluation component of the study.

Initiation of Policy Research

Evaluation of the Dropout Prevention Program was initiated by the school district official responsible for designing the program and acquiring the U.S. Department of Education funding. This official had a primary concern with developing programs to address the many educational, disciplinary, and resource problems that confronted a large inner-city school district. She had launched smaller-scale mentoring programs in the district and was convinced that if it could be expanded sufficiently, the mentoring approach would prove effective for reducing the district's excessive dropout rate. This advocate's personal commitment to the concept was emphasized by her own service as a mentor in the program.

This official saw program evaluation as a tool to document the success of the mentoring program and to secure further funding for continuing a strong mentoring program. The Department of Education funding source did not require a methodologically rigorous evaluation and it would allow the use of a modest amount of grant money for evaluation. To strengthen the credibility of study findings, the district official sought the involvement of experienced program evaluators in two major local universities. The result was a unique collaborative research effort involving faculty and graduate students in these institutions.

The budget for the study was modest, ranging from $7,500 to $15,000 per year for the duration of the program, but the participation of advanced graduate students from both institutions helped stretch these resources. The study proceeded in three phases, each lasting one year. Phase 1 documented the implementation of the program and piloted outcome-evaluation methods. Phase 2 focused on outcome evaluation, assessing the outcomes of the program for the full range of program participants. Phase 3 was devoted to elaboration, involving more in-depth, qualitative analyses of a small sample of participants. This section focuses on Phase 2.

The Policy Research Task

The task for the Dropout Prevention Program evaluation focused on outcome evaluation. From the perspective of the client, the task was to use limited available resources to produce a scientifically credible study that "proved" the effectiveness and value of the mentoring approach to reducing dropout rates. The evaluation team was solicited with this task in mind, and evaluators brought their own perceptions of an adequate approach to the research task to negotiations about the study scope and method. Given their experience with prevention programs, and with mentoring programs in particular, the evaluators argued strongly for a more balanced study that collected sufficient information on program implementation to assess the degree to which the "planned" program had been fully implemented. The final study method described below was a negotiated design with input from the client as well as the evaluation team, which consisted of faculty from two university research institutes.

Objectives

The Dropout Prevention Program in the St. Louis Public Schools was an ambitious attempt to provide mentoring and other services to at-risk students in district schools. As stated in the funding proposal, this program's goals included the following:

- Increasing the number of students who stay in school
- Increasing positive attitudes toward school among participating students in Grades 3 through 11
- Provision of trained adult mentors for each of 1,230 participating students
- Strengthening home-school-community collaboration for dropout prevention through the services of liaisons
- Pilot testing and dissemination of a mentoring model that could be replicated within the District and in other school systems.

The data gathered in the evaluation were central to the latter objective. Accordingly, pilot testing would focus on the degree to which the program had met its goals for matching students and mentors, for serving students with home-school liaisons, for reducing tardiness and absenteeism as indicators of staying in school, for improving self-concept, for improving attitudes toward school, and for improving performance in school.

Challenges

The Dropout Prevention Program evaluation brought challenges in several varieties—technical, implementation, and use. From a technical research point of view, the first challenge concerned adequate measurement of program outcomes. Whereas the program was intended to reduce school dropouts and to improve school performance, these ultimate outcomes were difficult to measure. For one thing, the younger students would have a very low probability of dropping out at any time during the life of the study—this benefit would come later in the students' education. School performance was also a difficult outcome to measure, particularly in a short study span. Grades are not a highly precise measure of performance, and they are made less sensitive by measurement "noise" introduced through differences in teachers, changes in class environment, and other sources of extraneous variation. Accordingly, an adequate design had to include other measures of attitudinal and behavioral outcomes that had to be constructed to be relevant for the program's primary plausible impacts.

Studies in school settings bring additional challenges of design and implementation. Typically, experimental design requirements like random assignment are not feasible—or ethically acceptable—in school settings. The resulting quasi-experimental designs, such as that used for this evaluation, raise technical challenges of analysis and interpretation. (These are discussed in more detail later in the design section.) School settings also can raise issues related to study implementation. In this study, for example, the quality of data collected in the first year was severely compromised because questionnaires were to be administered by classroom teachers, and some did not comply because of other priorities. The support of administrators had to be reiterated to improve compliance in the second year. Grade data were dropped as a dependent variable because there was no automated way to gather them in a timely fashion across all schools, and other forms of data collection met teacher resistance.

Finally, the evaluators in this case faced significant challenges in reporting findings that would be used in making program decisions. As noted above, the client had a very specific use scenario in mind when the project was initiated. There was little doubt in the client's perspective that the study would produce positive findings, and that they would be useful for promoting the program—*if* the evaluation team did a credible job in documentation. If the evaluation turned up anything other than a positive result, the evaluators would have a difficult time getting the client to take the study seriously.

The Decision Context

The decision context in this case is relatively simple. Only one organization was involved in decisions about letting the contract, and its size and funding status did not require involving other actors through a competitive bidding process or extensive review. The school board did have to approve the research, but this was routine because the study was being sponsored by a district office that has a strong research responsibility. The focus of institutional attention in one unit meant that the context was not complex and that interaction with stakeholders would depend almost exclusively on the relationship with the primary client.

The Institutional Context

The St. Louis Public School District is a large urban district that encompasses the entire city. The district had an independent evaluation unit, but its function was largely to monitor and make periodic recommendations concerning the quality and effectiveness of ongoing programs. The Dropout Prevention Project was administered through the district's Office of Federal Programs, a major center for responding to external funding opportunities available through federal programs. Since many federal programs are demonstrations that require independent evaluation, the office had ties to the local evaluation community.

Internally, office personnel were experienced not only with policy research but also with its use for purposes of assessment and argument. They were aware of the utility of credible documentation for influencing decisions about program expansion or reduction. The senior staff in the office were knowledgeable about the general nature of evaluation research, though they were not researchers themselves. In summary, the institutional environment for administering the project was focused within a subunit of the school district, and this subunit was experienced in directing and using program evaluations and planning studies.

School buildings and classrooms are also a relevant part of the institutional environment for this project. Data collection took place in the classroom setting, and required the cooperation and support of principals, teachers, and program staff. With the small project budget, the evaluation team was dependent on school personnel to ensure that data collection was organized and implemented. The negotiated contract for the study specified that a member of the office staff would coordinate the implementation of data collection procedures that involved school personnel or that took place in the schools. While this designated coordinator had experience working with evaluation data collection, the project was not always her highest priority, and lapses in data collection did occur in the first year of the study.

The Policy Cycle

The Dropout Prevention Project was ostensibly funded as a demonstration. The expectation was that the Department of Education funding supported a seed program that would provide guidance for development of future programs in the district. Formally, then, the project was clearly situated on the feedback loop between policy evaluation and policy planning. Evaluation research is an expected part of demonstrations so that the implementation and outcome effectiveness of the program can be documented and tested. The formal presumption is that the evaluation research will provide empirically based findings that will guide future action. Furthermore, that guidance may suggest that the approach is not effective and should be dropped, that it is promising but needs modification, or that it is very effective and should be expanded largely as implemented. Evaluation may also find that the program was poorly implemented, and that this demonstration does not provide a strong basis for decisions about the core program concept.

In the Dropout Prevention Project, the ideal operation of the demonstration concept as a "neutral test" was somewhat compromised by the realities of the decision setting. As noted above, the client was strongly committed to the program and was strongly disposed to discounting anything other than a positive result. Put simply, some outcomes from the evaluation would be more readily used than others if the feedback loop were to operate.

Clients and Stakeholders

The discussion to this point has emphasized that the evaluation team was working with one primary client. While the St. Louis Public School District was the formal client, the role was functionally focused in one small office within the district, primarily in the senior staff person who was the entrepreneur behind the program. The size and nature of the program meant that other stakeholders were distinctly secondary in influencing the project. The program was noncontroversial and had low visibility.

Within this caveat, other stakeholders for the project can be identified. Because school dropout is an important public education problem and mentoring is an intervention that was receiving increased attention in an era of public-private partnership, the project was potentially interesting to a broader audience. The Department of Education could be an audience for demonstration findings, but it would not be an aware stakeholder for program implementation. The school district and professional groups would be in a similar position of potential interest in findings that were effectively packaged and disseminated to them.

The immediate stakeholders with a vested interest in the actual conduct and immediate results of the study were teachers and program staff. Teachers may have had an interest in minimizing any work burden that the project placed on them, and program staff may have had an interest in a positive result. As in many evaluation studies, the dual role of staff as study subjects and interested stakeholders posed a challenge of data interpretation for the evaluation team.

Research Design and Implementation

The Dropout Prevention Evaluation was designed to focus on outcome data and analysis and to collect sufficient implementation data to prevent serious errors in interpreting program effectiveness. As is necessary in any applied research with very limited resources, the evaluation team had to be creative and resourceful in the design of the study, and in the analysis and reporting of results. The design features are highlighted in this section.

Information Needs

The client's insistence on a rigorous outcome evaluation meant that this study focused on causal information needs more than is the case with many examples of policy research, particularly those with small budgets. The client was also supportive of a quasi-experimental design that would focus on causal evidence and interpretation. The central information need was clearly to demonstrate the causal relation between mentoring activities and positive changes in attitudes and (less directly) behavior.

As is typical of policy research, the study involved not only exploratory research in identifying the purposes and strategies of the program from the standpoint of implementers, but also descriptive research in documenting the program intervention.

Design and Methods

Design

The Dropout Prevention Program used utilized a quasi-experimental design that compared attitudinal and behavioral changes in students participating in the program with changes occurring in similar students who were not participants in the program. The design also employed multiple methods to enhance interpretation and collect information on program implementation. The basic characteristics of the design were the following:

- The design included a treatment group composed of students in selected classrooms in the six schools participating in the program. Students in each of these classrooms were served by a liaison, and the program intent was to match each of them with a mentor.

- To provide a benchmark for identifying the effects of the program, the study also collected data on a comparison group composed of students in selected classrooms in six schools that did not participate in the program. These schools were chosen to be similar to the treatment schools in school and student characteristics.
- The Dropout Prevention Program design includes preprogram and postprogram measures on outcome variables for students in participating schools and those in comparison schools. If the program was effective, it was expected that students in the treatment schools would show more positive (or less negative) change than students in the comparison schools. Measurements for participant and comparison students were gathered early in the fall and late in the spring semesters.
- The participant and comparison samples were composed of intact classrooms (except for the high schools). In other words, students were not randomly (or individually) assigned to participant or comparison groups. Whole classrooms were designated. As is typical of evaluations conducted in school settings, this design had several limitations that had to be taken into account in the analysis and interpretation of the results.
- Most important, the use of intact classrooms raised the possibility of nonequivalence between participant and comparison students. The logic and power of the quasi-experimental design depended upon the similarity of students who participated and those who did not. Without this similarity, differences between the groups could be attributable to factors other than that of receiving program services. While efforts were made to select schools and classrooms that would be similar, the possibility that youth are systematically different in the two schools was a threat to validity.

Methods

The development of explicit measures of program outcomes is a critical point in any evaluation design. For the Dropout Prevention Program, measures were developed with the full consultation and review of program staff. The pre-post questionnaires were designed to measure several attitudinal areas that the program was expected to affect. These attitudinal dimensions are possible "proximal" outcomes linking intervention activities by mentors and home-school-community liaisons with behavioral change (such as finishing school). In the Phase 2 data, all the dimensions conformed to conventional standards of measurement reliability.

These dimensions included two major areas. First were scales measuring orientations and attitudes related to personal confidence and efficacy (for example, self-esteem, efficacy in planning for the future, or belief in a positive future). These reflected the Dropout Prevention Program's aim to develop a generalized sense of competence and an ability to attain positive personal accomplishments that will motivate a child to stay in school. The hypothesis embodied by the program was that home-school-community liaison contact, mentor contact, and the positively reinforcing behaviors issuing from these contacts would result in improvements in personal confidence and belief in personal efficacy.

Second, the instruments included scales measuring attitudes toward school and education, including school bonding and a sense of belonging at school, perceptions of support and encouragement in school, and belief in the relevance and importance of school. These measures were central to program expectations about motivation to stay in school. The hypothesis was that home-school-community liaison contact, mentor contact, and the positively reinforcing behaviors that issue from these contacts would result in more positive attitudes related to school and education. In addition, the postprogram test included questions asking about (1) the extent and nature of contact with home-school-community liaisons and mentors, (2) the perceived benefits of this contact, and (3) overall satisfaction with the program.

In Phase 2 of the study, 784 students completed preprogram questionnaires in the fall; 594 completed postprogram questionnaires in the spring, and 518 students completed both the preprogram and postprogram questionnaires. Of the students completing both questionnaires, 278 were in the participating schools, and 240 were in the comparison schools. Specific measures of change could be calculated for these 518 students, and they constitute the sample for the outcome results of the study.

In addition to the pre-post student questionnaires, the evaluation design incorporated other sources of data. Evaluation team members personally interviewed all home-school-community liaisons and all program administrative staff. The evaluation team also prepared a survey to elicit the experiences and perceptions of mentors in the program. The questionnaire, accompanied by a self-addressed return envelope, was mailed to 300 mentors in the dropout prevention program. Fifty-four mentors (a response rate of 18 percent) completed the survey and returned it. The survey included a series of closed-format and open-ended questions asking about contact with student partners, satisfaction with participation in the program, and perceived effectiveness.

Selected Findings

The evaluation was designed to test the program hypotheses that improved attitudes toward school, increased self-esteem, greater self-control (or efficacy), and positive changes in attitudes regarding personal behavior will lead to behavioral changes that may result in students remaining in school. The basic analysis to test this expectation was to compare change in attitudes between treatment and comparison groups. A finding of more positive change among treatment youth would tend to confirm program effectiveness.

Statistical comparisons of profiles were conducted to see whether the participant group and the comparison group, though not randomly assigned, approximated each other demographically. Participant and comparison groups were similar in their distributions on age, grade, gender, and race. No apparent problems of nonequivalence between participant and comparison groups would cloud the interpretation of results.

Analysis of Classroom Effects

Table 11.1 displays results of a regression analysis in which postprogram scores for youth were used as the dependent variable. Preprogram scores and membership in the participant group or the comparison group were entered as independent variables. (A positive relation for coefficients in the "Participant Classroom" column indicates that students in participating classrooms showed more positive change on the average than those in comparison classrooms, thus indicating a positive program effect.) Beta coefficients are standardized regression coefficients that represent variables in terms of standard deviations rather than raw scores, thus improving comparability of coefficients across variables with different measurement ranges. The figures in the R^2 column indicate the total amount of variance in the postprogram scores as explained by (a) the preprogram scores, and (b) whether the student was in the participant or comparison classroom.

Asterisks in the table indicate the level of statistical significance represented by results. A single asterisk indicates a probability level less than .05, the typical standard of acceptance for social sources.

TABLE 11.1

Multiple Regression of Program Effects on Change in Participant Attitudes (*n*=518)

Dependent Variable	Preprogram score beta	Participant classroom beta	R^2
Behavior	-.43*	.001	.18
Academics	.49*	-.006	.24
Hopefulness	.46*	.005	.20
Efficacy	.26*	-.06	.07
Attitude toward school	.47*	-.07	.22
Attitude toward authority	.41*	.001	.17
Total improvement	.55*	-.02	.30

* Statistically significant at the .01 level

The results underscore that no statistically (or substantively) significant difference was found between the average change in attitudes for students in participant classrooms as compared with students in comparison classrooms. In other words, being in a participating classroom had no apparent effect on the average change in scores from preprogram to postprogram, as compared with students in a group of comparison classrooms. The results of this analysis provided no evidence for program effectiveness in affecting student attitudes. This preliminary finding did not meet the client's expectations and engendered a very negative response. Indeed, the client immediately sought ways of discounting the null result, focusing on the weakness of measures and the lack of "hard" behavioral data (which were not available).

Documentation of Individual Contact

The evaluation team used additional information on program implementation and participation both to explicate the reasons for this finding of no program effect and to provide useful guidance for the program. The supplementary data gathered from other sources clearly indicated that the actual degree of contact with mentors or liaisons varied significantly between students in participating classrooms. Table 11.2 displays student responses concerning the amount of contact they had with the liaisons and their mentors.

As Table 11.2 illustrates, contacts with home-school-community liaisons

TABLE 11.2

Contact with Liaisons and Mentors

Frequency of Contact	Liaisons (*n*=261)	Mentors (*n*=278)
"A lot" (6 or more meetings)	48.7%	16.9%
Some (3 to 5 meetings)	29.5	12.6
Only one or two meetings	12.6	36.0
No meetings	9.2	34.5

were much more frequent than contact with mentors. Comments from the liaisons corroborated this student report. Significantly, more than one-third of the students had never met with a mentor, indicating that some students simply were not participating in the mentoring program. Results of the mentor survey were consistent with student reports. One-half of the mentors reported five or fewer meetings with students.

Another series of questions asked the students whether they ever met with their liaison or their mentor outside of school and whether the liaison or mentor ever visited the student's home, telephoned the home, or spoke to the student's parents. Table 11.3 displays the responses of those students who indicated having contact with a liaison or a mentor at least once.

The table indicates that many of the liaisons and the mentors became involved in the lives of their students beyond activities or meetings at school. Students reported extensive contact in their homes. In all areas, the liaisons were more likely than the mentors to have had some home contact with the student.

TABLE 11.3

Students' Reports of Contact with Liaisons and Mentors Outside of School

	Liaison (*n*=237)			Mentor (*n*=182)		
Question	Yes, more than once	Yes, once	No	Yes, more than once	Yes, once	No
Met outside of school?	Not Applicable			21.4%	18.1%	60.4%
Visited home?	15.2%	18.9%	65.9%	14.8	15.4	69.8
Telephoned home?	35.4	18.6	46.0	28.0	17.0	55.0
Talked to parents?	39.2	23.2	37.6	20.9	30.2	48.9

As these data indicate, liaisons and mentors often extended their efforts to contacting students at home. However, when the number of children who never had contact with a mentor was considered, only a small minority of children had a mentor who interacted with their family. Only two in ten (19.8 percent) had a mentor visit their home; slightly less than one-third (29.5 percent) had a mentor call their home; and just over one-third (33.5 percent) had a mentor talk to their parents. Most children in program classrooms had no interaction between mentors and their home.

More specifically, of 261 students in participating classrooms who provided information in their postprogram questionnaires, just 47 (or 18 percent) remembered having more than five meetings with a mentor, and 127 (or 49 percent) remembered having more than five personal meetings with a liaison. Just 34 (or 13 percent) had more than five meetings with both a mentor and a liaison. These findings indicate that just being in a participating classroom did not mean that a student was a meaningful participant in the program. The evaluation team elaborated on the implications of this issue by examining the effects of intensity of participation on change in student attitudes.

Analysis of the Effects of Individual Contact

To distinguish levels of participation among children in the participating classrooms, the evaluation team constructed intensity of participation indices for liaison contact and mentor contact. To construct this measure, students were simply divided into those who had more than five contacts with liaison or mentor, and those who had five or fewer contacts.

Table 11.4 displays mean change between preprogram and postprogram scores on all attitude measures for high-intensity and low-intensity contact with liaisons, mentors, or both. For example, students with high-intensity liaison contact had postprogram scores on the total improvement scale that were an average of .02 points *higher* than preprogram scores. Students with low-intensity contact had postprogram scores that were an average of .08 points *lower* than preprogram scores. The difference between change for students with high-intensity contact and those with low-intensity contact approached statistical significance (probability was between .05 and .10).

The data in Table 11.4 indicate a consistent pattern of more positive pre-post change for students with high intensity contact with liaisons than for students with low-intensity contact with liaison, except for attitude toward school. The individual changes were not, however, statisti-

TABLE 11.4

Average Change by Degree of Intensity (Total Sample)

	Liaison Contact		Mentor Contact		Combined Contact	
	High	**Low**	**High**	**Low**	**High**	**Low**
Hopefulness	.03	-.05	-.04	.05	.04	.03
Efficacy	.02	-.04	.08	-.05	.18	-.05**
Attitude toward school	.01	.02	-.02	.17**	.08	.15
Attitude toward authority	-.07	-.11	.00	-.09	.04	-.08
Total Scale	.02	-.08*	.008	-.01	.08	-.02

* Statistically significant at .05 level
** Approaches statistical significance at .05 level

cally significant. No clear pattern emerges for mentor contact, and results for several items indicate that students with high-intensity mentor contact experienced less positive change. Combined contact with both mentor and liaison shows a general pattern of positive effect, and a significant positive impact on attitude toward school. While these results are not strong, they do suggest a positive impact of high-intensity liaison contact.

Finally, Table 11.5 displays multiple regression results for several independent variables and each attitude dimension. These results do not account for the differences between schools identified earlier, and as interim results they require more detailed analysis in the final study report. Overall, however, these results indicate the following:

1. Students in participating classrooms in the aggregate did not experience more favorable attitude change than did students in comparison classrooms when intensity of participation is in the equation.
2. Intensity of mentor contact showed no pattern of positive impact on attitude change across the dimensions.
3. Intensity of contact with liaison did show a consistent pattern of slight positive relation to positive attitude change, approaching statistical significance for total improvement and hopefulness.

The suggested importance of liaisons was strengthened through self-report by the program youth. In response to questionnaire items concerning the perceived helpfulness of the program, a pattern of differences emerged in perceived effects between liaisons and mentors. Across the board, liaisons were perceived to have helped more than mentors. The liaisons also appeared to have been more effective in areas directly related to getting to school and getting along at school. This pattern was consistent with the focus of their activities on school-related issues.

The student postprogram questionnaires provided positive self-reports concerning program effects. In particular, these reports emphasized the key importance of liaisons to the program. Liaisons had more contact with students and were perceived to have had a more positive impact, particularly in areas directly related to school behavior. The pattern of pre-post change in attitude measures suggested that higher levels of contact with liaisons exerted a positive influence on attitude change. This pattern did differ significantly across schools, suggesting that some approaches to liaison activities may have been more important than others. Indeed implementation data were consistent with school differences, documenting that the most skilled and active liaisons were in the schools experiencing the most positive evaluation findings. Providing support to children is an endeavor that depends on personal skill and continuity.

TABLE 11.5

Program Effects on Change in Participants' Attitudes: Expanded Model (n=501)

Attitude	Pretest score beta	Participant classroom beta	Mentor intensity beta	Liaison intensity beta	Race beta	Gender beta
Behavior	.45*	-.03	-.02	.04	.03	.10
Academics	.48*	-.03	.04	.05	.12*	.03
Hopefulness	.49*	-.06	-.07**	.10*	.10*	.09*
Efficacy	.27*	-.10**	.003	.06	.06	.05
Attitude toward school	.46*	-.11*	.04	.06	.13*	.03
Attitude toward authority	.41*	-.02	.006	.005	.03	.08**
Total Change	.56*	-.08**	.00	.08**	.10*	.08*

* Statistically significant at the .10 level
** Statistically significant at the .05 level

The pattern of results for attitude measures supports observations by interviewees that the liaison and mentoring approaches are less suitable and less effective for older students.

In their own perception and in the perception of students, mentors brought strengths with respect to general outlook such as self-concept and thinking about the future. They were less helpful with respect to concrete issues and behaviors related to school. The results of pre-post comparisons of attitude change were thus consistent with a conclusion that mentor effectiveness in this program was limited. Dedicated mentors may have had a very positive impact on children, but the number of these instances was small, and many mentor relations were less productive. The study clearly documented that mentoring programs are difficult to implement. Few students received a level of mentor contact that could have been expected to have much impact on their attitudes or behavior.

The evaluation emphasized the fact that the program does not provide significant levels of contact, particularly mentoring contact, for large numbers of students in the participating classrooms. This shortfall in planned service intensity has occurred for understandable reasons (such as the difficulty of recruiting mentors and the limitations of liaison time). Nevertheless, they seriously complicated the analysis of evaluation results, and they lessened the potential impact of the program on the full range of students in participating classrooms. If mentoring approaches are to have much effect, they must be strongly implemented, with corresponding attention to recruitment, training, and retention of mentors.

Another unexpected result of the study was the suggested importance of the school liaisons. These program members tended to be very committed to students and had relatively high levels of contact with them. They focused on school issues and were on the scene to help and support young people. They were more likely to have contact with the student's home than were the mentors. The study suggests that the liaison role may be a more feasible and effective means of ameliorating immediate school problems in an inner city setting than is the more politically appealing mentoring strategy.

Communicating and Using Results

The evaluation team in this case worked closely with the program staff. Staff members agreed on the design, were involved in data collection, and were informed of emerging findings in face-to-face meetings. Still, the research findings were not consistent with the expectations of a determined client, and this presented an insurmountable challenge to full use of the study.

Reporting Results

Results of the study were presented in three annual reports. These reports were complete, presenting summary tables of analyses with full narratives in a clearly organized format. They did not stop simply at presentation of data. Instead, they reported on a series of analyses that explicated the relation between program implementation, differential exposure to the program for different students, and outcomes. The most comprehensive of these reports was the Phase 2 report that has been summarized in this chapter. This report included not only the basic findings reported here but also much more detail about individual schools and the satisfaction and perceptions of students, mentors, and liaisons. The client showed no interest in producing summaries or less technical reports suitable for more general distribution, and the audiences for the reports never went beyond the immediate staff and possibly the school district and funding agencies.

Results were also presented and discussed in person through periodic meetings with the client. While the evaluation team repeatedly emphasized the value of the findings for strengthening the program, and the suggested value of the liaison position, the client was persistently concerned about the lack of an unequivocally positive result.

Selected Recommendations

The Phase 2 report produced a number of recommendations, some of which were acted on in the third year. Many focused on the necessity for strengthened implementation of the mentoring program. The study clearly demonstrated that, despite impressive numbers with respect to mentor recruitment and assignment, the program had not been meaningfully delivered to most of the participants. Before a fair conclusion concerning the value of mentoring could be reached, it would be necessary to strengthen delivery of mentoring services. Recommendations for increased training and follow-up with mentors were partially implemented.

The evaluation team also recommended several improvements in the working conditions of liaisons. These were potentially important because of the promising findings regarding the effectiveness of liaisons. Indeed, the study suggests that this role is potentially productive independent of the mentoring component. Since liaison employment was governed by the school district, these recommendations went unheard because the program staff were not in a position to influence personnel matters.

Action

The overall use of the evaluation was discouraging. Even though the study's design and implementation provided focused information on the reasons for program weakness, little action resulted in the context of this program. The study's conclusions did not meet the expectations of the client and therefore were not considered suitable for the promotional use that the client had anticipated. Accordingly, the client had no commitment or motivation to disseminate the results, and the reports remained internal documents. While the study produced strong recommendations for management action in the program, the constraints of short-term funding and a large organizational environment prevented aggressive action to implement the recommendations. It may be that, as in many cases of policy research, the most direct effects on action will be in the altered awareness and expectations of decision makers in designing future programs.

Lessons for Policy Research

The Dropout Prevention Program evaluation exemplifies basic lessons in policy research. First, the study demonstrates the importance of balanced outcome and implementation designs in the evaluation of actual programs. A failure to collect adequate data on implementation will often result in a conclusion that a program is not effective when in fact it was never implemented. In this case, integrating information on liaison and mentor contact into the analysis helped explain the flat result of the simple outcome analysis and raised the possibility of further exploration of the liaison role as a countermeasure for school dropout.

The second point this study makes is that it exemplifies the marginal methodological strength of many policy studies. No strong measures of anticipated behavioral outcomes were feasible within the limited resources of the study, so intermediate attitudinal and perceptual measures became the focus. These are prone to measurement error and accordingly yield weak patterns of result. Interpretation of such weak findings must often involve multiple data sources and judgments about what is reasonable in the overall context of the study setting and the pattern of findings.

The third and final point is that the case highlights the importance of the expectations and orientation of the client for the use of the study results. Despite close cooperation between evaluators and the client, and despite careful attention to the concrete explanation of patterns of result, the study was of limited use because it did not fit the initial expectations and plans of the client.

Discussion Questions

1. How did the information needs of the client affect the outcome of this study?
2. In your opinion, how should the policy researcher have dealt with the client's demands?
3. What ethical questions about policy research does this case study raise? Are these questions commonly associated with policy research?
4. How were qualitative research methods used to enhance the usefulness of this study?
5. Why was a quasi-experimental, and not a classical experimental, design used in this study?
6. How could the use of the policy research findings been enhanced?

Assignments and Activities

1. Describe a strategy to maximize the use of policy research that contradicts a client's expectations.
2. Assuming that the client ordering this study had not had strong feelings for or against the program, suggest a research design that is more appropriate for this type of policy situation.

FOCUS ON RESEARCH METHODS

Measuring the Policy "Dose"

One prominent purpose of policy research is to assess the degree to which some policy intervention achieves its intended effects—thereby providing causal policy information. The study of the St. Louis Dropout Prevention Program indicates how important it is to measure the degree to which targets of a policy intervention (in this case, students) actually receive the planned intervention services (mentoring or contact with liaison). Policy researchers often refer to this degree of actual intervention or exposure to program efforts as the program "dose." Measures of contact are similarly referred to as "dosage data."

For the dropout study, dosage data were gathered through self-reports. That is, students were asked how much contact they had with their mentors or their home-school liaisons. This method of data collection is prone to error (respondents may forget or "selectively remember," based on what they feel the desired response is), but it was still critical to the analysis of program outcomes.

When resources allow, policy research can be strengthened through careful collection of dosage data from primary sources such as attendance records or service logs. Collecting consistent and accurate dosage information typically requires close cooperation with program staff because policy researchers rely on them to complete data collection forms.

CASE STUDY AT A GLANCE

Program Title and Policy Area The Dropout Prevention Project

Program and Policy Background This St. Louis program used a mentoring strategy to encourage students to stay in school. Liaisons and mentors from an urban community monitored attendance; communicated with parents, teachers, and school administrators; and provided assistance to students after school as needed. Mentors were recruited from public agencies, businesses, universities, and other organizations. The goal of the program was to prevent students from dropping out of local schools.

Client and Other Primary Stakeholders The St. Louis Public School District was the formal client, although a single senior staff member was the entrepreneur behind the program. Other stakeholders included the U.S. Department of Education, which funded the program; local teachers; students; parents; and program staff.

Information Needs The client explicitly sought rigorous causal information and advocated a quasi-experimental research design. However, the study also used exploratory methods to help identify purposes and strategies behind the program, and descriptive research in documenting the program's implementation.

Research Design and Methods The central research method was a quasi-experimental design that compared changes among program participants with changes occurring in similar students who were not in the program. Qualitative research activities, such as interviews with program staff and participants, were used to complement this technique.

Findings and Recommendations The study found little reason to believe that the program was having its intended impact on school dropout rates; few differences were identified between the comparison and experimental groups. This finding was clarified with process evaluation data that identified and described weaknesses in the program's design and implementation.

(continued on next page)

(continued)

Program Jargon and Acronyms

liaisons School employees who facilitated student-mentor relationships

mentors Community figures who served as advisers to school children

Office of Federal Programs An agency of the St. Louis Public School District that administered the Dropout Prevention Mentor Project

CHAPTER 12

Housing Sales in Urban Neighborhoods

Using Policy Research to Inform Planning

With Liz Sale, M.A., EMT Associates, Inc.

Introduction

Land-use planning, including residential development, is largely the province of local governments in the United States, a traditional responsibility that some critics cite as a contributor to the decline of many older core cities. While no clear national urban policy has been developed in the United States, federal agencies like the U.S. Department of Housing and Urban Development (HUD) have instituted programs designed to encourage local governments to address urban problems. This case demonstrates the interaction of federal government, local government, and policy researchers in developing planning information concerning housing. As is often the case, research is an indirect but potentially important contribution to the policy process.

The Policy Problem

The need for effective residential redevelopment policy in the nation's older core cities is clear. The loss of population in central cities has been well documented (Spain 1980), and in cities like St. Louis the lack of residents in downtown areas has become a major impediment to continued commercial revitalization. The clarity of the need, however, has not reduced the difficulty of the policy problem facing declining cities. Despite several decades of efforts to entice suburban dwellers back to the city, or to increase the availability of adequate housing for the urban poor, positive results have been limited.

The City of St. Louis is the prime example of residential decline in the nation, having lost more than half of its population in five decades—from 857,000 people in 1950 to fewer than 400,000 in 1990. This decline in city population is largely attributable to movement within the metropolitan area, largely into St. Louis County, which surrounds the city west of the Mississippi. As the city has declined, St. Louis County has boomed.

Whereas the residential focus of the metropolitan area has moved to the west into St. Louis County, the city has maintained some of the elements of the core city of the metropolitan area. It has remained a strong cultural center, with a world-class symphony, a fine art museum, and a resurgent arts district in the mid-town area. Its zoo (free to the public) and science center are popular family destinations. The City of St. Louis has avoided losing its major sports franchises to suburban facilities, and city development efforts in the 1960s and 1970s placed a high priority on downtown business and building development, with some success. The downtown area experienced a substantial building spurt in the 1980s.

This progress in arresting decline and revitalizing the city as a work and leisure destination has made the need for residential revitalization even more glaring. In the 1980s the city gave renewed attention to encouraging residential development through home ownership as one major theme in revitalization. St. Louis is a city of neighborhoods, and the clear identity and character of its different residential neighborhoods became a natural focus for attempts at encouraging residential redevelopment. Within the neighborhood focus, different strategies for neighborhood revitalization were pursued. A second major theme has focused more on strengthening neighborhood environments than on home ownership itself. While neither of these has been clearly articulated as "policy" by the city, the threads of these policy approaches clearly run through the variety of city-sponsored physical redevelopment efforts and programs.

A major thrust of Mayor Vincent Schoemehl's housing policy during his tenure from 1980 to 1992 was a gentrification strategy—"the physical renovation and social-class upgrading of inner-city neighborhoods" (Kerstein 1990:620). City and citizen efforts in this area included encouragement of household-led gentrification by urban resettlers in select neighborhoods with historic structures (Spain 1980:28). However, the major manifestation of conscious gentrification efforts in St. Louis was developer-led renovation of select neighborhoods (Tobin and Judd 1982). In the early 1980s, the city supported this developer-led process through its condemnation and tax abatement procedures and focused infrastructure development in several focused development neighborhoods at strategic points in the city. These areas were characterized by the architectural interest, proximity to major recreational and entertainment centers, or proximity to major employers in the city that studies of gentrification have shown to facilitate the process.

Specific areas of the city, particularly within the central corridor, were targeted for gentrification. Housing that was either abandoned or occupied by lower-income residents was condemned to allow developers to rehabilitate entire neighborhoods. Promotional campaigns, such as a "City Living" public relations effort stressed the attractiveness of city neighborhoods, multiple options for schooling, and the safety of particular neighborhoods, all oriented toward attracting residents into the city of St. Louis.

Proponents of gentrification foresee numerous benefits assumed to accompany the influx of more affluent residents.

> As a general rule, cities and people living in them benefit from the presence of stable households. An increase in relatively high-income households tends to aid the community, both economically and psychologically. Long-time owner-occupants affected by decreasing property values in their neighborhood, deterioration, and increased crime—or the fear of increased crime—are the most likely beneficiaries. (Schill and Nathan 1983:138)

Gentrification in St. Louis has had its critics, as it has in other cities. Critics argued that gentrification, particularly developer-led gentrification, drains excessive public resources to attract and support the physical rehabilitation and infrastructure necessary to attract the more affluent target population. Furthermore, critics say, the more politically astute and vocal gentrifiers will continue to demand a level of city services that will detract from more balanced development of other geographic areas (Laska and Spain 1979). Other concerns are equity-related, in particular, that gentrification funding competes with affordable housing efforts. Finally, critics argue that the number of gentrifiers is simply too small to make a major impact on urban revitalization (Spain 1980).

A second theme in neighborhood development is less focused on creating residences that appeal to a specific targeted population of buyers and more concerned with developing the general physical, social, and political infrastructure of city neighborhoods. Proponents of balanced neighborhood development in the city have always seen efforts at infrastructure development as less prominent than the focused physical development of targeted neighborhoods, but a number of initiatives in the 1980s reflected this theme.

Early programmatic efforts reflected concern with the physical appearance and safety of city neighborhoods. Operation Brightside, initiated in the mayor's office, was a visible campaign to clean up and sod vacant lots, reduce trash and litter, and brighten thoroughfares with plantings. Operation Safestreet was a companion program aimed at neighborhood security. This program included subsidized installation of home security measures, neighborhood watch organization, and a more controversial program of installing street barriers to channel traffic flow and more clearly delineate neighborhood boundaries.

More recently, the focus on infrastructure development in specific neighborhoods was intensified through Operation Conserve. This program sought to coordinate services and development programs in selected neighborhoods through city Conserve officers who served as conduits, organizers, and ombudspersons for local citizens and neighborhood associations.

By the end of Mayor Schoemel's tenure in office, the dual strategy of targeted, developer-led gentrification and revitalization of selected neighborhoods had not reversed the downward trend in numbers of city residents. Citizen surveys commissioned by the mayor's office suggested that movement into the city was often temporary, with younger professionals and families moving in only until they had children. There was no systematic information on who was willing to invest their future in the city through home ownership, however. Information on the pattern of citizen response to the city's efforts at residential rejuvenation would be helpful in planning future efforts to revitalize the city's residential base.

Initiation of Policy Research

As a distressed urban area, the City of St. Louis was not in a position to finance detailed research into home buying in the city. However, the city's Community Development Agency (CDA) administered various grants-in-aid from the federal government concerning housing and urban development programs, and these grants often supported or required policy research for planning or evaluation purposes. For example, at the time of this study, CDA was required to produce a housing plan indicating how the agency would promote diversity in the housing market through their use of funds from the Department of Housing and Urban Development (HUD). CDA staff were given both the responsibility for producing this plan and a modest budget for generating information to support plan preparation.

Discussions among CDA staff focused on the lack of explicit information about recent home buyers in the city. A basic tenet of marketing research is that future buyers will resemble past and current buyers. Staff felt that to promote future home ownership in the city, they needed to know more about recent purchasers. To get this information, CDA negotiated with local universities to get proposals for conducting a survey of recent home buyers. A contract to conduct the study was written with the Public Policy Research Centers at the University of Missouri in St. Louis. This organization had worked with city agencies on a number of prior urban development studies, including the series of annual citizen surveys commissioned by the former mayor.

The Research Task

The research task defined by CDA was straightforward. However, the information that would be produced was significant because it addressed a crucial issue for the future of the city and provided clearly relevant data that had not been available before this effort. This kind of concrete and relevant information had clear implications for a range of decision making, including assessments of past city efforts to stimulate home ownership and planning for future efforts.

Objectives

The major objectives of the research task defined by CDA staff were to document accurately (a) the socioeconomic and demographic characteristics of persons buying homes in various city neighborhoods, (b) the location and housing status of buyers before their city purchase, (c) their motivations for buying in the city, (d) the degree and sources of satisfaction with their housing purchase, and (e) home buyers' plans for holding and improving the property. CDA was also interested in the observations of real estate agents and urban developers concerning the reasons for the difficulties in the urban housing market and what might be done about them.

The Decision Context

The housing survey provides an example of a piece of policy research that was initiated for a specific purpose mandated by a federal agency. However, the information that would be generated by the study had important implications for policy decisions of core importance to the City of St. Louis. Thus, the information generated to meet a paper planning obligation might generate useful information for decision makers in city government and for interest groups active in city development and neighborhood revitalization issues.

The Institutional Context

St. Louis is an old city with an unreformed, strong mayor system. The legislative branch of city government consists of a precinct-based city council that gives strong voice to the diverse neighborhood areas in the city. The city itself is financially strapped, having lost much of its residential tax base through urban decline and low housing value. Generous tax abatements have been part of the strategy for spurring businesses to locate downtown. Therefore, as are many older urban areas, the City of St. Louis is heavily dependent on federal funds for community development initiatives. The Community Development Agency (CDA), the agency responsible for administering many of these funding programs, has major responsibility for developing funding proposals, generating information concerning urban development in St. Louis, and carrying out development planning.

The evaluation team, headed by a professor at the University of Missouri and a senior staff analyst at the Public Policy Research Centers, worked directly with CDA staff. The working relationship was collaborative, with CDA staff involvement in developing the sampling plan and the questionnaire and in interpreting results. No representatives from the larger institutional environment were directly involved in any of these activities. As in any specialized policy area agency, the CDA staff had a desire to influence city development and many were particularly concerned about ways of revitalizing the residential housing market in the city. CDA staffers were aware of the attractive and affordable older housing stock in many parts of the city, and they were concerned about ways in which the city might better use this resource in the process of residential rejuvenation. Thus, this project represented an opportunity for them to develop information that might demonstrate the value of the older housing stock for spurring home ownership and to suggest ways of promoting that resource.

The Policy Cycle

The housing study was formally part of a planning process, providing information on past conditions to inform the development of plans for future action. However, as noted above, CDA was a major source of information for community development policy in the city, and the housing survey would become a general source of information on housing sales that the agency could draw on in other tasks. In other words, the study could provide an opportunity for CDA input to decisions in other parts of the policy cycle.

Clients and Stakeholders

The evaluation team had only one involved client: CDA—more particularly, a few staff from the CDA research and planning component. Since the study was mandated to meet external requirements for receiving HUD funding, it did not attract a lot of attention from other actors. The evaluation team and CDA staff were free to shape the study without constraints from a broader scope of active participants. HUD was an indirect client and stakeholder, but this had little influence on the detailed content of the study because the general planning requirement could be met in a great variety of ways. Furthermore, the plan would neither receive much scrutiny nor generate feedback to the city once it was submitted to HUD. Like many funding requirements of this type, the HUD requirement served to motivate local funding recipients to go through a planning process that hopefully would make their local policy decisions more informed. Once it was done, HUD would do little with the plan.

Of course, the utility of the study results as a tool for CDA depended on the degree to which the study anticipated the concerns and information needs of other stakeholders and participants in the community development policy community within the city. As noted earlier, the policy initiatives of the 1980s had created an active and diverse set of interests within this policy community, ranging from large residential developers to neighborhood associations and affordable-housing activist groups.

The politically appointed head of CDA and the St. Louis mayor's office were key among these stakeholders in study results. In this strong-mayor city, the immediate utility of any information for effecting city policy would depend most directly on its reception by these policy makers. The residential development and real estate industries are important voices in this community, and they were explicitly brought into data collection for the study both for their key role in shaping the housing market and for the insight they might have into the dynamics of this market. Neighborhood associations and strongly organized local residential groups were other stakeholders who would be vocal participants in future policy discussions about housing availability and promotion in the city.

Research Design and Implementation

In terms of research methods, the task before the research team was quite straightforward. There were two basic types of data collection tasks—a telephone survey, and several focus groups. Both were research tasks with which the evaluation team had extensive experience. The Public Policy Research Centers included a survey research unit that regularly implemented telephone surveys using trained interviewers. There were no difficult sampling issues, and the information to be collected in the survey was largely informational and nonsensitive, presenting no difficult measurement issues. While the analysis of survey data can be simply descriptive, the real implementation challenge to making this a useful study was in the analysis area. As the discussion of findings will show, conducting and presenting analyses in a way that was relevant to policy issues and positions required creativity from the evaluation team.

Information Needs

The basic information needs for the research tasks were descriptive—accurately portraying the characteristics of past home buyers. The client's information needs were to estimate the characteristics and motivations of potential home buyers in the city, and the study generated information useful for this estimation task. In fact, as is the case in many planning applications, the estimation function was not built into the policy research task. The writers of the plan would perform this analytic function and would probably rely more on experience and intuition than on formal technical (that is, statistical) methods of projection or forecasting. As noted above, this descriptive information base had the potential for meeting other information needs in the community development policy community. For example, it could be used to support evaluative purposes by shedding some light on the possible effects of former housing policy. This information would not support formal technical evaluation of past policy, but it would provide a strengthened base for reasoned discussion among policy makers.

Design and Methods

The study of St. Louis home buyers was a straightforward descriptive study. The design objective was to draw a sample that would provide a precise and unbiased estimate of all city home buyers during the study period, and to use a questionnaire that would accurately elicit the desired information. Accordingly, the design was centered on a representative survey, enriched through focus groups. Using the marketing research principal that future consumers are most likely to be similar to current consumers, this descriptive design was expected to provide a solid base for understanding and appealing to future home buyers. The major source of data for this study was a telephone survey of 1062 single-family home buyers in the city of St. Louis. The research was conducted in the fall of 1992, under contract to the City of St. Louis's Community Development Agency. To implement the telephone survey, a list of all single-family residential purchases in the city from 1989 to 1991 was obtained from the city's assessor's office. Proportionate random sampling was conducted and responses were weighted after the survey was completed to account for differing response rates by area. The samples of focus group participants were gathered from the city's Community Development Agency with requirements that participants working in different parts of the city (north, south, and central) all be represented.

The intent of the survey was to gain a greater understanding of the home-buying market in the city. Specifically, the survey asked questions regarding the characteristics of the current and previous residents, the physical characteristics of the dwellings, the primary factors considered by the respondents during the search and purchase processes, and their current satisfaction with their homes and neighborhood.

The survey was augmented by five focus groups of lenders, developers, appraisers, brokers, and realtors who work in the city, and one focus group of persons who had recently sold their homes in the city. The intent of the focus groups was to gain a greater understanding of the issues facing those who participate in supplying housing to potential purchasers in the city. Specifically, the focus group participants were asked to discuss current market trends in different parts of the city, including the characteristics of buyers and sellers, perceived barriers to prospective buyers in the city, and recommendations for future housing policy.

Data gathered through the survey and focus groups produced a multidimensional picture of current patterns of home buying in the city of St. Louis. This information is unusual among studies of residential redevelopment in core cities. Most existing surveys of home buyers concerning urban revitalization are focused on particular neighborhoods or specific categories of buyers. This survey provides self-report information on the full range of buyers in the city, and it is therefore ideally suited to the interest of policy makers in a larger pattern of policy options for encouraging neighborhood stability through home ownership.

Selected Findings

The survey and focus groups provided a volume of specific findings that were reported back to CDA staff in descriptive fashion—that is, through straight presentation and summaries of responses. However, discussion between CDA staff and policy research team members had identified areas in which the findings might have larger implications for residential development policy in St. Louis. The selected findings presented here summarize some of the analyses the evaluation team conducted to address these more speculative, yet highly relevant, issues.

In-Movers and City Dwellers

The housing redevelopment strategies of the Schoemehl administration, and the gentrification strategy generally, were based on the expectation that higher income home buyers can be attracted to the city, largely from surrounding suburbs. The responses of recent home buyers allowed an assessment of the importance of back-to-the-city buyers to the overall

TABLE 12.1

Place of Residence Prior to Purchase

Place	Percentage of Total Buyers	Number of Buyers
City of St. Louis	63.0	669
St. Louis County	21.9	233
St. Charles County	0.4	4
Elsewhere in Missouri	4.1	44
Illinois	2.7	29
Elsewhere in the United States	7.8	83

housing market in St. Louis. They also allowed an indirect assessment of the degree to which this back-to-the-city movement was fueled by gentrification strategies.

Just over one-third (37%) of the respondents in the survey of recent home buyers had previously lived somewhere other than the city prior to their purchase. The largest percentage of home buyers who did not previously live in the city came from St. Louis County (21.9%)—an area that the Schoemehl administration specifically targeted through public relations campaigns (see Table 12.1). This pattern of movement from near suburbs is consistent with in-migration patterns in other U.S. cities (LeGates and Hartman 1986:180).

If the downward trend in city population is to be reversed, increasing housing sales to city in-migrants is an important objective. The evaluation team used the survey information to provide information on characteristics of buyers from outside the city and how they differed from city-dwellers who had purchased homes. Table 12.2 illustrates the demographic characteristics of those who moved into the city (the "in-movers") compared with those home buyers who had previously owned in the city (the "city dwellers"). At the request of CDA staff, percentages for the in-movers did not include those who moved to the city from elsewhere in the United States because the people specifically targeted for city living through CDA promotions were St. Louis metropolitan area residents.

The profile indicated that the great majority of recent home buyers, whether in-movers or city dwellers, had previously been renting—implying they were first-time home buyers. There were few differences between the two groups. The sample of in-movers was slightly younger and better educated than the previous city dwellers. Fewer in this group had chil-

TABLE 12.2

Demographic Comparisons Between "In-Movers" and "City Dwellers"

Characteristic	In-movers (n = 310)	City dwellers (n = 669)
Age		
18–34	57.7%	49.2%
35–54	31.6%	39.9%
55+	10.8%	10.5%
Marital status		
Married	63.2%	71.7%
Never married	24.3%	14.9%
Divorced/separated/widowed	12.2%	12.3%
Education		
High school graduate or less	22.2%	32.5%
Some college/Associates degree	28.3%	26.1%
Bachelor's degree	34.1%	26.0%
Masters/professional/Ph.D.	15.1%	14.7%
Family		
Children at home	39.4%	51.8%
No children at home	59.9%	47.9%
Occupation		
Professional/managerial	48.7%	44.0%
Clerical/sales/service	20.1%	22.8%
Other	31.2%	33.2%
Income		
Less than $30,000	22.5%	23.5%
$30,000–59,999	42.3%	45.7%
$60,000 or more	18.4%	12.7%
Race		
African-American	7.9%	11.7%
Caucasian	91.4%	86.6%
Other	0.5%	1.2%
Prior place of residence		
Previously a renter	67.1%	73.9%
Previously a home owner	32.9%	26.1%

dren, a higher percentage had never been married, and slightly more had previously owned homes. There were no major income or occupational differences between the two groups. These findings illustrate that for the most part, home ownership in the city was attractive not to upper-middle class residents from outside the city limits, but rather to young, middle-class, well-educated people who had not yet started a family. In terms of residential development strategy, the in-mover profile does not fit the presumed buyer who would be attracted to a gentrification strategy.

If gentrification was not the magnet drawing buyers to the city, what was? To explore this question, the evaluation team looked for information that might explain the reasons for buying in the city. The most important consideration for both groups was the affordability of the housing (44.3% of in-movers, 44% of city dwellers). The next most important considerations were location in the city, and safety and security—cited by only about 10 percent of each group of buyers.

Further evidence of the attractiveness of affordable housing to the in-movers was found when the respondents were asked if the home they purchased would have been more attractive, less attractive, or about the same if it had been located somewhere other than the city of St. Louis. Almost one-third (32.2%) of the in-movers said they would have found their home to be more attractive if it were located elsewhere, compared with only 19.4% of the city dwellers. A substantial number of in-movers were apparently purchasing in the city largely because they could find affordable housing, and they would rather have purchased elsewhere. Contrary to findings in studies of gentrifiers, many of the St. Louis in-movers are not simply city lovers. They are attracted by the housing value they can achieve in the city context.

Finally, to further substantiate the finding that the majority of in-movers moved to the city because it provided affordable housing, the evaluation team looked at where the in-movers located. Just 11.6 percent of the respondents who moved into the city located in gentrified neighborhoods, where for the most part, median housing prices are $100,000 or more. Rather, most moved into more affordable neighborhoods, primarily in the southern part of the city, where median housing values range between $32,250 (the "Patch" neighborhood) to $94,575 (the "St. Louis Hills" neighborhood), with most neighborhoods in the $40,000 to $70,000 range. Most in-movers, therefore, moved into areas with affordable housing, not into gentrified areas.

Analysis by Neighborhood

The data on recent home purchases clearly demonstrated that most of the home purchasing was not related to gentrification strategies. When the full home-buying market was considered, it became clear that understanding the characteristics and preferences of the home buyers who purchased in more affordable, nongentrified areas was crucial to comprehending the current housing market in the city of St. Louis. Following the premise that neighborhood environment was an important link between home-buying decisions and neighborhood revitalization policy, city neighborhoods were divided into three groups.

- Housing development policies of the 1980s had produced clearly identifiable city neighborhoods that had been targeted for focused residential development. These neighborhoods, identified as "focused development neighborhoods," were initially identified through discussions with informed observers and review of development patterns. Their distinctness was confirmed through examination of the socioeconomic characteristics of the households in the areas. The focused development neighborhoods were the areas in which gentrification was expected to occur.
- A second set of neighborhoods was defined as "stable." They had low vacancy rates (fewer than 10% of units were vacant), a low percentage of very poor people (fewer than 12% were very poor), and a low percentage of unemployed persons (less than 10%). These neighborhoods lie largely in the southwest corner of the city. Most residents were white, and participants in industry focus groups identified these neighborhoods as the strongest housing market areas in St. Louis.
- A third set of neighborhoods identified as "less stable" were outside the focused development areas. They had higher percentages than the stable neighborhoods on at least one of the indicators identified above (i.e., vacancy rates, percentage of very poor persons, and unemployment as identified through analysis of census data).

The stable neighborhoods were almost all in the southern part of the city, and the gentrified neighborhoods were all in the central part of the city. The less stable areas were in the north and in parts of central and south St. Louis.

This categorization of neighborhoods created a context for understanding the patterns of home buying in the city. These different neighborhood groupings reflected the approaches taken to revitalizing the city through home ownership. The focused development areas reflected the

TABLE 12.3

Demographic Profile of Respondents

Characteristic	Stabilizers ($n = 354$)	Stability Seekers ($n = 616$)	Gentrifiers ($n = 92$)
Age			
18–34	45.3%	57.0%	29.3%
35–54	41.2%	33.0%	60.4%
55+	13.0%	9.8%	10.4%
Marital status			
Married	65.6%	72.0%	65.0%
Never married	16.0%	17.8%	24.1%
Divorced/separated/widowed	17.5%	10.0%	10.3%
Education			
High school graduate or less	32.6%	28.2%	8.6%
Some college/Associates' degree	27.9%	26.0%	20.1%
Bachelor's degree	22.7%	32.0%	33.8%
Master's+	16.6%	13.2%	37.4%
Children at home			
Yes	56.6%	45.4%	31.1%
No	42.8%	54.4%	67.8%
Children under age 5			
Yes	32.9%	33.3%	20.1%
No	67.1%	66.7%	79.9%
Occupation			
Professional	29.6%	33.7%	39.1%
Managerial	12.6%	14.3%	12.6%
Skilled labor	8.1%	8.8%	2.2%
Clerical/sales/service	22.1%	21.5%	10.9%
Homemaker	5.2%	7.0%	13.3%
Retired	6.0%	4.3%	5.8%
Other	16.4%	10.4%	16.1%
Income			
Less than $30,000	29.7%	21.9%	4.6%
$30,000–$59,999	42.6%	47.0%	20.0%
$60,000 or more	12.9%	13.0%	50.1%
Refused to state	14.7%	18.2%	25.3%
Race			
African-American	26.1%	1.5%	8.1%
Caucasian	72.6%	97.0%	88.5%
Other	1.0%	1.1%	2.3%

significant attention paid to creating environments that were expected to appeal to higher income persons, and to enticing purchasers back to the city. The stable neighborhoods had a healthy housing market and did not demonstrate a great need for ameliorative policy. The less stable areas were those that had either become dilapidated or that were in danger of losing their viability as strong residential neighborhoods. Operation Conserve neighborhoods, for example, were found in these areas.

The evaluation team conducted analyses that grouped respondents according to the neighborhoods in which they purchased a home. Respondents who purchased homes in focused development areas were referred to as *gentrifiers;* respondents who purchased in "stable" neighborhoods were labeled *stability seekers;* and purchasers in less stable neighborhoods were called *stabilizers.* In the three years covered by the study, well more than half (58%) of the home purchases in St. Louis were made in the stable areas, confirming the observations by realtors that these areas were the strongest housing market in the city. One third of the sales were in the less stable areas, and just 8.7 percent were in the gentrification areas. Again, it is clear that gentrification accounted for only a small part of the housing market. Table 12.3 outlines the demographic characteristics of stabilizers, the stability-seekers, and the gentrifiers.

- *The gentrifiers* Not surprisingly, the gentrifiers were significantly older than the other two groups, with a higher percentage of people who had never married. They also had a higher percentage of high educational and income levels and occupational status, and relatively few had children at home. This information confirmed that the persons sampled represented those who had typically gentrified in urbanized areas across the country.
- *The stability seekers* The stability seekers—those living in "stable" neighborhoods, were significantly younger, with over half of the respondents less than 35 years old. Most were white and married, and around half had children at home, with a large percentage with children under the age of 5. Educational and income levels and occupational status were significantly lower than those of the gentrifiers. This group appeared to be a mix of blue-collar and white-collar home owners who were mainly young and either childless or just starting a family.
- *The stabilizers* The stabilizers—those living in "less stable" neighborhoods, were slightly older than the stability seekers, with a

> lower percentage of married persons, slightly lower educational and income levels, and a higher percentage of children at home, though fewer had children under the age of 5. Significantly, 31.9 percent of the stabilizers were African Americans, compared with only 1.3 percent of African Americans in the stable neighborhoods and 11.6 percent in the gentrified neighborhoods. The stabilizers were the least affluent of the three groups, and they may not have had the means to move into some of the more stable (and more expensive) neighborhoods in the city.

For purposes of arresting neighborhood decline in the city, stabilizers had particular importance. They were the buyers who were making a home-buying commitment to areas that were important to reversing the historical trend of residential flight from the city. Comparisons of the home-buying considerations and other characteristics of stabilizers with other home buyers would provide insight into who was buying in the less stable areas and why. To understand differences in home-buying preferences, researchers asked respondents to rank the importance of various factors in their decision to purchase a home and to indicate which factor was the most important. Table 12.4 displays the results for the three groups.

Again, price was considered *very important* by the greatest portion of buyers in each of the three groups. However, stabilizers specified it more often than did gentrifiers. Safety and security ranked second for both stabilizers and stability seekers, but those considerations ranked fifth for the gentrifiers. The percentage of stability seekers who felt safety and security were very important was highest by a substantial amount, and they had purchased in neighborhoods with lower crime rates. This finding suggests that the gentrifiers were least motivated by a fear of crime, and the stability seekers were most concerned about crime. Stabilizers placed midway between those groups.

An attractive neighborhood and a location convenient to work were also very important to the stabilizers. Access to quality education, architectural style, diversity in people and neighbors, access to family and friends, and access to entertainment and culture were ranked lower as concerns for both the stabilizers and the stability seekers. In contrast, the gentrifiers ranked architectural style, diversity in people and neighbors, and access to entertainment and culture considerably higher. This suggested that the gentrifiers were the group most tolerant of and attracted by urban living conditions, including urban ambiance, diversity in people, and access to

TABLE 12.4

Ranking of Various Factors in Purchasing Decisions of Three Groups of Home Buyers

Consideration	Stabilizers ($n = 354$)	(Rank)	Stability Seekers ($n = 616$)	(Rank)	Gentrifiers ($n = 92$)	(Rank)
Good price	86.9%	(1)	81.8%	(1)	67.2%	(1)
Safety and security	66.4%	(2)	80.6%	(2)	48.9%	(5)
Attractive neighborhood	54.8%	(3)	70.0%	(3)	59.7%	(3)
Location in city	49.6%	(4)	63.5%	(4)	64.3%	(2)
Convenience to work	48.5%	(5)	40.6%	(5)	45.4%	(7)
Architectural style	37.5%	(6)	29.5%	(8)	48.2%	(6)
Access to quality education	34.8%	(7)	37.4%	(6)	16.8%	(9)
Diversity in people and neighbors	32.9%	(8)	21.8%	(9)	50.6%	(4)
Access to family and friends	23.6%	(9)	29.6%	(7)	12.1%	(10)
Access to entertainment and culture	19.3%	(10)	13.1%	(10)	37.3%	(8)

entertainment and culture. The stabilizers were attracted by the opportunity to own a home and were tolerant of an urban environment, though they expressed some concern about the characteristics of the environment in which their homes were located. This concern was reflected in answers to questions regarding satisfaction with their new purchase and whether their home would have been more attractive if located elsewhere.

When asked if they would have found their home to be more attractive if it were located somewhere other than the city, both the stabilizers (56.1%) and the stability seekers (57.9%) were more likely than the gentrifiers (25.9%) to say it would have been just as or more attractive if located outside the city. This finding, which suggested that many of the stabilizers might relocate if they had the means, reinforced the importance of continuing policy efforts to upgrade neighborhood environments in the less stable areas.

If home buyers were to serve as stabilizers in less-than-stable neighborhoods, their future plans for housing were important. Three fourths (74.3%) of the gentrifiers saw their purchase as adequate for the future, reflecting the substantial nature of the housing they had purchased. More than half of the stabilizers (59%) also saw their purchase as adequate for the future, as did stability seekers (58.4%). With respect to housing alone, many stabilizers saw their purchase as adequate for long-term housing.

Another indication of the stabilizing potential of home buyers is their plans for upgrading their homes. Again, the striking finding was the similarity in plans between stabilizers and other categories of buyers. Stabilizers were just as likely as others to plan on complete rehabilitation (10.7% versus 8.3% and 10.9% for stability seekers and gentrifiers respectively), and just a little less likely (24.9% versus 29.6% and 29.3%, respectively) to plan major rehabilitation. Stabilizers planned to upgrade their homes, demonstrating an economic commitment to the neighborhood.

Neighborhood commitment is also demonstrated through active involvement in neighborhood organizations and activities. Gentrifiers were most likely to belong to a neighborhood association (57.4%), reflecting their general commitment to city living as well as the strong organizations in their neighborhoods. However, stabilizers (38.0%) were nearly twice as likely as stability seekers (19.1%) to report belonging to a neighborhood association.

Communicating and Using Results

The summary of findings presented here has focused on elaborations of the basic data set produced by the survey. These analyses would not necessarily have been conducted if the use of the survey had been restricted to the simple descriptive purposes required by the HUD planning mandate. They were prompted by the interaction of CDA staff and members of the evaluation team. This group of analysts had a larger interest in housing policy and residential development in the city, and they saw the opportunity to provide useful information in this area through additional analysis of the home-buyers survey. The communication and use of the findings reflects this expanded vision of the potential utility of the information.

Reporting Results

The basic findings of the housing survey were presented to the CDA in a final report prepared by the evaluation team. This report presented profiles of recent home buyers in the city and summarized their reasons for buying, their satisfaction with the purchase, their plans for improving their home, and their planned length of stay in the home. The report also included comparison information on in-movers and city dwellers. In addition to the report, the evaluation team made an in-person presentation of findings to members of the CDA staff. The final report became an information base for preparing the required HUD plan for promoting housing diversity in the city, and it was included in the plan as an attachment.

The analysis of buyers by neighborhood of purchase was not included in the final report. This analysis was not clearly related to the core purpose of the contract for the survey, although it did reflect the interests of CDA staff. Members of the evaluation team conducted the analyses and wrote up a paper for presentation at a Sociology of Housing Conference (Sale and Springer 1993). The paper was shared with CDA staff, and its implications for housing development policy were discussed informally.

Selected Recommendations

Recommendations were not an appropriate part of the final report to CDA because the focus of the contract was simply to provide new information relevant to plan preparation. However, the data set had clear implications for policy concerning residential development in the city—a core area of CDA responsibility. Some of these implications were spelled out in the conference paper prepared by members of the evaluation team and were shared with CDA staff through the paper and informal discussion. The breakdown of home buyers into three broad categories served as a useful heuristic device for linking stabilization strategies to home-buying patterns. Implications of the analysis included the following:

- *Recent gentrifiers in St. Louis reflected the pattern identified in studies of gentrification in other cities.* They had a higher income than other categories of buyers and were less likely to have a family with small children. They were more frequently committed to city living as a matter of lifestyle, were less likely to be motivated by issues of affordability concerning their home purchase, and were relatively "risk oblivious" in their buying decision. The St. Louis gentrifiers also reflected the finding elsewhere that gentrification is not predominantly a "back to the city" movement. Many of the purchasers in these neighborhoods were already city dwellers.

- *Gentrifiers were a small portion of total city home buyers.* This was perhaps the most important finding for redevelopment policy. Gentrifiers are city lovers, and thus the potential for this movement depends on the pool of city lovers in the immediate suburban environs. Furthermore, tax law changes after 1986 have reduced the supply-side incentives to renovation and correspondingly reduced the supply of developer-led gentrification opportunities. While a piece of the revitalization puzzle, gentrifiers were a relatively small piece, and they are likely to remain that way for the immediate future.
- *The largest group of recent home buyers in St. Louis fell into the stability seekers category.* This designation simply indicated that these purchasers located in the stable neighborhood areas in the southwest corner of the city, and did not imply that stability was their top concern in searching for a home. The neighborhoods in which this group bought were not experiencing rapid migration and were not plagued by the high rates of vacancy, crime, and other social problems found in the less stable areas.

Stabilizers were an important group for the prospect of reversing migration and decline in the less stable areas of the city. They were a sizable group, representing one third of the purchasers in the city. A significant number of them were in-movers, and one third were African Americans. The less stable neighborhoods represented the most significant opportunity for home ownership for minorities in the city. Stabilizers tended to be people of modest income, many of whom had postponed their first home purchase until later in life. They were just as committed to staying in their homes and upgrading them as were the stability seekers. They had made a home owner's commitment to living in and improving the neighborhoods where they lived.

From a public policy standpoint, the stabilizers are a forgotten component of neighborhood revitalization. Policies aimed at home ownership have been targeted at the more affluent through gentrification, or at the very poor. For cities like St. Louis, a modicum of policy attention to stabilizers may pay great returns in revitalizing some city neighborhoods. The findings in the home-buyers survey, and the comments of participants in the focus groups conducted for the study, suggested that the greatest impediment to home buyers in the stabilizer category is the attainment of housing finance. The combination of modest household income and neighborhood location made stabilizers marginal to the housing finance markets. Simple and modest assistance in acquiring home mortgages could be a strong impetus to stabilizing home ownership in less stable neighborhoods. As the forgotten piece of the urban housing policy puzzle, the stabilizing buyer of modest existing housing represents an important policy opportunity.

Action

The housing study represents a common pattern of linkage between policy research findings and policy decisions. The study had direct relevance for meeting information needs at CDA, and it contributed to their complying with HUD requirements for continued funding. However, this direct contribution to action (writing the HUD plan) probably produced very little in the way of policy decisions or resource allocations for strategies to revitalize housing in St. Louis. The analyses and conversations regarding gentrification or neighborhood stabilization strategies had more salience for the policy debates surrounding community development in St. Louis, and these implications were not part of the direct mandate for the survey report. The evidence supporting the importance of stabilizers and the opportunities for facilitating home ownership for stabilizers did become part of the information base at CDA, and it may have influenced the perspectives of key staff members with the ability to affect the policy process in St. Louis. Thus, the most important link between this study and policy action was indirect. The study injected new perspectives and new evidence into the community development policy community, and it may help tilt the scales in weighing future policy options.

Lessons for Policy Research

This case demonstrates the inexact correspondence between the logic of analysis in a focused piece of policy analysis and the logic of decision making to which it may be applied. In this case, the policy research task was clearly descriptive. CDA perceived an opportunity to gather relevant information that had never been available about city home buyers and had an opportunity to fund a survey of these prior home buyers. The constraints of the survey technique and the limits of the budget meant that this task was designed to meet descriptive information needs. It described the characteristics and perceptions of recent home buyers. However, the policy decisions for which it was relevant required assessment of the efficacy of past policy choices (such as gentrification strategies) and estimation of the desirability of future policy choices (such as housing development plans). Neither resources nor available data would support rigorous methods of research to address these causal and estimation information needs directly, and these logical inferences would still be accomplished through the reasoned judgment of actors in the policy community. Nevertheless, the provision of new and highly relevant descriptive information provides a basis for improving these policy judgments and inferences.

The case also demonstrates the potential utility of facilitating the production of relevant information through reporting and planning requirements from higher levels of government. Local governments typically operate in an environment of fiscal scarcity with strong demands for using resources to meet direct service needs. Finding resources for conducting policy research is difficult, and the requirement to use funds from higher levels of government (typically federal) for research accounts for a major portion of the policy research conducted at local levels. Many critics of federal research requirements focus on the perception that much of what is reported to the federal level does not lead to direct federal action. In many instances, the greater value of much of the federally required policy research may be its relevance for, and influence on, the perceptions and judgments of local decision makers.

Discussion Questions

1. Descriptive information needs were paramount in this study; what other kinds of information needs did the policy research client have, and how were they met? What kinds of additional policy research activity would have been useful in meeting these needs?
2. Why did the policy research team use focus groups? How did they enhance the findings of the study?
3. This study provides another example of policy research generating new concepts as a by-product of data collection and analysis. Why and how did the policy researchers develop new concepts and terminology in conjunction with this study?
4. Why were no recommendations associated with this study?
5. How and why did the policy research team expand the research problem beyond the immediate needs of the decision-making client?

Assignments and Activities

1. Propose an appropriate research design for planning housing development policy in your city. Be sure to check for existing data by consulting with local housing officials.
2. After becoming familiar with relevant planning documents and existing data for your city, write a request for proposals that calls for data to address the information needs associated with city housing policies.

FOCUS ON RESEARCH METHODS

Using Focus Groups in Policy Research

A focus group is a "carefully planned discussion designed to obtain perceptions on a defined area of interest in a permissive, nonthreatening environment" (Krueger 1988:18). The St. Louis housing study described in this chapter used focus groups as one means of learning about the preferences of home buyers in the city. The use of focus groups originated as a technique of basic social science in the late 1930s, but it has gained more widespread recognition as a tool of market researchers in the private sector. Typically, focus groups consist of seven to ten people discussing an issue of concern with a skilled interviewer; discussion is intended to be relaxed and informal, with the possibility that group members will influence one another in an interactive fashion (Krueger 1988).

Focus groups are popular among market researchers because they can provide credible, in-depth information about consumer perceptions, attitudes, and preferences at a minimal cost. Although the information that focus groups typically yield is not necessarily generalizable to large populations, they may provide greater detail than a conventional survey would. For this reason, focus groups have also become increasingly popular as a tool for policy researchers.

Krueger (1988:31–37) suggests several possible settings in which focus groups may be a useful tool in policy-related research:

- Before a program begins—Focus groups can be used to assist in projects designed to assess needs, research markets, or inform program design.
- During a program—Focus groups can help provide information for formative "process" evaluations.
- After a program has been completed—focus groups can help illuminate outcome-oriented assessments.

As Krueger (1988:37) noted, focus groups, like other qualitative policy research techniques, can be used to complement more quantitative data collection methods, such as surveys of larger populations. The St. Louis housing study used such a combined approach—a systematic sample of home buyers was comple-

(continued on next page)

(continued)

mented with focus group interviews of buyers from different regions of the city.

However, the use of focus groups must be limited to settings for which they are appropriate and valid. Krueger also noted: "*Focus groups are valid if they are used carefully for a problem that is suitable for focus group inquiry*" (1988:41; emphasis added). Moreover, policy researchers must be careful not to overgeneralize from focus group results. For additional information about how to use focus groups in policy research, see, for example, Krueger (1988), Goldman and McDonald (1987), and Advertising Research Foundation (1985).

CASE STUDY AT A GLANCE

Program Title and Policy Area Housing Policy in St. Louis

Program and Policy Background As part of an effort to rejuvenate the city's residential base, a survey was commissioned by the Community Development Agency (CDA) of the City of St. Louis to learn about recent home buyers.

Client and Other Primary Stakeholders The client was the CDA; the study did not receive a great deal of outside attention. The project helped the agency meet external requirements for receiving HUD funds.

Information Needs The project was designed primarily to provide quantitative descriptive information—the characteristics of past home buyers—that could be used to help plan future policy.

Research Design and Methods The primary data collection activity was a telephone survey of 1,062 single-family home buyers in the city of St. Louis. Focus groups that represented home buyers from different parts of the city were also convened.

Findings and Recommendations The study produced a volume of specific findings that were augmented through discussion between the CDA staff and the policy research team. Among other things, the survey results shed light on the perceived effect of the city's gentrification strategy. It revealed, for example, that those moving into the city did not fit the profile of buyers who would be attracted by such a strategy. Formal recommendations were not part of the contract between the CDA and the policy researchers, but implications from the findings could and would be drawn.

Program Jargon and Acronyms

CDA City of St. Louis Community Development Agency
city dwellers Survey respondents (recent home buyers) who reported previously owning homes in the City of St. Louis
gentrification The physical and social-class upgrading of inner-city neighborhoods
gentrifiers Survey respondents who purchased homes in focused development areas

(continued on next page)

(continued)

HUD U.S. Department of Housing and Urban Development

in-movers Survey respondents (recent home buyers) who reported moving into the City of St. Louis

Operation Conserve St. Louis program to coordinate services and development programs in selected neighborhoods using Conserve officers who served as conduits, organizers, and ombudspersons for local citizens and neighborhoods

stability seekers Survey respondents who purchased homes in stable neighborhoods

stabilizers Survey respondents who purchased homes in less stable neighborhoods

CHAPTER 13

Lessons from Case Studies in Policy Research

The cases presented in this text were intended to illustrate at least some of the variety of real conditions under which policy research is conducted. These cases reinforce many of the general assertions made in Part One. Several themes run through the case study materials, making important points about the way policy researchers fulfill clients' information needs.

Policy Research Is Conducted During Different Parts of the Policy Sequence

The cases illustrate that policy research is required by decision makers before, during, and after the decision to enact a given policy or program. Among the cases discussed here, the housing survey (Chapter 12) was intended as a planning document. The demonstration/pilot projects—Ignition Interlock (Chapter 6), SWTHRY (Chapter 10), POWER (Chapter 9), and Dropout Prevention (Chapter 11)—were intended to precede a policy choice. All of these cases demonstrate the complex and multidimensional nature of information needs prior to policy decisions. Different actors in the policy process will want information to match their perspective on policy issues. Other cases demonstrate situations where decision makers required information in the middle of the policy sequence—after key policy choices were made and the programs were being implemented. Perhaps surprisingly, several of these cases involve essentially exploratory research, including the ADTR (Chapter 5), ENYSP

(Chapter 7), and Deinstitutionalization (Chapter 8) projects. These cases reflect the importance of day-to-day implementation for shaping policy. Even after a policy choice has been made, decision makers need to know "what's going on" (Murphy 1980:3).

The cases also include more conventional causal evaluation projects that seek to evaluate program outcomes after the program has been implemented. These cases include the SWTHRY High-Risk Youth Project (Chapter 10), Ignition Interlock (Chapter 6), and Dropout Prevention (Chapter 11). It is interesting that each of these was consciously designed to test pilot projects in order to decide whether policy experiments should be expanded, demonstrating that policy research is ideally part of a continuing feedback loop that uses program results for planning purposes.

Students of policy research need to be alert to the fact that policy research can and does become necessary at all points of the policy sequence and that appropriate research approaches and methods may need to be adjusted accordingly.

Policy Research Generally Relies on the Use of a Multiplistic Approach

Each of the projects embraced a multiplistic approach to policy research. Indeed, none of the projects could have been completed effectively without the combination of data collection efforts, multiple measures, and various research perspectives (Cook 1985).

Several studies might have ended with incorrect or misleading findings had they been limited to a single method or data source. For example, without the interviews of judges and other criminal justice officials, neither the reasons behind the sentencing decisions, nor the problem of circumvention of the interlock device, would have come to light in the Ignition Interlock project (Chapter 6). Process information, gathered primarily during a series of site visits, was a critical addition to the standard surveys of program staff and participants in the ENYSP project (Chapter 7).

The policy research process proposed in Chapter 4 emphasizes fitting research methods to information needs, so that multiple issues and information needs of decision makers are addressed. Forcing information needs to fit a single, or "preferred" research method opens the doors to bias and partial information. The decision to use multiple research methods and other elements of multiplism is important if policy researchers are attentive to the real information needs of their clients.

Policy Research Relies on Basic Research Methods

Despite the emphasis of many policy-research–related texts on formal, rigorous, quantitative methods (such as cost-benefit analysis and experimental designs), many research situations require the use of basic methods found in many of the case studies. Among the methods commonly used in these cases were interviews, site visits and observations, process analysis techniques, and document analysis. Interviewing program staff, stakeholders, and participants was particularly important to many of these projects. These methods are important for policy researchers to get an accurate, holistic, and cost effective view of program or policy arenas.

All of the case studies include fairly extensive use of quantitative techniques and analyses, but these were primarily straightforward descriptive statistics, contingency tables, and simple displays. Only two of the studies—Ignition Interlock (Chapter 6) and SWTHRY High-Risk Youth Project (Chapter 10) hinged upon more sophisticated quantitative analyses. Indeed, studies that rest solely on sophisticated statistical analysis often lack the grounded relevance that is important to lay actors in the decision-making process. Such analyses are often more likely to find their way into academic journals than into the hands of decision makers.

Policy Research Serves the Needs of a Variety of Types of Clients

Although many academic accounts of policy research refer to federal policies and programs, many of the cases described in this text involved state, local, or nonprofit agencies. Though several were partially or entirely funded by federal money, they were implemented more locally. Given their relatively more modest resources, such agencies tend to have (a) fewer staff dedicated to policy research activities and (b) less existing data amenable to rigorous quantitative analysis. Fewer policy researchers working in-house translates into a frequent need for the use of outside consultants, and most of these cases involved consultants. The lack of high-quality data contributes to the need for the use of alternative research methods such as use of available information or lower cost data collection methods.

As policy researchers move from the more sophisticated and general environs of policy research at the federal government to the more concrete and specific world of state and local government, they may find increased demand for immediately applicable research results. Stakeholders may be closer to the policy research process, necessitating a sensitive and inclusive approach to conducting the research process. They may be rewarded with a more tangible impact on the decision-making process.

Constraints of the "Real World" Shape Policy Research Activities and Products

In a perfect world with limitless resources, the case study projects recounted here might have been much more ambitious with respect to producing definitive information about program and policy effectiveness. For example, the ADTR evaluation (Chapter 5) might have included an in-depth analysis of the impact of the federal block grant on the well-being of individual clients—perhaps coupled with a cost-benefit analysis. With more resources, it might have been possible to create control groups and conduct a rigorous experiment on the effectiveness of ENYSP drug-prevention activities on disadvantaged youth (Chapter 7). Limited resources, however, preclude such grandiose research designs. Moreover, as argued earlier, rigorous quantitative designs don't necessarily create the kind of information that decision makers really want. Furthermore, decisions can often be placed on stronger empirical grounds with much simpler research designs. The case studies in this text, for the most part, shared an emphasis on producing relatively simple information about *why* and *how* programs work or fail to work. In any case, as students of policy research enter the "real world" of analyzing public programs and policies, they quickly learn that their tools are sharply circumscribed by limited resources.

Use of Policy Research Varies Situationally and with the Initiation of Research

The ways in which the information produced by the studies was used, and the means by which that use occurred, varied widely and unpredictably. Whereas several projects (Interlock and POWER, for example) were clearly structured elements of a decision system (as described in Chapter 3), and hence more likely to be integrated into the policy process, others arose from *ad hoc* requests (as did the Deinstitutionalization project) or were required by federal grant regulations (such as ADTR or SWTHRY).

The extent to which projects were integrated into the decision system seemed in turn to affect patterns of research use. Generally, the projects that were planned as parts of a decision system enjoyed greater access to decision makers and/or the decision-making process. For example, the Ignition Interlock study was central to the debate about continuing and expanding the use of the interlock device—the legislature had demanded policy research to help inform their decision. The POWER study was influential in affecting decisions about how to implement and expand an innovative welfare-to-work strategy. At the other end of the usage scale, studies conducted primarily to fulfill grant regulations—such as ADTR and the SWTHRY High-Risk Youth Project—did not have a direct impact on the decision-making process, although they may have had more or less noticeable impacts on other audiences.

Policy Research Requires Flexibility

Chapter 4 presented a model for designing, conducting, and implementing policy research projects. The model suggests that policy research entails a linear, step-by-step process—each stage completed sequentially. In reality, most of the projects described in the case studies were the product, to varying degrees, of adjustment and modification as the projects developed. Typically, the conditions envisioned during the problem definition stage are somewhat different from the true conditions affecting a program or policy. Often, the information needs of clients—as articulated by the clients themselves—impinge on the choices that policy researchers make. For example, the SWTHRY project (Chapter 10) was originally conceived with a quasi-experiment underpinning the research design. When it became apparent that the number of clients available for the study was insufficient for this approach, the design was changed to reflect a nonexperimental design, with added emphasis on describing program processes. The Ignition Interlock study (Chapter 6) was originally planned as a classic experiment, but it became a quasi-experiment when county judges insisted on controlling who would be sentenced to interlock—thereby making random assignment impossible. The protocols for the site visits described in the ENYSP evaluation project (Chapter 7) were modified after lessons learned from initial visits suggested how to structure them more effectively. Nearly every policy research project undergoes various changes in approach, methods, and implementation at some stage of the policy research process.

Use of Policy Research Must Be Planned and Incorporated into the Research Process

The studies described here represent a wide range of contexts in which policy research results were disseminated to and used by decision makers. To a large extent, the use is dictated by conditions beyond the direct control of policy researchers. Some clients, for example, are quite demanding in their desire to control study outcomes. The client in the Dropout Prevention study (Chapter 11), for example, had specific expectations about the results of that study and tended to ignore results that ran counter to these expectations. The client in the POWER study (Chapter 9), on the other hand, was eager to work with the policy researchers to maximize the usefulness of the study. Other studies are characterized by fairly rigid processes for dissemination of study findings; the SWTHRY demonstration project (Chapter 10), for example, was part of a highly structured series of studies funded by the national funding body, CSAP. Dissemination of study results proceeded primarily through established professional channels.

Many of the studies included here, however, featured conscious efforts on behalf of the policy researchers to work with decision makers to optimize the utility and use of research findings. An obvious first step toward optimizing usability is to plan research activities that are suited to the actual management information needs of decision makers, as emphasized in the policy research model described in Chapter 4. However, regardless of the specific research activities involved in a project, policy researchers may do a variety of things to promote the use of their research findings. The case studies included the following strategies:

- Consult with decision makers and stakeholders about study design and implementation.
- Release quarterly and other interim reports that facilitate feedback from clients and other stakeholders.
- Meet personally with clients to discuss the relevance of study findings to ongoing issues of program design and implementation.

- Participate in staff, decision maker, or public discussion about the meaning of research findings.
- Whenever possible, use nontechnical language to clearly explicate the significance of findings to the appropriate audiences.

Policy Research Raises Challenging Ethical Questions

Because it often addresses politically sensitive issues of resource allocation, policy objectives, and policy effects, policy research frequently presents ethical questions for policy researchers. Creation of policy experiments, for example, excludes some individuals from potentially beneficial policy or program actions. In the SWTHRY study (Chapter 10), the policy researchers had to abandon an experimental approach, in part because it would have entailed withholding program benefits from some clients. Here are some other potential ethical dilemmas encountered in policy research:

- Struggles with clients over divulging study results that disappoint them
- Observation of unethical or possibly illegal activities at program sites
- Balancing the need for scientific rigor with resource limitations posed by policy research

Conclusion

Policy research is a relatively recent arrival in the world of public decision making. As the problems facing politicians and public servants have become more complex, their need for accurate information and relevant analysis has grown. As social science methods and information analysis techniques have improved, the ability of policy researchers to meet this need has also grown.

Still, policy research is a fledgling profession, and much remains to be learned and to be institutionalized before the promise of clearly planned, needs-based public programs is realized, or the prospect of improved policy performance through outcome evaluation comes to fruition. The benefits of a decision system are just becoming understood across the intergovernmental system, and the slow process of institutional change is largely before us.

Nevertheless, the cases presented here demonstrate that meaningful policy research regularly takes place throughout our government—in legislatures and public agencies, at federal, state, and local levels. The cases also demonstrate that the utility of that research depends on the ability of the researcher to combine perceptiveness concerning the interests surrounding a problem, skills in research and analysis, and the ability to cooperate and communicate with decision makers. As our understanding of these requirements of good policy research continues to grow, future public policy decisions will increasingly benefit from a solid foundation of relevant information and analysis.

Discussion Questions

1. Take any two case studies and compare them along the following dimensions:
   - Which best exemplifies the model for policy research described in Chapter 4?
   - Which provided the most useful information in terms of improving the policy or program it addressed and why?
   - Which was ultimately used the most, and why?
   - How was multiplism a part of each study?
2. Which research methods were most effective in producing the findings and recommendations in each case study?

Assignments and Activities

1. Reexamine the research proposal you completed for Chapter 4. Using the principles and lessons you have learned from the case studies, try to improve on your original proposal.
2. See if you can locate a policy research study that addresses a policy or program similar to one or more of those described in the case studies. How is it different, and why?

APPENDIX

Example of a Request for Proposals

Interrater Reliability in Determining Levels of Severity in Order of Selection

California Department of Rehabilitation, 1996

Introduction

The California Department of Rehabilitation is soliciting proposals for contractual services to evaluate current interrater reliability; to make recommendations for improving interrater reliability; and to develop a plan by which the Department can continue to monitor and evaluate interrater reliability in the determination of level of severity and priority category for eligible applicants for the Vocational Rehabilitation Program of the Department of Rehabilitation as a component of the Order of Selection for Vocational Rehabilitation Services process. This process involves vocational counselors throughout the state determining levels of severity of disability to assure that first priority for services is given to individuals with the most severe disabilities. There are numerous models of implementation being used that must be factored into the evaluation.

The rehabilitation Counselor assesses each eligible applicant through a systematic method of setting a numerical value within a Significance Scale, in each of 10 functional capacity areas, as a means of quantifying the impact of the limitations presented by an individual's disability considered in a full range of environments. Counselors possess a wide range of educational and professional experience and serve individuals from very diverse populations (disability, ethnic, urban/rural, age, etc.). Throughout the *17 districts* and more than 100 branch offices within the state, various models of implementation have developed. Consequently, there is concern with the consistency of scoring by counselors in the use of the "severity of disability" significance scale.

Background

The mission of the California Department of Rehabilitation is to assist individuals with disabilities, emphasizing those with the most severe disabilities, toward informed choice and success in education, vocational training, career opportunities, independent living, and in the use of assistive technology to improve their employment opportunities and their lives. Included in the Department's goals are the delivery of effective services, accessible by all groups, particularly to those who have been unserved or underserved in the past.

In the Rehabilitation Act of 1973, as amended in 1992, Congress requires states unable to serve all eligible applicants to first serve those with the most severe disabilities through an Order of Selection procedure. The California Department of Rehabilitation has determined that its funds are not adequate to serve all persons eligible for services. Consequently the Director has declared the Department under Order of Selection.

Implementation of an Order of Selection requires the Department to assess each eligible applicant's level of severity, and to establish priority categories that assure that eligible applicants with the most severe disabilities are assured priority. The Department has developed an organized and equitable method for prioritizing individuals with disabilities. The tool used by the Department to determine the impact of an individual's disability/ies on the 10 functional capacity areas, as they impact an employment outcome, is the Significance Scale.

It is the intent of this system to assure that determinations of severity of disability are consistent throughout the state. The Department has developed definitions of "almost severely disabled," "severely disabled," and "disabled" and has established procedures for determining an individual's level of severity. Persons eligible for services are assigned a priority score based on the level of severity of their disability and placed on a statewide waiting list based on their level of severity, Significance Scale score, and their date of application.

Project Objectives/Deliverables

1. Assess current interrater reliability in the assessment of level of severity and determination of priority category for eligible applicants for Vocational Rehabilitation services including, but not limited to, consideration of:
   a. Issues that impact individual counselors conducting the assessment, including their education, knowledge, experience, etc.
   b. Variations of implementation models in the district and branch offices (e.g., all counselors, an assessment unit, a panel process)
   c. Impacts related to
      (1) Any geographic location of residency within the state
      (2) Type of disability
      (3) Sex, race, religious creed, color, ancestry, national origin, sexual orientation, or marital status
      (4) Source of referral
      (5) Type of expected employment outcome
      (6) The particular service needs or anticipated cost of services required by an individual
      (7) The income level of an individual or an individual's family
2. Develop recommendations for improvement of interrater reliability in the assessment of level of severity and determination of priority categories including, but not limited to:
   a. Models of implementation
   b. Training
   c. Modifications to the Significance Scale
   d. Regulatory changes
3. Provision of a written plan for ongoing monitoring and evaluation of interrater reliability. The plan must include recommendations for internal and/or external monitoring and estimation of associated costs and/or staffing requirements.

Resources Available

The contractor will have access to central office and field staff, including counseling personnel. Records, which include individual consumer information; medical documentation of disability; identification of primary and secondary disabilities; and client demographic information and assessment information will be provided. Statistical information, including data from the Department's internal review conducted to date of the scores of all consumers placed on waiting lists, is also available. The internal review is primarily focused on consistency related to medical diagnosis.

Evaluation Criteria

A committee of three evaluators will independently review each proposal meeting minimum requirements. Points will be assigned to each area of the RFP with a total of 100 points as identified below:

1. Organizational/Individual Capacity to Complete Project	10
2. Methodology/Investigative Process	50
3. Interpretive/Statistical Techniques	20
4. Report Formats	10
5. Project Timeline	10
Total	100

Proposals scoring below 70 points will be eliminated from competition. The separately submitted budget will be opened only for the applicants with the three top-scoring proposals. Qualifying budgets will be screened to determine that minimum requirements are met. Budgets that do not meet the requirements listed below will be eliminated from competition. The Department reserves the right to reject any and all bids/proposals. The contract will be awarded to the qualified applicant with the lowest bid of the three top-scoring proposals.

Proposal Format

1. Cover Sheet—signed by an authorized individual (*must be a signature on all copies*)
2. Narrative—in the following format:
   a. *Organizational/Individual Capacity to Complete Project:* Must include descriptions of comparable projects completed; length of time organization/individual has been conducting research; experience of staff proposed to complete the project; and other pertinent information that speaks to the organization/individual's capacity to complete the project. Resumés/vitae of staff proposed to complete the project and letters of recommendation related to former projects must be included in the appendices.
   b. *Methodology/Investigative Process:* A complete work plan for the project including proposed data collection, interviews, and/or other investigative techniques.
   c. *Interpretive/Statistical Techniques:* Proposed manner in which data will be analyzed.
   d. *Report Formats:* Proposed manner in which data, recommendations, and continuing evaluation will be presented.
   e. *Project Timeline:* Timeline for completing each phase of the project related to the work plan in (b) above.

   The narrative must be typed in a print size comparable to that used in this RFP, double spaced, and limited to twenty-five (25) pages (8 1/2" x 11") in length.
3. Appendices—prior work and qualifications in evaluation of social service programs/services:
   a. Letters of Reference (minimum of two)
   b. Resumés
4. Statement of Compliance—signed by an authorized individual
5. Budget and Budget Narrative—All line items in the budget section require a specific narrative statement providing the budget rationales. The total budget may not exceed $70,000.

Terms

The contract shall be effective from April 1, 1996, through December 31, 1996. The contract may be terminated by either party upon written notice of at least thirty (30) days prior to such termination.

Payment Schedule

In consideration of the services provided by Contractor, State agrees to reimburse Contractor monthly, in arrears, ninety percent (90%) of actual expenses. Upon satisfactory completion of contract work, Contractor will submit an invoice for the remaining ten percent (10%) of actual expenses. All payments shall be in accordance with the approved items in the Contract Budget, provided, however, that:

1. Any major line item may not be increased by more than ten percent (10%) through corresponding dollar reduction in other line items.
2. All other major line items increased/decreased in excess of ten percent (10%) shall not be made except upon written request to and approval by the Department of Rehabilitation's Contract Administrator.
3. Reimbursement for travel expenses shall not exceed the rates established for the State's nonrepresented employees. All out-of-state travel for the purpose of bringing in consultants or for attendance by project staff at meetings and/or conference presentations requires prior written approval of the Department of Rehabilitation's Contract Administrator.
4. Invoices for reimbursement shall be submitted monthly in arrears in triplicate to the Department of Rehabilitation's Contract Administrator.

References

Part One

Ascher, William. 1978. *Forecasting: An Appraisal for Policy Makers and Planners.* Baltimore: Johns Hopkins University Press.

Bingham, Richard D., and Claire L. Felbinger. 1989. *Evaluation in Practice.* New York: Longman.

Box, G. E. P., and G. M. Jenkins. 1969. *Time Series Analysis: Forecasting and Control.* San Francisco: Holden-Day.

Burman, Peter J. 1972. *Precedence Networks for Project Planning and Control.* London: McGraw-Hill.

Carley, Michael. 1980. *Rational Techniques in Policy Analysis.* London: Policy Studies Institute.

Cook, Thomas D. 1985. Postpositivist critical multiplism. In R. Lance Shotland and Melvin M. Mark (editors). *Social Science and Social Policy.* Beverly Hills, Calif.: Sage Publications, pp. 21–62.

Dunn, William N. 1994. *Public Policy Analysis,* 2nd ed. Englewood Cliffs, N.J.: Prentice-Hall.

Fink, Arlene. 1985. *How to Conduct Surveys: A Step-by-Step Guide.* Beverly Hills, Calif.: Sage Publications.

Fitz-Gibbon, Carol Taylor, and Lynn Lyons Morris. 1987. *How to Design a Program Evaluation.* Newbury Park, Calif.: Sage Publications.

Folz, David H. 1996. *Survey Research for Public Administration.* Thousand Oaks, Calif.: Sage Publications.

Fowler, Floyd J., Jr. 1987. *Survey Research Methods.* 1984. Beverly Hills, Calif.: Sage Publications.

Gass, Saul I., and Roger L. Sisson. 1974. *A Guide to Models in Governmental Planning and Operations.* Washington, D.C.: Environmental Protection Agency.

Giventer, Lawrence L. 1996. *Statistical Analysis for Public Administration.* New York: Wadsworth.

Gordon, Raymond. 1992. *Basic Interviewing Skills.* Itasca, Ill.: Peacock.

Gramlich, Edward M. *Benefit-Cost Analysis of Public Programs,* 2nd ed. Englewood Cliffs, N.J.: Prentice-Hall.

Hatry, Harry P., Richard E. Winnie, and Donald M. Fisk. 1981. *Program Evaluation for State and Local Government,* 2nd ed. Washington, D.C.: Urban Institute.

Herman, Joan L., Lynn Lyons Morris, and Carol Taylor Fitz-Gibbon. 1987. *Evaluator's Handbook.* Newbury Park, Calif.: Sage Publications.

Kress, Guenther, Gustav Koehler, and J. Fred Springer. 1981. Policy drift: An evaluation of the California Business Enterprise Program. In Dennis J. Palumbo and Mavin Harder (editors). *Implementing Public Policy.* Lexington, Mass.: Lexington Books.

Kress, Guenther, and J. Fred Springer. 1988. Service utilization in public sector consulting. *American Review of Public Administration,* 18 (2), 327–342.

Langbein, Laura. 1980. *Discovering Whether Programs Work: A Guide to Statistical Methods for Program Evaluation.* Glenview, Ill.: Scott Foresman.

Lavrakas, Paul J. 1987. *Telephone Survey Methods: Sampling, Selection, and Supervision.* Newbury Park, Calif.: 1987.

Linstone, Harold A., and Murray Turroff. 1975. *The Delphi Method: Techniques and Applications.* New York: Addison-Wesley.

MacRae, Duncan Jr., and James Wilde. 1979. *Policy Analysis for Public Decisions.* North Scituate, Mass.: Duxbury Press.

Matlack, William F. 1993. *Statistics for Public Managers.* Itasca, Ill.: F. E. Peacock.

Meyer, Kenneth, and Jeffrey Brudney. 1993. *Applied Statistics for Public Administration,* 3rd ed. New York: Wadsworth.

Miller, Thomas I., and Michelle A. Miller. 1985. *Citizen Surveys: How to Do Them, How to Use Them, What They Mean.* Washington, D.C.: International City Management Association.

Mohr, Lawrence B. 1988. *Impact Analysis for Program Evaluation.* Chicago: Dorsey Press.

Morris, Lynn Lyons, Carol Taylor Fitz-Gibbon, and Marie E. Freeman. 1987. *How to Communicate Evaluation Findings.* Newbury Park, Calif.: Sage Publications.

Mowitz, Robert. 1980. *Design of Public Decision Systems.* Baltimore: University Park Press.

Murphy, Jerome T. 1980. *Getting the Facts: A Fieldwork Guide for Evaluators and Policy Analysts.* Santa Monica, Calif.: Goodyear Publishing.

Nachimas, David. 1979. *Public Policy Evaluation: Approaches and Methods.* New York: St. Martin's Press.

O'Sulivan, Elizabeth Ann, and Gary R. Rassel. 1995. *Research Methods for Public Administrators.* White Plains, N.Y.: Longman Publishers.

Patton, Carl V., and David S. Sawicki. 1993. *Policy Analysis and Planning: Theory and Practice,* 2nd ed. Englewood Cliffs, N.J.: Prentice-Hall.

Patton, Michael. 1987a. *How to Use Qualitative Methods in Evaluation.* Newbury Park, Calif.: Sage Publications.

Patton, Michael Quinn. 1987b. *Utilization-Focused Evaluation.* Newbury Park, Calif.: Sage Publications.

Pressman, Jeffrey, and Aaron Wildavsky. 1975. *Implementation.* Berkeley: University of California Press.

Putt, Allen D., and J. Fred Springer. 1989. *Policy Research: Concepts, Methods, and Applications*. Englewood Cliffs, N.J.: Prentice-Hall.

Quade, E. S., and Grace Carter. 1989. *Analysis for Public Decisions,* 3rd ed. New York: North-Holland.

Rossi, Peter H., and Howard E. Freeman. *Evaluation: A Systematic Approach,* 4th ed. Newbury Park, Calif.: Sage Publications.

Rothman, Jack. 1980. *Using Research in Organizations: A Guide to Successful Application.* Beverly Hills, Calif.: Sage Publications.

Rutman, Leonard, and George Mowbray. 1983. *Understanding Program Evaluation.* Newbury Park, Calif.: Sage Publications.

Scriven, Michael. 1972. Pros and cons about goal-free evaluation. *Evaluation Comment,* 3:1–14.

Sharp, Elaine B. 1994. *The Dilemma of Drug Policy in the United States.* New York: Harper-Collins.

Springer, J. Fred, and Joël L. Phillips. June 1994. Policy learning and evaluation design: Lessons from the Community Partnership Demonstration Program," *Journal of Community Psychology.* Special Issue, pp. 117–139.

Starling, Grover. 1988. *Strategies for Policy Making.* Chicago: Dorsey Press.

Sylvia, Ronald D., Kenneth J. Meier, and Elizabeth M. Gunn. 1985. *Program Planning and Evaluation for the Public Manager.* Monterey, Calif.: Brooks-Cole.

Weikart, David P. 1984. *Changed Lives.* Ypsilanti, Mich.: Scope Educational Research Foundation.

Weimer, David L., and Aidan R. Vining. *Policy Analysis: Concepts and Practice.* Englewood Cliffs, N.J.: Prentice-Hall.

Weiss, C.H. 1972. *Evaluation Research: Methods of Assessing Program Effectiveness.* Englewood Cliffs, N.J.: Prentice-Hall.

Weiss, Carol H., and Michael J. Bucuvalas. 1980. *Social Science Research and Decision Making.*

Welch, Susan, and John Comer. 1988. *Quantitative Methods for Public Administration,* 2nd ed. Pacific Grove, Calif.: Brooks-Cole.

Whitaker, Gordon P., Charles David Phillips, Peter J. Haas, and Robert F. Worden. 1985. Aggressive policing and the deterrence of crime, *Law and Policy* 7 (April): 395–416.

Part Two

Advertising Research Foundation. 1985. *Focus Groups: Issues and Approaches.* New York: A. R. S.

Bardach, Eugene. 1977. *The Implementation Game.* Cambridge, Mass.: MIT Press.

Benard, B. 1991. *Fostering Resiliency in Kids: Protective Factors in Family, School, and Community.* Portland, Ore.: Northwest Regional Educational Laboratory.

Brook, J. S., M. Whiteman, A. S. Gordon, and D. W. Brook. 1988. The role of older brothers' drug use viewed in the context of parent and peer influences. *Journal of Genetic Psychology,* 151, 59–75.

Butterfoss, F. D., R. M. Goodman, and A. Wandersman. 1993. Community coalitions for prevention and health promotion. *Health Education Research*, 8 (3), 315–330.

Cottage Programs International. 1988. *The Families in Focus Handbook*. Provo, Utah: Cottage Industries.

Donelson, Alan C. 1988. The alcohol-crash problem. In M. D. Laurence, J. R. Snortum, and F. E. Zimring (editors), *Social Control of the Drinking Driver*. Chicago: The University of Chicago Press, pp. 3–42.

EMT Group. 1990. *Evaluation of the California Ignition Interlock Pilot Program for DUI Offenders (Farr-Davis Driver Safety Act of 1986): Final Report*. Sacramento, Calif.: EMT Group.

EMT Group. 1991a. *Evaluation of the Emergency Substance Abuse Treatment and Rehabilitation Block Grant (Anti-Drug Abuse Act of 1986): Final Report*. Sacramento, Calif.: EMT Group.

EMT Group. 1991b. *An Evaluation of the Extended National Youth Sports Program (ENYSP) 1990–91: Final Report*. Sacramento, Calif.: EMT Group.

Frankfort-Nachmias, Chava, and David Nachmias. 1996. *Research Methods in the Social Sciences*, 5th ed. New York: St. Martins.

Goldman, Alfred E., and Susan S. McDonald. 1987. *The Group Depth Interview: Principles and Practice*. Englewood Cliffs, N.J. Prentice-Hall.

Gusfield, Joseph R. 1988. The control of drinking-driving in the United States: A period in transition? In M. D. Laurence, J. R. Snortum, and F. E. Zimring (editors), *Social Control of the Drinking Driver*. Chicago: The University of Chicago Press, pp. 109–135.

Hansen, W. B. 1992. School-based substance abuse prevention: A review of the state of the art in curriculum, 1980–1990. *Health Education Research*, 7 (3), 403–430.

Hansen, W. B., J. W. Graham, J. L. Sobel, D. R. Shelton, B. R. Flay, and C. A. Johnson. 1987. The consistency of peer and parent influences on tobacco, alcohol, and marijuana use among young adolescents. *Journal of Behavioral Medicine*, 10, 559–579.

Hawkins, D. J., R. R. Catalano, and Y. J. Miller. 1992. Risk and protective factors for alcohol and other drug problems in adolescence and early adulthood: Implications for Substance Abuse Prevention. *Psychological Bulletin*, 112 (1), 64–105.

Hawkins, J. D., and J. G. Weiss. 1985. The social development model: An integrated approach to delinquency prevention. *Journal of Primary Prevention*, 6 (2), 73–79.

Jacobs, James B. 1989. *Drunk Driving: An American Dilemma*. Chicago: The University of Chicago Press.

JLARC (Joint Legislative Audit and Review Commission, Commonwealth of Virginia). 1979. *Deinstitutionalization of the Mentally Ill and Mentally Retarded*. Richmond, Va.: Joint Legislative Audit and Review Commission.

JLARC (Joint Legislative Audit and Review Commission, Commonwealth of Virginia). 1985a. *Deinstitutionalization and Community Services*. Richmond, Va.: Joint Legislative Audit and Review Commission.

JLARC (Joint Legislative Audit and Review Commission, Commonwealth of Virginia). 1985b. *State and Local Services for Mentally Ill, Mentally Retarded and Substance Abusing Citizens*. Richmond, Va.: Joint Legislative Audit and Review Commission.

Kaufman, E. 1986. A contemporary approach to the family treatment of substance abuse disorders. *American Journal of Drug and Alcohol Abuse, 12* (3), 19–211.

Kaufman, E., and L. Borders. 1988. Ethnic family differences in adolescent substance use. *Journal of Chemical Dependency Treatment, 1*, 99–121.

Kerstein, R. 1990. Stage models of gentrification: An examination. *Urban Affairs Quarterly*, 25, 620–638.

Kettl, Donald F. *Government by Proxy*. Washington, D.C.: CQ Press.

Krueger, R. A. 1988. *Focus Groups: A Practical Guide for Applied Research.* Newbury Park, Calif.: Sage Publications.

Kumpfer, K. L., and R. Alvarado. 1995. *Strengthening Families to Prevent Drug Use in Multi-Ethnic Youth*. University of Utah, Health Education Department.

Kumpfer, K. L., R. Alvarado, C. Turner, and E. Griffin. March 1993. A preliminary predictive model of alcohol and other drug use for Hispanic adolescents. Paper presented at the Center for Substance Abuse Prevention's 1993 National/International Prevention Conference, "New Dimensions in Prevention: Sharing Today, Shaping Tomorrow," Washington, D.C.

Kumpfer, K. L., and D. P. DeMarsh. 1988. *Recruitment and Attrition Issues*. Paper presented at the Office for Substance Abuse Prevention Conference, San Antonio, Texas.

Kumpfer, K. L., and C. Turner. 1990. The social ecology model of adolescent substance abuse: Implications for prevention. *International Journal of the Addictions,* 25 (4A), 435–462.

Laska, S., and D. Spain. October 1979. Urban policy and planning in the wake of gentrification. *Journal of the American Planners Association*, 523–531.

LeGates, R., and C. Hartman. 1986. The anatomy of displacement in the United States. In N. Smith and P. Williams (editors). *Gentrification of the City*. Boston: Allen and Unwin.

Lucas, William A. 1974. *The Case Study Method: Aggregating Case Experience.* Santa Monica, Calif.: Rand Corporation.

Mohr, Lawrence B. 1988. *Impact Analysis for Program Evaluation.* Chicago: Dorsey Press.

Moos, R. H., and A. G. Billings. 1982. Children of alcoholics during the recovery process: Alcoholic and matched-control families. *Active Behaviors,* 7, 155–163.

Newcomb, M. D., E. Maddahian, and P. M. Bentler. 1986. Risk factors for drug use among adolescents: Current and longitudinal analyses. *American Journal of Public Health, 76*, 525–531.

Richardson, G. E., B. L. Neiger, S. Jensen, and K.L. Kumpfer. 1990. The resiliency model. *Health Education,* 21, 33–39.

Rohrbach, L. A., W. B. Hansen, and M. A. Pentz. 1992. Strategies for involving parents in drug abuse prevention: Results from the Midwest Prevention Program. Paper presented at the 120th Annual Meeting of the American Public Health Association, November 8–12, Washingon, D.C.

Rutter, M. 1990. Psychosocial resilience and protective mechanisms. In J. Rolf, A. S. Masten, D. Cicchetti, K. H. Neuchterlien, and S. Weintraub (editors). *Risk and Protective Factors in the Development of Psychopathology*. New York: Cambridge University Press, pp. 181–214.

Rutter, M., and D. Quinton. 1984. Long-term follow-up of women institutionalized in childhood: Factors promoting good functioning in adult life. *Journal of Developmental Psychology,* 18, 225–234.

Sale, E. W. and J. F. Springer. May 1993. Neighborhood stabilization through home ownership: Patterns of recent home buying in the City of St. Louis. Paper presented to the Sociology of Housing Conference, St. Paul, Minn.

Schill, M., and R. Nathan. (1983). *Revitalizing America's Cities*. Albany, N.Y.: SUNY Press.

Schuckit, M.A. 1992. A clinical model of genetic influences in alcohol dependence. *Journal of Studies on Alcohol*, 55 (1), 5–17.

Shorr, L., and D. Shor. 1988. *Within Our Reach: Breaking the Cycle of Disadvantage*. New York: Anchor Press.

Spain, D. 1980. Indicators of urban revitalization: Racial and socioeconomic changes in central-city housing. In S. Laska and D. Spain (editors). *Back to the City: Issues in Neighborhood Renovation*. New York: Pergamon Policy Studies.

Springer, J. F., and J. L. Phillips. 1992. Extended National Youth Sports Program Evaluation: Individual Protective Factors and Risk Assessment Study. Submitted to the National Collegiate Athletic Association and the Office of Family Services, U.S. Department of Health and Human Services, November 1992.

Springer, J. F., and J. L. Phillips. 1995. The individual protective factors index: A comprehensive measure of adolescent resiliency. Paper presented at the Annual Meetings of the American Evaluation Association, Vancouver, Canada, November.

Springer, J. F., J. L. Phillips, L. C. Cannady, L. Phillips, and E. Kerst-Harris. 1992. CODA: A creative therapy program for children in families affected by abuse of alcohol and other drugs. *Journal of Community Psychology*, CSAP Special Issue, pp. 55–74.

Springer, J. F., L. S. Wright, and G. J. McCall. 1997. Family interventions and adolescent resiliency: The Southwest Texas State High-Risk Youth Program. *The Journal of Community Psychology*. CSAP Special Issue, pp. 78–101.

Stern, A. 1992. A Review of the Research on Family Influences on Alcohol and Other Drug-Taking Behavior: Implications for Prevention Programming. Prepared for the Southwest Regional Center for Drug-Free Schools and Communities.

Swaim, R. C., E. R. Oetting, R. W. Edwards, and F. Beauvais. 1989. Links from emotional distress to adolescent drug use: A path model. *Journal of Consulting and Clinical Psychology*, 57, 227–231.

Tobin, G., and D. Judd. 1982. Moving the suburbs to the city: Neighborhood revitalization and the 'amenities bundle.' *Social Science Quarterly*, 63, 771–779.

Tobler, N. S. 1993. Updated meta-analysis of adolescent drug prevention programs. In C. F. Montoya, C. Ringwalt, B. E. Ryan, and R. Zimmerman (editors). *Evaluating School-linked Prevention Strategies*. San Diego: University of California, San Diego Extension, pp. 71–86.

Werner, E. E. 1986. Resilient offspring of alcoholics: A longitudinal study from birth to age 18. *Journal of Studies on Alcoholism*, 47, 34–40.

Wolin, S. J., L. A. Benett, and D. L. Noonan. 1979. Family rituals and the recurrence of alcoholism over generations. *American Journal of Psychiatry*, 136, 589–593.

Yin, Robert K. 1985. *Case Study Analysis*. Beverly Hills, Calif.: Sage Publications.

Yin, Robert K., and Kenneth Heald. 1975. Using the case study method to analyze policy studies. *Administrative Science Quarterly*, 20 (3), 371–381.

INDEX

Page numbers for figures and tabular material are in italic.